CRITICAL INSIGHTS

The Poetry of Baudelaire

CRITICAL
INSIGHTS

The Poetry of Baudelaire

Editor

Tom Hubbard

University of Edinburgh, Scotland

SALEM PRESS

A Division of EBSCO Information Services, Inc.

Ipswich, Massachusetts

GREY HOUSE PUBLISHING

∞ The paper used in these volumes conforms to the American National Standard for Permanence of Paper for Printed Library Materials, Z39.48-1992 (R1997).

Library of Congress Cataloging-in-Publication Data

The poetry of Baudelaire / editor, Tom Hubbard, University of Edinburgh, Scotland. -- [First edition].

pages : illustrations ; cm. -- (Critical insights)

Includes bibliographical references and index.
ISBN: 978-1-61925-395-7

1. Baudelaire, Charles, 1821-1867--Criticism and interpretation. 2. French poetry--19th century--History and criticism. I. Hubbard, Tom, Dr. II. Series: Critical insights.

PQ2191.Z5 P64 2014
841/.8

First Printing

PRINTED IN THE UNITED STATES OF AMERICA

Contents _____

Overcoming Despair: "Le Voyage" and its Ethical Implications,
  Edward K. Kaplan

Resources _____

Acknowledgements

I would like to thank all contributors for their splendid essays, and for their kindness and patience during sometimes complicated editorial processes. I've enjoyed the spontaneous seminars that have developed by e-mail, and in some cases, personal meetings in Edinburgh and St. Andrews. For generous advice at the planning stages of this book, I'm indebted to Ellen S. Burt, David Carrier, Peter France, Francesco Manzini, and Maria Scott.

My daughter, Claire Hubbard, a graphic designer and computer whiz kid, rescued me during my frequent bouts of techno-neurosis, whenever my laptop just felt like usurping my role of control-freak.

About This Volume

Tom Hubbard

As befits a poet with a strong engagement with the other arts—particularly painting and music—books on Baudelaire require an awareness of his multifaceted career. Moreover, his many roles are intimately related: he believed that, while a critic may not be also a poet, a poet must be also a critic. Indeed, it was possible for a sonnet to be both a well-crafted poem and a piece of art criticism.

Accordingly, the present work has been designed to cover a wide range of Baudelaire's output—including the translations of Edgar Allan Poe; the essays on topics that make reference to such diverse figures as the Spanish painter and caricaturist Francisco Goya and the German composer Richard Wagner; Baudelaire's philosophical, theological, and ethical concerns—while anchoring the whole in the actual poetry. When all is said and done, Baudelaire was primarily a poet.

The first section of the present volume offers multiple birds' eye views of the poet, situating him in key contexts, while swooping in on precise details that vividly illustrate the wider expanse of his vision—what I would call his integrative vision. The sign of a great writer is that the whole of his or her work is illuminated by its constituent parts, and vice versa: the macrocosm and the microcosm, as it were, are interdependent.

The second section hones in on particular poems as foci for close reading, or rather *explication de texte*. Again, the variousness of approach reflects that of the poet himself: as well as detailed analysis of a poem as a verbal construct, we have discussion of how composers have teased out a poem's detail in order to guide their non-literary treatment of it, as also considerations of how translators match (or mismatch!) one language with another as they negotiate the "transcreation" of the French original into English—and not necessarily "standard" English at that, but also into those registers (such as the Scots language and its own dialects), which deviate significantly from the standard.

All in all, this book aims to serve as both an introduction to the poet for those approaching his work for the first time—albeit with an existing level of competence in reading French—and a compendium of fresh and even unexpected insights. We have been fortunate in being able to assemble a team of established and distinguished Baudelaire scholars, as well as relative "newcomers" (though with expertise in adjacent fields). In many cases, our contributors are here extending and augmenting their earlier published scholarship, making it available to the new generations of readers who will be coming to the present volume.

In many ways, this book may be viewed as a complementary work to *The Cambridge Companion to Baudelaire* (2005), edited by Rosemary Lloyd, who in the present volume provides its first "context" essay, in a lucid and entertaining account of Baudelaire's place in the cultural matrix of his day. Lloyd is also the author of the acclaimed *Baudelaire's World* (2002), to which we would refer readers for further detail. One of the most surprising and striking allusions in Lloyd's essay is the reference to Jacques Offenbach's comic opera *Orphée aux enfers*, which dates from 1856, the year after Baudelaire's *Les Fleurs du mal*. One would not make an immediate and obvious association of Offenbach's rollicking vulgarity, the very essence of the Second Empire culture-lite that Baudelaire so despised, and the lofty refinement of our poet. But as Rosemary Lloyd shows, Baudelaire's call for art to deal with "la vie moderne" caused him to reject the stuffy traditional French neo-classicism which Offenbach, for his part, subjected to a hilarious send-up. (We should remember, too, that Baudelaire wrote an essay about the essence of laughter and recorded his appreciation of caricature, about which more is observed at the end of this preface.)

My own survey of the critical reception of Baudelaire's poetry points to those instances of calm percipience amidst the frenzy of establishment objection (and persecution of) *Les Fleurs du mal* from 1857 on. My account takes in responses to Baudelaire by later French poets, writers, and critics from Georges Rodenbach to Jean-Paul

Sartre and their successors, while noting the first stirrings of interest in the Anglo-Saxon world from the likes of Algernon Swinburne (an admirer) and Henry James (a detractor). There is also allusion to the German-speaking world and Rainer Maria Rilke's enthusiasm for Baudelaire and for the poem "Une Charogne" in particular, as well as to Russia and the strictures of a stern, aging Leo Tolstoy. Octavio Paz is quoted on Hispanic countries and their take on our poet.

In the first of her two essays in this volume, Beryl F. Schlossman takes, as a "critical lens" on the poet, perhaps his most often cited critic, Walter Benjamin, who interpreted Baudelaire "as a vector of history." Benjamin focused on Baudelaire as the pioneer poet of "la vie moderne," of that phenomenon we call the city, the metropolis, whose growth was accelerated by nineteenth-century capitalist development (which Baudelaire himself would have summed up as the realized concept he so loathed, "Progress"). In a rich and detailed argument, Schlossman pays particular attention to Benjamin's analysis of the poem "A une passante," with its vision of fleeting transcendence of human contact, not actual but merely potential, of loneliness and alienation in a crowd whose individual components lack common purpose and significance. Beryl F. Schlossman includes her own translation of "A une passante": she is a professor who—as Baudelaire would have put it—is promoted to the rank of poet. Another seasoned Baudelaire scholar, she is well-known for her books *The Orient of Style* (1991) and *Objects of Desire* (1999), where she deals with Baudelaire as a modernist in the company of his French contemporaries and those who came after him.

One of those contemporaries was the novelist Gustave Flaubert, and Kathryn Oliver Mills, who has written a book on Baudelaire and his great counterpart in the novel, is concerned with the ways in which the two writers advanced a modern aesthetic. The very title of her book, *Formal Revolution in the Work of Baudelaire and Flaubert* (2012) more than hints at just such an approach. For her essay in the present volume, Mills addresses Flaubert's major novels, *Madame Bovary* and *L'Education sentimentale*, but is especially concerned to advance his short story collection, *Trois contes* (1877) and Baudelaire's *Le Spleen de Paris* as two works that mark a distinct cultural turning point. Moreover, in discussing together a novelist and a poet, Mills is able to explore the relationships between poetry and prose within the work of both writers: Flaubert wrote "poetic" prose and Baudelaire wrote prose poems, one could say poems "reinvigorated" by prose. Intriguingly, she comments on Baudelaire's punning on vers (poetry) and vers (the plural form of ver, worm), in "Le Soleil"—with implications for "Une Charogne," where the poet (notoriously) ponders the decomposition of the future corpse of his lover.

We move into the section devoted to close readings with another crucial relationship between Baudelaire and another writer—this time, not so much a contemporary as an antecedent: Edgar Allan Poe. Lois Davis Vines' study of this literary pedigree comes first in this section, not only because of the tremendous cultural resonances that Baudelaire's Poe would generate, but also in view of the fact that the Frenchman's translations of the American were the first substantial marker of the former's career. Vines cites the dramatic nature of Baudelaire's discovery of Poe during his mid-twenties, when he experienced a "commotion singulière" on encountering an American writer who was otherwise unknown in France. Baudelaire went on to make versions of forty-five tales by Poe; they remain the standard French translations.

Beryl F. Schlossman returns with her explication de texte of "Le Cygne," that quintessential poem of the modern city. Here, she adds further detail to the theme she has pursued in her essay on Benjamin's Baudelaire. She draws attention to the poem's abrupt, dramatic beginning; its juxtaposition of modernity and antiquity (an antithesis, incidentally, that would be taken up by another poet of a metropolis, T. S. Eliot, who would go on to write a canonical essay on Baudelaire); displacement and exile. "Le Cygne" also raises questions of female experience and of "distant" cultures: readers can be referred to Schlossman's books *The Orient of Style* (1991) and *Objects of Desire* (1999)—see the Bibliography at the end of the present volume for details.

The next two chapters turn to abiding themes in Baudelaire's work, as summed up in single words—"spleen," "idéal," "correspondances"—and while these terms are examined here in specific poems, readers would be advised to think about how such motifs pervade other areas of Baudelaire's œuvre, in both the poetry and the prose. Maria Scott, the award-winning author of Baudelaire's *"Le Spleen de Paris": Shifting Perspectives* (2005), addresses herself to "spleen" and "idéal" in a concise, but probing, exploration of several poems, including some lesser-known pieces as "Le Parfum." Scott deploys a sound theoretical foundation derived from Jacques Lacan and linguist Roman Jakobson. For those of us who have agonized over what distinguishes metonymy from metaphor, Scott provides the most lucid explanation (with a wealth of examples) that we are ever likely to encounter.

David Evans presents a forensic analysis of the sonnet "Correspondances," whose title concept has served as a major entry point for many readers of Baudelaire and of those poets, especially the Symbolists, who came after him. However, Evans avoids such well-explored (and often oversimplified) lines of enquiry, preferring to treat the poem as a well-made work of art in its own right, and ingeniously demonstrates the complexities and subtleties of its versification. When Evans and I discussed his topic at the planning stage, it seemed to us that what he had in mind promised to be an invaluable pedagogic exercise, and so it has proved. Evans' essay (and, in a wider sense, his method) will yield considerable benefits to students and—dare we say it—to their professors.

To complement Evans' essay, readers are advised to consult Stanley Burnshaw's short line-by-line analysis of "Correspondances" in his *The Poem Itself* (1960); Evans, though, is far more probing and detailed.

Evans helpfully cites those scholars who have been best-placed to situate the poem in its wider contexts, such as its resonances elsewhere in Baudelaire's work and its influences on the later poets. Evans is himself the author of a 2004 book, which discusses Rimbaud and Mallarmé, both major post-Baudelairean figures, as well as Baudelaire himself: again consult the bibliography at the end of this volume.

"[…] Les couleurs et les sons se respondent": this, from a line in "Correspondances," signals Baudelaire's active interest in the visual arts and in music. Eminent Baudelaireans, such as Alison Fairlie, David Kelley, James Hiddleston, and David Carrier in his provocative *High Art: Charles Baudelaire and the Origins of Modern Painting* (1996), have drawn on their deep knowledge of Baudelaire's art criticism. Baudelaire displayed special affinities with the painter Eugène Delacroix, as in a stanza of his poem "Les Phares" and in much prose devoted to the artist. It is said that criticism analyzes, but that poetry (and, by extension, art) synthesizes: never the twain can meet. Such an attitude would reject Oscar Wilde's view of "the critic as artist." It would also reject Baudelaire's firm belief that poetry and criticism could be one—that (as mentioned earlier) even poetry and art criticism could be one:

> Je crois sincèrement que la meilleure critique est celle qui est amusante et poétique; non pas celle-ci, froide et algébrique, qui, sous prétexte de tout expliquer, n'a ni haine ni amour, et se dépouille volontairement de toute espèce de tempérament; mais,—un beau tableau étant la nature réfléchie par un artiste,—celle qui sera ce tableau réfléchi par un esprit intelligent et sensible. Ainsi le meilleur compte rendu d'un tableau pourra être un sonnet ou une élégie ("Salon de 1846," Baudelaire, *Ecrits esthétiques* 103).

It was in commenting on the sonnet form, in a letter to Armand Fraisse of February 18, 1860, that Baudelaire made one of his most memorable remarks on how a visual image could be most effectively represented. Here, there seems to be no frontier between the verbal and the visual:

> Parce que la forme est contraignante, l'idée jaillit plus intense. Tout va bien au Sonnet, la bouffonnerie, la galanterie, la passion, la rêverie, la méditation philosophique. Il y a là la beauté du métal et du minéral bien travaillés. Avez-vous observé qu'un morceau de ciel, aperçu par un soupirail, ou entre deux cheminées, deux rochers, ou par une arcade, etc., donnait une idée plus profonde de l'infini que le grand panorama vu du haut d'une montagne? (Baudelaire, *Correspondances* 196).

That Scottish doyenne of Baudelaire studies, Alison Fairlie (Fairlie 31), as well as subsequent scholars, have linked this passage to Baudelaire's perceptions, in his "Salon de 1859":

Je ne veux pas quitter cet aimable artiste [the now little-known Penguilly d'Haridon], dont tous les tableaux, cette année, sont également intéressants, sans vous faire remarquer plus particulièrement les Petites Mouettes : l'azur intense du ciel et de l'eau, deux quartiers de roche qui font une porte ouverte sur l'infini (vous savez que l'infini paraît plus profond quand il est plus resserré) (Baudelaire 328).

In our volume, Frances Fowle, who is a much-published curator at the National Galleries of Scotland, where she specializes in nineteenth- and twentieth-century French and Scottish art, guides us through "Les Phares," Baudelaire's praise-poem to the great artists: indeed, the poem is the verbal equivalent of an art gallery, a *catalogue raisonné* in verse. Delacroix in particular was a great example of what Baudelaire called "l'universalité," not only "un peintre complet" but "un homme complet," who embraced the "ténébreuse et profonde unité" of that line in "Correspondances," who possessed an integrative vision in contrast to the fashionable trivialities of so much prevailing Second Empire art. Delacroix was indeed a role model for Baudelaire—a true "phare." The English novelist E. M. Forster (of *A Passage to India*) adapted Baudelaire's poem to his own gentler vision: for him, art "is the one orderly product which our muddling race has produced. It is the cry of a thousand sentinels, the echo from a thousand labyrinths; it is the lighthouse which cannot be hidden" (Forster 100). Forster liked to posit his "aristocracy of the sensitive, the considerate and the plucky" against "the vast armies of the benighted."

Our second art-historical perspective is contributed by Juliet Simpson, a specialist in French art, visual culture, and art criticism; she has a particular interest in Symbolism, which, as observed above, owed so much to Baudelaire. Simpson's essay focuses on Baudelaire's best-known piece of art criticism, "Le Peintre de la vie moderne," where the poet concentrates on the work of Constantin

Guys. Simpson argues that Baudelaire "places Guys as innovator at the limits of a Romantic view of art, who takes trivial materials and ephemera only to transfigure them into experiences that are not merely transient, but synthetic and visionary." This point, in particular (as indeed Simpson's discussion generally), is crucial to an understanding of Baudelaire as art critic—and as poet.

Randolph Paul Runyon addresses himself to those of Baudelaire's poems which have music as their theme or at least as a major theme. His discussion proceeds in the context of Baudelaire's insights into the music of Richard Wagner, the subject of an essay from 1861. Baudelaire, who corresponded with the composer, was intrigued by the visual suggestiveness of Wagner's aural art. Runyon's book *Intratextual Baudelaire: The Sequential Fabric of the Fleurs du mal and Spleen de Paris* (2010) argues for the unity and cohesion of *Les Fleurs du mal* as against those who persist in seeing the book as a rag-bag of unrelated pieces. Baudelaire's collection, then, even when one takes into account the poems added to later editions, can reveal (on closer examination) what Barbey d'Aurevilly called an "architecture sécrète." In this volume, Runyon develops his ongoing argument that Baudelaire's discussion of the subtle structural and thematic patterns to be discerned in music (and in the visual arts) can be related to Wagner's "leitmotifs" (as they came to be called)—musical phrases, I would add, that suggested certain psychological conditions—that corresponded, as it were, to emotional temperatures. The "leitmotif," the sequence of notes, would undergo metamorphoses, according to the substantial or slight changes in those psychological / emotional temperatures. All this gave coherence—"concaténation," as conceptualized by Baudelaire, to a work of art (in essence, what Barbey meant by "architecture secrete"—or, for that matter, what I have been calling integrative vision in relation to both Baudelaire and Delacroix).

I would add further that this is strikingly and ironically echoed, in effect, by the Russian novelist Leo Tolstoy. Ironically—because Tolstoy despised the works of both Baudelaire and Wagner, dismissing them as variously perverse, decadent, pretentious if not downright pernicious. In his private correspondence during the

1870s (after Baudelaire's death and during the period when Wagner's masterpiece, *The Ring of the Nibelung* cycle, was premièred), Tolstoy spoke of a "labyrinth of linkages," of connections, which to him was the essence of art (Greenwood 95). Moreover, in answer to a correspondent who, otherwise admiring, had felt that *Anna Karenina* lacked a coherent structure, Tolstoy protested: "On the contrary, I am proud of the architecture—the arches have been constructed in such a way that it is impossible to see where the keystone is. And that is what I was striving for most of all. The structural line is not the plot or the relationship of the characters [...], but an inner link" (Christian 202).

This digression on Tolstoy is essentially a footnote to Randolph Paul Runyon's argument. His essay demonstrates that, every so often, we can profitably read Baudelaire through the lenses of other great figures in the arts of the nineteenth century.

Helen Abbott continues the musical theme, if from the other direction: after music's impact on Baudelaire, we have Baudelaire's impact on musicians. Abbott guides us along both the highways and byways of Baudelaire-based song-settings, through Henri Duparc's much performed (and much recorded) "L'Invitation au voyage" from his several settings of the poet, Claude Debussy's *Cinque poèmes de Baudelaire*, the chansonnier Léo Ferré's mid/late- twentieth century versions (and performances), to—fascinatingly—Alexander Gretchaninov's two versions of "Harmonie du soir" (one in the original French, the other in a Russian translation!), the American experimental composer Ruth White and the contemporary French musican BabX ("La Mort des amants," of 2010). In Abbott's essay we gain a better understanding of French song as both mélodie and chanson (which might be crudely rendered in English as "art" and "popular" song, respectively, though the distinction can often be happily blurred, not least in the case of Léo Ferré). This essay also provokes us into thinking more generally about the relationships between words and music. For further reading, please consult Abbott's two recent books, cited in the bibliography.

Song-settings are a form of "translation," other than the more usual verbal-to-verbal relationships by which we normally understand that term. Mario Relich and James W. Underhill address themselves to translation as more conventionally defined, but both scholars offer us no shortage of surprises and are intent on widening the range of concepts—and examples—for this particular area of Baudelaire studies.

In choosing for his examples of translators—a South African (Roy Campbell), a New Englander (Robert Lowell), and a Scot (James Robertson)—Mario Relich draws on a wide range of cultural backgrounds; there is the Catholicism of converts along the way, and, intriguingly, Relich points to a transposition from a French Catholic culture to a Scottish Calvinist one in Robertson's Scots versions of Baudelaire. Relich considers such concepts as metaphrase, paraphrase, and imitation, as well as their modulation into "translation with latitude" and "translation with attitude." Early in his essay, Mario Relich cites Laurence Lerner's rendering of Baudelaire's lines "Je suis un vieux boudoir plein de roses fanées / Où gît tout un fouillis de modes surannées" ("Spleen II") as "I am the room in which Miss Havisham / Sits brooding and remembering." The reference is to the abandoned bride who became a faded, crazy old maid in Charles Dickens' novel *Great Expectations*, which appeared only a few years after *Les Fleurs du mal*. Dickens and Baudelaire are not often invoked together, perhaps largely due to their very different cultural backgrounds, but it is otherwise odd that comparisons are so rarely made. After all, they were the great portrayers of the nineteenth-century city, be that Paris or London. In his *Romantic Image* (1957), however, Frank Kermode has made this valuable observation:

> [Baudelaire's] mythology is of the perversion, the ennui, the metaphysical despair of men and women subjected to what Dickens (in this respect Baudelaire's English equivalent—compare *Le crépuscule du matin* with certain passages in *Little Dorrit*) called 'the shame, desertion, wretchedness and exposure of the great capital (Kermode 17).

James W. Underhill writes as a practicing translator who, like James Robertson, has gone back to his native Scots tongue; it's a question of being able to capture something of what can elude standard English in attempts to get to grips with both the horror and humor of Baudelaire's poetry. Underhill demonstrates a particular interest in tackling the prose poems. He has robust points to make about where translation (and interpretation) can go wrong, as well as where it (they) can go right—note, in particular, his introduction of the term "the Swinburne syndrome." He can praise those translators who manage to avoid "mistakenly elevating and intellectualizing Baudelaire," who offer us an Englished Baudelaire "that sings with the angels while strolling in the gutters." Like Helen Abbott, Underhill cites the translation theorist Lawrence Venuti; to follow this up, one should check out Underhill's published work on translation in general and Venuti in particular.

The last poem in the later editions of *Les Fleurs du mal* is "Le Voyage," the subject of Edward K. Kaplan's closing essay. In his monograph on Russian novelist Nikolai Gogol (1944; 1961), Vladimir Nabokov—always vigorous in his judgments—declared: "I have a lasting grudge against those who like their fiction to be educational or uplifting, or national, or as healthy as maple syrup or olive oil" (Nabokov 42). It's hard to imagine Baudelaire favoring such worthy natural fare over his *paradis artificiels*. He'd have endorsed Nabokov's comment, as applied to poetry (well, almost). Baudelaire, notably, recoiled at moral intention in art; in his *William Blake* (1868), Algernon Swinburne—Baudelaire's loquacious English admirer—quoted "the heresy of instruction (*l'hérésie de l'enseignement*): one might call it, for the sake of a shorter and more summary name, the great moral heresy." However, in his breathless zeal to accommodate Baudelaire to his own less subtle agendas, Swinburne oversimplified Baudelaire: "Art is not like fire or water, a good servant and bad master; rather the reverse. [...] Handmaid of religion, exponent of duty, servant of fact, pioneer of morality, she cannot in any way become; she would be none of these things though you were to bray her in a mortar" (Swinburne 90–92). Baudelaire's position was far more nuanced and sophisticated. In his writings on Baudelaire, in the present volume and going as far back as 1978, Kaplan has been concerned with matters of ethics and faith and how these are negotiated in the poetry. "Le Voyage" is that poem, above all, where Baudelaire can be reclaimed for existentialism, albeit of the Christian variety, which the poet's notorious twentieth-century detractor, Jean-Paul Sartre, would have scorned. Indeed, the very title of Kaplan's study, *Baudelaire's Prose Poems: The Esthetic, the Ethical and the Religious in "The Parisian Prowler"* (1990), indicates the famous three "stages" on life's way as propounded by the great Christian existentialist Søren Kierkegaard. In his essay for the present book, together with much else of considerable depth, Edward K. Kaplan suggests further the enharmonics, as it were, of Baudelaire's poetry and Kierkegaard's philosophical (many would say, anti-philosophical) essays and journals.

Baudelaire and Kierkegaard are also linked by virtue of the former's concept of "le grotesque comique absolu" in his essay "De l'essence du rire," his admiration of caricature, and the latter's ever-evident sense of irony. The two men did not come into their own until well into the twentieth century, with its particular anxieties, its need to find faith in an increasingly faithless world, its desperation in "overcoming despair." German writer Thomas Mann, in a 1926 essay on the novelist Joseph Conrad, made this arresting comment:

> I feel that, broadly and essentially, the striking feature of modern art is that it has ceased to recognise the categories of tragic and comic, or the dramatic classifications, tragedy, and comedy. It sees life as tragi-comedy, with the result that the grotesque is its most genuine style—to the extent, indeed, that to-day that is the only guise in which the sublime may appear (Mann 106).

He could have been talking about the writings of Kierkegaard—and of Baudelaire.

Note
Readers are advised to take note of emerging Baudelaire scholars: among the names to watch are Damian Catani, Greg Kerr, and Francesco Manzini.

Works Cited

Baudelaire, Charles. *Correspondances. Choix et présentation de Claude Pichois et Jérôme Thélot*. Paris: Gallimard, 2000.

_____. *Ecrits esthétiques. Préface de Jean-Christophe Bailly*. Paris: 10/18, 1986.

Carrier, David. *High Art: Charles Baudelaire and the Origins of Modernist Painting*. University Park, PA: Pennsylvania State UP, 1996.

Christian, R. F. *Tolstoy: A Critical Introduction*. Cambridge, England: Cambridge UP, 1969.

Fairlie, Alison. "Aspects of Expression in Baudelaire's Art Criticism." *French Nineteenth Century Painting and Literature*. Ed. Ulrich Finke. Manchester, UK: Manchester UP, 1972: 40–64.

Forster, E. M. *Two Cheers for Democracy*. Harmondsworth, UK: Penguin, 1965.

Greenwood, E. B. *Tolstoy: The Comprehensive Vision*. London: Methuen, 1980.

Kermode, Frank. *Romantic Image*. London: Collins Fontana, 1971.

Mann, Thomas. "Joseph Conrad's The Secret Agent." *Conrad: The Secret Agent: A Casebook*. Ed. Ian P. Watt. London: Macmillan, 1973: 99–112.

Nabokov, Vladimir. *Nikolai Gogol*. Corrected ed. New York: New Directions, 1961.

Swinburne, Algernon. *William Blake: A Critical Essay*. London: Heinemann, 1925.

THE BOOK
AND
AUTHOR

On Charles Baudelaire

Tom Hubbard

Sometimes, in offering an overall account of a writer's career, it can be helpful to indicate not so much what kind of a writer he is, but what kind he is not.

So let's start there. In the present volume, Kathryn Oliver Mills has made illuminating comparisons of Baudelaire with his great contemporary in the novel, Flaubert; we can take a briefer look at a writer whose debut came in the year of Baudelaire's death. Émile Zola's first novel *Thérèse Raquin* was published in 1867; he would go on, over succeeding decades, to chronicle—albeit retrospectively— the years of the Second Empire, that period within which Baudelaire made his (troubled) reputation. Baudelaire and Zola have in common an unflinching response to the mediocrity and corruption of Napoléon III's France, but the resemblances don't go far.

Thérèse Raquin tells the story of a sexual triangle—of the fiercely sensuous Thérèse, her weak, mama's-boy husband Camille, and her lover, the brutal, bull-like Laurent. During a boating trip, Laurent—with the collusion of Thérèse—disposes of Camille in the waters of the Seine. Unbridled erotic delights seem to be in prospect for the murderous pair who, however, end up as savagely hostile to each other, ultimately agreeing only in their choice of a double suicide.

Zola sought to write novels with a new, professedly scientific method that would come to be called Naturalism, and which he himself described as the undertaking of "le roman expérimental." For Zola, the novelist was working in a virtual laboratory, analyzing the biochemical nature of his characters; observing their interactions like the experimental scientist with his specimens, test-tubes, and microscopes; and coolly and objectively noting the results.

In the grip of a neurotic uncertainty as to whether Camille is really dead, and, as if impelled by psychological forces over which he has no control, Laurent visits the morgue where his victim is laid out:

Camille était ignoble. Il avait séjourné quinze jours dans l'eau. Sa face paraissait encore ferme et rigide; les traits s'étaient conservés, la peau avait seulement pris une teinte jaunâtre et boueuse. La tête, maigre, osseuse, légèrement tuméfiée, grimaçait; elle se penchait un peu, les cheveux collés aux tempes, les paupières levées, montrant le globe blafard des yeux: les lèvres tordues, tirées vers un des coins de la bouche, avaient un ricanement atroce; un bout de langue noirâtre apparaissait dans la blancheur des dents. Cette tête, comme tannée et étirée, en gardant une apparence humaine, était restée plus effrayante de douleur et d'épouvante. Le corps semblait un tas de chairs dissoutes; il avait souffert horriblement. On sentait que les bras ne tenaient plus; les clavicules perçaient la peau des épaules. Sur la poitrine verdâtre, les côtes faisaient des bandes noires; le flanc gauche, crevé, ouvert, se creusait au milieu de lambeaux d'un rouge sombre. Tout le torse pourrissait. Les jambes, plus fermes, s'allongeaient, plaquées de taches immondes. Les pieds tombaient (119–120).

Apart from such intrusions of subjectivity as "ignoble," "atroce," or "horriblement," the tone is on the whole detached, telling it as it is and no more. Contrast this with these opening stanzas from Baudelaire's "Une Charogne," where the poet/lover and his mistress also find themselves in an encounter with death in all its physicality:

Rappelez-vous l'objet que nous vîmes, mon âme,
  Ce beau matin d'été si doux:
Au détour d'un sentier une charogne infâme
  Sur un lit semé de cailloux,

Les jambes en l'air, comme une femme lubrique,
  Brûlante et suant les poisons,
Ouvrait d'une façon nonchalante et cynique
  Son ventre plein d'exhalaisons.

Le soleil rayonnait sur cette pourriture,
  Comme afin de la cuire à point,
Et de rendre au centuple à la grande Nature
  Tout ce qu'ensemble elle avait joint;
                    (Baudelaire 1975-76: 31, Lines 1-12)

And here are the concluding stanzas:

— Et pourtant vous serez semblable à cette ordure,
  À cette horrible infection,
Etoile de mes yeux, soleil de ma nature,
  Vous, mon ange et ma passion!

Oui! telle vous serez, ô la reine des grâces,
  Apres les derniers sacrements,
Quand vous irez, sous l'herbe et les floraisons grasses,
  Moisir parmi les ossements.

Alors, ô ma beauté! dites à la vermine
  Qui vous mangera de baisers,
Que j'ai gardé la forme et l'essence divine
  De mes amours décomposés!
(32, Lines 37-48)

This is not "objective" observation so much as unashamedly subjective transformation. The very corpse itself is an actor in this drama, unlike Zola's Camille lying inertly on a slab: images tumble over each other, with a kind of life-in-death; obscene similes ("comme une femme lubrique") pervade the poem. The final stanzas can still shock, as much as by the boldness of that conflation of beauty and corruption as by the sheer horror: any writer can do horror, but boldness is rarer. When we compare "Une Charogne" with the passage from *Thérèse Raquin*, we note in the former a greater power of—imagination.

That's a key word in the mind and art of Charles Baudelaire. The English poet Coleridge had referred to "the shaping spirit of imagination"; Baudelaire, in essence, includes that concept, but goes further. Of all our human resources, imagination reigned quite regally supreme:

Mystérieuse faculté que cette reine des facultés! Elle touche à toutes les autres; elle les excite, elle les envoie au combat. Elle leur ressemble quelquefois au point de se confondre avec elles, et cependant elle est toujours bien elle-même, et les hommes qu'elle n'agite pas sont facilement reconnaissables à je ne sais quelle malédiction qui dessèche leurs productions comme le figuier de l'Évangile.

Elle est l'analyse, elle est la synthèse ; et cependant des hommes habiles dans l'analyse et suffisamment aptes à faire un résumé peuvent être privés d'imagination. Elle est cela, et elle n'est pas tout à fait cela.

Elle est la sensibilité, et pourtant il y a des personnes très-sensibles, trop sensibles peut-être, qui en sont privées. C'est l'imagination qui a enseigné à l'homme le sens moral de la couleur, du contour, du son et du parfum. Elle a créé, au commencement du monde, l'analogie et la métaphore. Elle décompose toute la création, et, avec les matériaux amassés et disposés suivant des règles dont on ne peut trouver l'origine que dans le plus profond de l'âme, elle crée un monde nouveau, elle produit la sensation du neuf (Baudelaire, "Salon de 1859," *Curiosités esthétiques* 274).

The possessor of imagination is not content simply to point out, dully and literal-mindedly, that which already exists: "En décrivant ce qui est, le poète se degrade et descend au rang de professeur" (Baudelaire, "Victor Hugo," *L'Art romantique* 314).

It is curious that, by this line of reasoning, Baudelaire could dismiss the emerging art of photography as no art at all. Curious, because he was friendly with one of the great photographers of his day, Nadar; and another photographer, Eugène Carjat, has left us the most haunting image of Baudelaire—much stronger, surely, than Courbet's painted portrait: black-and-white, too, winning out over that which was so prized by the poet—color. Baudelaire could not have foreseen how, by the end of the nineteenth century, photography would indeed call for as much compositional skill, as much visual ingenuity, as was traditionally associated with painting. But his point, in 1859, was that photography merely captured the surface of things; it lacked the shaping spirit; it could not probe, it could not create; it limited itself to "ce qui est." Similar charges, after Baudelaire's death, would be laid against Zola and the Naturalists; yet Zola did, after all, possess, and indeed deploy, a powerful imagination—in spite of his dogmatic pronouncements on sticking to "scientific" transcription. After reading *Germinal* (1885), his novel of the lives of those who toiled and struggled in the coalfields of northern France, no-one could easily forget this image of the pit:

> Au loin, les hauts fourneaux et les fours à coke avaient pâli avec l'aube. Il ne restait là, sans un arrêt, que l'échappement de la pompe, soufflant toujours de la meme haleine grosse et longue, l'haleine d'un ogre dont il distinguait la buée grise maintenant, et que rien ne pouvait repaître. [...] ce dieu repu et accroupi, auquel dix mille affamés donnaient leur chair, sans le connaître (78).

It's as strong as Charles Dickens' vision, in his earlier industrial novel *Hard Times* (1854), of the piston of a steam-engine working "monotonously up and down like the head of an elephant in a state of melancholy madness." Zola's mine as a god, to which men and women (and children) are sacrificed is surely as much a product of "imagination [...] cette reine des facultes" as, say, Baudelaire's evocations of "le gouffre," of nineteenth-century despoliation and alienation in a poem like "Le Cygne." Baudelaire's hapless birds— his swan, his albatross—are also sacrificial victims offered up to a brutally uncomprehending, narrowly materialistic world. Perhaps Baudelaire and Zola are not so far apart after all. Literary argument, like literature itself, can take strange turns.

Strange indeed. "*Le beau*," declared Baudelaire, "*est toujours bizarre.*" (Baudelaire, *Curiosités esthétiques* 224). The italics are his. He continues:

> Je ne veux pas dire qu'il soit volontairement, froidement bizarre, car dans ce cas il serait un monstre sorti des rails de la vie. Je dis qu'il contient toujours un peu de bizarrerie, de bizarrerie naïve, non voulue, inconsciente, et que c'est cette bizarrerie qui le fait être particulièrement le Beau (Baudelaire, *Curiosités esthétiques* 224).

In a prose passage of the following year, 1856—i.e. a year before the appearance of *Les Fleurs du mal*, that *cause célèbre* of all poetry collections: "[...] l'irrégularité, c'est-à-dire l'inattendu, la surprise, l'étonnement sont une partie essentielle et la caractéristique de la beauté" (Baudelaire, *Œuvres complètes* 656). Such statements of aesthetic faith would explain why Baudelaire became a guru for the Symbolist poets who would come after him (they also anticipate the Surrealists); it is of more immediate interest, though, that they reflect his enthusiasm for Edgar Allan Poe, whose tales he had recently translated and whose critical essays he took as almost holy writ. But the bizarre, the irregular, and the shocking all mark the artist as an awkward cuss who thumbs his nose at the humdrum predictability of that philistine bourgeoisie, which so smugly flourished during the reign of Napoléon III (as under the previous régime, hardly less meretricious, of Baudelaire's early years). Poe served as a useful analog, as the American writer was seen by Baudelaire as having been martyred by the crass, go-getting *mœurs* of his own country.

The poet, like the albatross in one of Baudelaire's best-known pieces, is an exile (a key concept, to which we must return): his gifts disable him from fitting comfortably into the quotidian round of mid-century capitalism, with those who—as Oscar Wilde was to put it—know the price of everything and the value of nothing. Baudelaire had been on the barricades, a revolutionary of 1848, but had come to despise democracy altogether: the working-class and socialism were as grubbily materialistic as the bourgeoisie and capitalism. Such sentiments were shared by his friend and fellow-sufferer from the censors, Gustave Flaubert, who, writing to the Russian novelist Turgenev in 1872, confessed that "J'ai toujours tâché de vivre dans une tour d'ivoire. Mais une mare de merde en bat les murs, à la faire crouler" (Flaubert 605). Baudelaire was ambivalent towards another great contemporary: conscious of the power of Victor Hugo's work, he could not share the belief in "Progress" of such a supremely *engagé* writer. Hugo was the target of much sarcastic comment by Baudelaire. Here was one exile who yet had become a national institution, an impossible status for another exile, Baudelaire, to attain even if he wished it. Every substantial French town has its Place Victor-Hugo; one searches with difficulty for a Place Charles-Baudelaire.

Baudelaire is generally recognized as the first poet of what we call modernity, especially in his representation of the city in its metropolitan complexity, the loneliness of the crowd, and its individual members. Poe, virtually imprisoned in "une grande barbarie éclairée au gaz" (Baudelaire, *Histoires extraordinaires* ix), dying drunk and alone in Baltimore, was a precursor (though as prose-writer rather than poet). The American writer set his "The Man in the Crowd" not in the more obviously lonely spaces of the prairie (which, of course, lacks crowds) but in London, which in turn became the locus of Dickens' novels; St. Petersburg would likewise be located on the literary map by Dostoyevsky, whose fictional murderer Raskolnikov in *Crime and Punishment* (1866) is a haunted intellectual, the solitary holder of a dark secret, wandering neurotically through teeming streets of folk going about their everyday banalities. As for Poe's "man of the crowd," he inhabits one of the *Limbos* (border areas, No-Man's-Lands), the term Baudelaire used for the original title of *Les Fleurs du mal* (Keogh 27).

Throughout the present volume, critic Walter Benjamin is much invoked, in particular by Beryl F. Schlossman; he is the Baudelaire commentator who, above all, has presented the poet to us in all his urban modernity. Benjamin's celebrated analysis of "À une passante," for many, reinforces the visual analog that can be discerned in the paintings of the Impressionists; these came to the fore in the decades following Baudelaire's death—in particular, the Parisian scenes of Camille Pissarro, with their bustle of horse-drawn traffic and faces never seen clearly that seem to flicker and are gone. "Ailleurs, bien loin d'ici! trop tard! jamais peut-être! / Car j'ignore où tu fuis, tu ne sais où je vais, / Ô toi que j'eusse aimée, ô toi qui le savais!" ("A une passante," Baudelaire, *Œuvres complètes* 92–3, lines 12–14). Baudelaire had set out these views in "Le Peintre de la vie moderne": "La modernité, c'est le transitoire, le fugitif, le contingent, la moitié de l'art, dont l'autre moitié est l'éternel et immuable." (*L'Art romantique* 66). He did not live to see and judge the example offered by the Impressionists.

There is also the ambivalent nature of his relationship to romanticism. English Romantic poets, such as William Wordsworth, lauded nature in both its grand and small manifestations—his poem "Daffodils" is an example of the latter. For his part, Baudelaire drily remarked that he could not get sentimental about vegetables. Baudelaire preferred the artificial to the natural, dedicated as he was to stressing the first syllable of the former. And of course, as a city poet, he was more concerned with the grim lives represented in such poems as "Les Petites vieilles" and "Les Sept vieillards" than with the grandeur of mountains and villages. For Baudelaire, "La Nature" was rather a dictionary where the poet could look up "confuses paroles," where man could wander through "forêts de symbols" (*Œuvres complètes* 11, line 3) rather than forests in a literal sense.

What, though, of the figure of the archetypal "poet" as articulated in the decades preceding Baudelaire? Again, we can turn to the English Romantics. In his "Kubla Khan," Samuel Taylor Coleridge saw the poet as bard, seer, prophet, almost a god to be worshipped: "Weave a circle round him thrice / And close your eyes with holy dread / For he on honey-dew hath fed / And drunk the milk of paradise." For Percy Bysshe Shelley, a more earthly political trope is preferred: poets, he asserts, are "the unacknowledged legislators of the world." ("Defence of Poetry," 1821, the year of Baudelaire's birth.)

Baudelaire's view of the poet / artist as "Exilé sur le sol au milieu des huées" ("L'Albatros," *Œuvres complètes* 10, line 15), echoes Shelley—that is to say, in the sense of those who are "unacknowledged" rather than able to attract the closed-eyed "holy dread" due to Coleridge's venerable, bard-like figure. The mid-nineteenth century Parisian "foule" isn't going to buy such unprofitable goods. Baudelaire provides a link, a bridge, between the Shelleyan-Romantic poet-icon and the modern notion of the artist/intellectual as an alien in society, an outsider, in a distinctly grimmer, unromantic and even anti-romantic sense. In his book on the twentieth-century French writer Albert Camus in the present "Critical Insights" series, Steven G. Kellman quotes from Edward Said's 1993 public lectures, "Representations of the Intellectual." An intellectual is not quite the same thing as a poet, of course, but the most challenging poets have tended also to be intellectuals. Said describes "the intellectual as outsider" as someone who is in a plight that "is best exemplified by the condition of exile, the state of never being fully adjusted, always feeling outside the chatty, familiar world inhabited by natives, so to speak, tending to avoid and even dislike the trappings of accommodation and well-being. Exile for the intellectual in its metaphysical sense is restlessness, movement, constantly being unsettled, and unsettling others. You cannot go back to some earlier and perhaps more stable condition of being at home, and, alas, you can never fully arrive, be at one with your new home or situation" (Said 373; Kellman 4). As more than hinted above, this is a condition closer to the experience of Baudelaire than to Hugo. Baudelaire was not only an *exil* but also an *étranger*.

It would be fair to say that Baudelaire was both a romantic and an anti-romantic: fascinating for us, but painful for him. That said, as he grew older, he became more of the latter and less of the former—a commonplace experience, one might say: most of us lose our illusions as we get older and settle down into a safe, if moderately boring, lifestyle, sharing our neighbors' opinions on this and that. Some of us don't, though, and it's difficult to imagine Baudelaire sinking into bourgeois contentment and grey-haired venerability. Whether his was a late-romantic or anti-romantic form of dissent is probably irrelevant: Beryl F. Schlossman (1991) prefers to call his poetry *trans-romantic*, that is to say that Baudelaire took the basic terms of romanticism but transformed them. The revolutionary of 1848 became the dour prophet of *spleen* and *ennui*; the *idéal* remains as part of that trinity, against which the other two serve as counterfoil. *Spleen* and *ennui* have in common a spirit-sapping lassitude; the *idéal* involves energy (the ideal woman, for the poet, is not some anaemic, conventionally pretty fashion model, but a sexily-wicked force, such as Lady Macbeth ["L'Idéal," *Œuvres complètes* 22]). All three parts of Baudelaire's "trinity" operate in a manner that's dark and deep. *Ennui* means more than an everyday, banal boredom; it's rather a spiritual condition, a disease of the soul. (Edward K. Kaplan, a contributor to the present volume, has pointed out that "mal" in the title of Baudelaire's collection can mean not only "evil," but also "affliction" [Kaplan 93]).

In the opening chapter of his book, *In Bluebeard's Castle: Some Notes Towards a Redefinition of Culture* (1971), George Steiner argues that "a corrosive ennui" is as much a feature of nineteenth-century culture as the "dynamic optimism" of the believers in Progress—of those earlier romantics and revolutionaries on the one hand, and the ever-triumphalist, industrializing technocrats and entrepreneurs on the other. Steiner sees the disillusionment of the intelligentsia setting in much earlier than 1848—in 1815, rather, following Napoléon I's defeat at Waterloo:

> How can an intellectual bear to feel within himself something of Bonaparte's genius, something of that demonic strength [see Lady Macbeth, above—TH] which led from obscurity to empire, and see before him nothing but the tawdry flatness of bureaucracy? Raskolnikov [in Dostoyevsky's *Crime and Punishment*] writes his essay on Napoleon and goes out to kill an old woman (22).

Steiner continues by drawing attention to Baudelaire's so often like-minded contemporary, Flaubert, and to that novelist's obsession with a savage, even sadistic past, as a welcome antidote to the sheltered tedium of the affluent present. "One should have known," writes Steiner in a tone that might be described as retrospectively ominous, "that *ennui* was breeding detailed fantasies of nearing catastrophe. Most of what has occurred since has its specific origins in the tensions of nineteenth-century society [...]" (26). Though it homes in (17–18) illuminatingly on Baudelaire's *Spleen* poem beginning "J'ai plus de souvenirs que si j'avais mille ans," George Steiner's book is not a monograph on our poet, but it doesn't need to be: it rather provides an expansive context, in which we can profitably read Baudelaire in (and beyond) his poetry.

Spleen—Baudelaire uses the English word—is, as often as not, coupled with *ennui*, not necessarily in company with the third part of the trinity: as the term for a part of the body notorious for nasty sensations (real or imagined), it suggests a certain physicality to complement the vaguer, more abstract notion of *ennui*. Baudelaire's best-known *spleen* poem is the one beginning "Je suis comme le roi d'un pays pluvieux" (*Œuvres complètes* 74). It can serve as a fitting companion piece to the *spleen* poem discussed by George Steiner, as cited above. The imagery, however, is very different. "J'ai plus de souvenirs" commences with musty, domestic details—a chest of drawers stuffed with documents—before it proceeds to more sinister or exotic tropes, though the chest of drawers is likened to a "pyramide," as if in anticipation of the "Saharah brumeux" and "vieux sphinx ignoré du monde insoucieux" at the poem's conclusion (*Œuvres complètes* 73, lines 6, 21, 22). Certainly, "Je suis comme le roi" continues "l'humeur farouche" (line 23) associated with the sphinx, but in this poem we're presented with the trappings of the Middle Ages—falconry, the court jester, the gold-making alchemist—as also with a backward glance at the horrors of imperial Rome. The king, old before his time, cannot relieve his weariness even with sadistic decrees or lustful congress with the ladies of the court. "Ce jeune squelette" (line 12) may link intertextually with the hanged man, in "Un Voyage à Cythère," whose rotting corpse is consumed, bit by bit, by predatory birds: the poet / king in "Je suis comme le roi" may be (to quote another Baudelaire poem, "L'Héautontimoroumenos") both "victime" and his own "bourreau" (Baudelaire, *Œuvres complètes* 78, line 24).

There has been much comment on how Hugo and Baudelaire compare in the way they represent the medieval world—albeit the mythical rather than the actual medieval world. There are suggestions that, in the smaller-scale compass of his poetic *œuvre*, Baudelaire achieves this more intensely than does Hugo on the ample canvas of his novel *Notre-Dame de Paris*, with the great cathedral looming larger than it does in actual fact, Quasimodo with his bells, the teeming, stinking alleyways of the old city long before the demolition work of the mid-nineteenth century. One might suggest, at the very least, that "Je suis comme le roi" offers a distillation of the sinister Gothic ambience of Hugo's famous novel. Behind this poem, though, is not so much the still-living example of Hugo as the ghost of Poe. Had Poe been as accomplished a poet as he was short-story writer, and had French rather than English been his native language, "Je suis comme le roi" is the poem he would have written.

In this volume, Mario Relich discusses James Robertson's inventive version—in the Scots language—of the poem. There is much in the corpus of Scottish literature that reveals striking affinities with Baudelaire's sensibility. The most original and influential Scottish poet of the twentieth century, Hugh MacDiarmid (1892–1978), is the third subject of my short book *The Integrative Vision* (1997), which I based on lectures at Glasgow School of Art; it dealt with poets who enjoyed a significant relationship with the visual arts. The MacDiarmid chapter followed those devoted to Baudelaire and Rilke. In a 1923 essay, MacDiarmid wrote of "the unique blend of the lyrical and the ludicrous in primitive Scots sentiment [...] the reconciliation it effects between the base and the beautiful, recognizing that they are complementary and indispensable to each other." (MacDiarmid, *Thistle Rises* 130–31). It's not that "unique"— leave out the reference to the Scots and you are in the territory of Baudelaire's critical theory and poetic practice. MacDiarmid tacitly admits the universality of his own aesthetic in citing his appreciation of a number of German poets "for the sake of a certain Gothicity on the role of *grotesquerie* in revitalizing phases of literature [...] (MacDiarmid, *Lucky Poet* 46–47). Again, MacDiarmid–who was not unfamiliar with Baudelaire's poetry—could have been describing the Frenchman's work. MacDiarmid was often given to quoting G. Gregory Smith's *Scottish Literature: Character and Influence* (1919), where that critic refers to a "medieval" quality in Scottish literature, in its juxtaposition of extremes: "a gargoyle's grinning at the elbow of a kneeling saint" (Smith 35). Certainly in the poetry of the medieval Scottish writers, such as Robert Henryson, we can discern a laconic blend of humor and horror. In Baudelaire, that derives from Poe and also from his own "medieval" awareness of the transitoriness of sinful human lives.

To cite the Scottish affinities is not to deny that the features in question may also link Baudelaire with the greatest of Englishmen, Shakespeare. We've encountered "L'Idéal" and the poet's erotic-sadistic interest in Lady Macbeth; writing to Baudelaire in 1862, the dying poet Alfred de Vigny expressed general admiration for *Les Fleurs du mal* but found it "empoisonné quelquefois par je ne sais quelques émanations du cimetière de Hamlet" (Pichois 382). This refers to Hamlet holding the skull of the court jester Yorick and uttering his own grim jests of the graveyard, its stinks, and its warnings. The first American essay (1869) on Baudelaire, by Eugene Benson, made a passing reference to Hamlet (171). Hamlet: Baudelaire; they're a pair of brooding, sardonic dissidents. Baudelaire himself had written on Delacroix's lithographs, which were inspired by Shakespeare's play, and this appreciation even carried over into a poem (Baudelaire did not recognize a rigid boundary between his art criticism and his poetry). In "La Béatrice," a troupe of malign dwarfs compares the poet to Shakespeare's prince in terms that refer to one of Delacroix's images:

> Contemplons à loisir cette caricature Et cette ombre d'Hamlet imitant sa posture, Le regard indécis et les cheveux au vent.
> N'est-ce pas grand'pitié de voir ce bon vivant, Ce gueux, cet histrion en vacances, ce drôle, Parce qu'il sait jouer artistement son rôle, Vouloir intéresser au chant de ses douleurs Les aigles, les grillons, les ruisseaux et les fleurs, Et même à nous, auteurs de ces vieilles rubriques, Réciter en hurlant ses tirades publiques? (Baudelaire, *Œuvres complètes* 117, lines 13–22).

Jeffrey Coven comments: "Baudelaire saw himself in Delacroix's Hamlet and then, in his poem, transferred the vision to the demons who mock him" (36). In this medieval grotesquerie directed towards himself, the poet is also, in effect, offering a variation on the *spleen* poem: "Je suis comme le roi."

"Tu sais que je suis très laid," says Gwynplaine, the deformed fairground entertainer, to his beloved Déa, who has been blind from infancy. She replies: "Je sais que tu es sublime." (Hugo 289). That exchange is from Victor Hugo's novel *L'Homme qui rit*, which was published in 1869, two years after Baudelaire's death; Gwynplaine is a variant on the great-hearted hunchback Quasimodo in *Notre-Dame de Paris*. It was such a juxtaposition—of the grotesque and the sublime—that attracted Hugo (and also Baudelaire) to the work of Shakespeare. In the course of his art criticism, Baudelaire devoted an important chapter to the work of the Spanish painter and engraver Francisco de Goya and demonstrated that it was possible to transfigure the hideous and misshapen into moving works of art: "Ses monstres sont nés viables, harmoniques. Nul n'a osé plus que lui dans le sens de l'absurde possible. Toutes ces contorsions, ces faces bestiales, ces grimaces diaboliques sont pénétrées d'*humanité*. Même au point de vue particulier de l'histoire naturelle, il serait difficile de les condamner, tant il y a analogie et harmonie dans toutes les parties de leur être; en un mot, la ligne de suture, le point de jonction entre le réel et le fantastique est impossible à saisir; c'est une frontière vague que l'analyste le plus subtil ne saurait pas tracer, tant l'art est à la fois transcendant et naturel" (Baudelaire, *Curiosités esthétiques* 439–440). "Transcendant" is the word: in Goya, Baudelaire found evidence for his view that no subject-matter is off-limits for art, for his very modern idea—to become so prevalent in the twentieth century and beyond—that a kind of beauty can be shaped from that which is ugly.

If the sublime and the grotesque can be interdependent, one might reasonably infer that anything can be interdependent. In our time, that interdependence underlies environmentalism, "green" issues, biodiversity and so on; we talk of "holistic" approaches. There is the well-known question: "Does the flap of a butterfly's wings in Brazil set off a tornado in Texas?" For Baudelaire, this operated rather in dimensions that were aesthetic, spiritual, religious, even Catholic (bearing in mind that his Catholicism was idiosyncratic). This brings us to the vexed question of synesthesia: in his art criticism, such as in his writings on Delacroix and in the sonnet "Correspondances," Baudelaire dwells on how sounds can suggest colors, colors can suggest sounds, how indeed our preceptions deriving from our human senses (including smell and taste, as well as sight and hearing) can "correspond" to our perceptions deriving from all the others. Baudelaire sees this as evidence of God's design, of "une ténébreuse et profonde unité" (*Œuvres complètes* 11, line 6). As inherited by Baudelaire's would-be disciples, such as the Symbolists, as well as modulated by painters, composers and writers in the late nineteenth century and beyond, synesthesia loses its religious aspect and often becomes a matter for fashionable, even parodic and trivial, discourse. Baudelaire's English admirer Algernon Swinburne, who was given to oversimplifying Baudelaire's aesthetic, once described a painting in terms of its "melody of colour, [its] symphony of form" (Swinburne 360), and the American Whistler called his pictures symphonies and nocturnes (the latter term borrowed from piano pieces by Chopin and other composers). The Symbolist movement seized on the "Correspondances" sonnet, with its "forêt des symboles" as some kind of retrospective validation for its bargain-basement Baudelaireanism, which Baudelaire himself might well have characterized not so much as "bizarre" (a quality he favored) as perverse for perversity's sake, as well as distant from his serious theological concerns.

Actually, the association of synesthesia with diverse but interrelated forms of art was not an intellectual monopoly belonging to Baudelaire. Théophile Gautier, for example, entitled one of his poems "Symphonie en blanc majeur." Moreover, the theory of "correspondances" was not original to Baudelaire, but was borrowed by him from the philosopher and mystic Emanuel Swedenborg; there is some irony in Baudelaire's Catholic-inflected theology having been influenced by someone from Swedish Protestant culture. Moreover, the complex structure of vertical and horizontal relationships between earthly phenomena as reflexive of their celestial counterparts informs key themes and images in the plays of Shakespeare. In that context, what for Swedenborg and Baudelaire would be summed up as "correspondances" has been variously called "the Great Chain of Being" or "The Elizabethan World Picture"—earthly music being our perception of the music of the spheres, the workings of the human body corresponding to the governance of a kingdom, and so on.

We can say, at least, that Baudelaire was a conduit of "correspondances" and synesthesia to the Symbolists and other later figures. Certain operas, which are Symbolist or Symbolist-derived in character, such as Claude Debussy's *La Chute de la maison Usher* or Erich Wolfgang Korngold's *Die tote Stadt* (*The Dead City*, based on Georges Rodenbach's 1892 novel *Bruges la Morte*) would not have existed without the influence of Baudelaire along the way;

the Debussy work is based on an Edgar Allan Poe story which, by means of his translation, Baudelaire introduced to the French-speaking world.

However, it can be strongly argued that Baudelaire's poetry has its affinities with the Parnassianism of his contemporaries rather than with the Symbolism which came after him. According to this view, Baudelaire's verse is as finely chiselled, as coolly precise as the work of the Parnassian poets, such as Leconte de Lisle, and that is all far from the misty, miasmic quality of much Symbolist poetry and art.

It remains that post-Baudelairean literature, music, and art—the Symbolists included—pursued not so much the "Other" (which seems to me too vague a term to mean very much), as the "Elsewhere." That takes its cue partly, even largely, from Baudelaire. "Anywhere Out of the World" is the title (in English in the original) of one of his prose poems: anywhere, at least, that isn't Second Empire France. Could not that "elsewhere" be anywhere north or south of sick, corrupt Paris? Lisbon, perhaps; Rotterdam; the East Indies; the Arctic even, with the splendor of the Aurora Borealis? (Baudelaire, *Œuvres complètes* 356–7). There are the "voyage" poems - "L'Invitation au voyage," with its promise of a mysterious land where all is "ordre et beauté / Luxe, calme et volupté" (Baudelaire, *Œuvres complètes* 53, lines 13–14); the prose poem with the same title, with its vision of somewhere rather homelier and cozier, and Dutch (Baudelaire, *Œuvres complètes* 301–303); the concluding poem of *Les Fleurs du mal*, "Le Voyage," opening with a child, so curious that he must be an artist-in-the-making, "amoureux de cartes et d'estampes," to whom "L'univers est égal à son vaste appétit." (Baudelaire, *Œuvres complètes* 129, lines 1–2). Towards the end of the nineteenth century and well into the twentieth, French artists would discover the new perspectives suggested by Japanese prints. Debussy would be influenced in his compositions by the Javanese gamelan, which he heard at the Paris Exhibition. Odilon Redon, who produced many images inspired by the works of Poe and Baudelaire, portrayed Buddha in a dream-like landscape around the same year (1906) that Pierre Bonnard borrowed Baudelaire's title "Le Voyage" for his painting of an exotic-erotic sea-and-landscape, with its Chinaman squatting on the shore. Further in the distance appears a pagoda-crowned city, which invites the spectator to explore it (Baudelaire's "gloire des cités" [131, line 62]), the monkeys, and the mermaids at play.

The East: anywhere out of monochromatic Paris, so long as it was East. Colonial and postcolonial perspectives have long challenged the ideological innocence (whether real or pretended) of the West's obsession with the "elsewheres" it plundered, whose realities it distorted or discarded to fit its own fantasies, the "elsewheres" that should never be allowed to speak with the voices of its authentic residents (the "voyage," as it were, in search of dark-skinned ventriloquists' dummies). It may seem odd that Baudelaire is mentioned only in passing by Edward Said in his pioneering book *Orientalism: Western Concepts of the Orient* (1978): he devotes several pages to Flaubert. That could be because Flaubert, in real life, traveled much in Egypt, Lebanon, Palestine and Turkey, whereas Baudelaire never reached India, stopping only at Réunion and Mauritius before returning to France. The poem "A une malabraise" (*Œuvres complètes* 173–4) represents no known *actual* dusky beauty among the pineapples and bananas. Nevertheless, there's as much association of sultry sex and distant lands in Baudelaire as in Flaubert, if much augmented in the former's case by lively imagination. That, in turn, should lead us to expect an encounter with a plethora of fused feminist and postcolonial readings of the poet. Until the appearance of books by Beryl F. Schlossman (1991) and Melvin Zimmerman (2009), such perspectives were not conspicuous in Baudelairean studies, relatively speaking, though they weren't absent. The terms of debate are now set and may well guide future discussion of the poet.

All of which may not necessarily invalidate the strongly existential urgency of the poet's departure at the end of "Le Voyage," in which death—even death!—could promise a fresh start. For the Marxist critic Ernst Fischer, that provided an (unlikely?) metaphor for revolutionary possibility in a world devastated by capitalism ("Baudelaire reacts subjectively to an actual social situation"

[Fischer 180]). Implicit in such a reading is an insistence that Baudelaire cannot be simplistically reduced to the status of one who formerly manned the barricades then became merely a disillusioned reactionary. It is of note that in the year of the poem's composition (1859), Charles Darwin brought out his *On the Origin of Species*. On the aesthetic level, those concluding stanzas of "Le Voyage" say farewell to an outgoing poetics and hail all that we understand as the "modern." Encompassing all that is the broader insight that in life as well as in art, and a little beyond its mid-point, the nineteenth century has reached its most crucial turning point:

> Ô Mort, vieux capitaine, il est temps! levons l'ancre!
> Ce pays nous ennuie, ô Mort! Appareillons!
> Si le ciel et la mer sont noirs comme de l'encre,
> Nos coeurs que tu connais sont remplis de rayons!
>
> Verse-nous ton poison pour qu'il nous réconforte!
> Nous voulons, tant ce feu nous brûle le cerveau,
> Plonger au fond du gouffre, Enfer ou Ciel, qu'importe?
> Au fond de l'Inconnu pour trouver du *nouveau*!
> (134, lines 143–4).

Works Cited

Baudelaire, Charles. *Correspondances*. 2 vols. Eds. Claude Pichois & Jean Ziegler. Paris: Gallimard, 1975.

_____. *Œuvres complètes*. 2 vols. Ed. Claude Pichois. Paris: Gallimard, 1975–76.

_____. *Œuvres completes. L'Art romantique*. Ed. Jacques Crépet. Paris: Conard, 1925.

_____. *Œuvres compèetes. Curiosités esthétiques*. Ed. Jacques Crépet. Paris: Conard, 1923.

_____. *Œuvres complètes. Histoires extraordinaires par Edgar Poe*. Ed. Jacques Crépet. Paris: Conard, 1932.

Benson, Eugene. "Charles Baudelaire, Poet of the Malign." *The Atlantic Monthly* 23: 136 (February 1869): 171–177.

Coven, Jeffrey. *Baudelaire's Voyages: The Poet and his Painters*. Boston: Little, Brown, 1993.

Fischer, Ernst. *The Necessity of Art: A Marxist Approach.* Trans. Anna Bostock. Harmondsworth: Penguin, 1963.

Flaubert, Gustave. *Correspondances.* Ed. Jean Bruneau. Vol. 4. Paris: Gallimard, 1998.

Hugo, Victor. *Romans.* Vol. 3. Paris: Editions du Seuil, 1963.

Kaplan, Edward K. "Baudelairean Ethics." *The Cambridge Companion to Baudelaire.* Ed. Rosemary Lloyd. Cambridge, England: Cambridge UP, 2005. 87–100.

Kellman, Steven G., ed. *Albert Camus.* Hackensack, NJ: Salem Press, 2012. Critical Insights Ser.

Keogh, J. G. "The Crowd as No Man's Land: Gas-light & Poe's Symbolist Effects." *The Antigonish Review* 58 (Summer 1984): 19–31.

MacDiarmid, Hugh. *Lucky Poet.* Berkeley and Los Angeles: U of California P, 1972.

MacDiarmid, Hugh. *The Thistle Rises.* Ed. Alan Bold. London: Hamish Hamilton, 1984.

Pichois, Claude, ed. *Lettres à Baudelaire.* Neuchâtel: Etudes Baudelairiennes 4–5, 1973.

Said, Edward. *The Edward Said Reader.* London: Granta, 2001.

Schlossman, Beryl F. *The Orient of Style: Modernist Allegories of Conversion.* Durham: Duke UP, 1991.

Smith, G. Gregory. *Scottish Literature: Character & Influence.* London: Macmillan, 1919.

Steiner, George. *In Bluebeard's Castle: Some Notes Towards the Redefinition of Culture.* London: Faber, 1971.

Swinburne, Algernon. *Essays and Studies.* London: Chatto & Windus, 1875.

Zimmerman, Melvin. *Baudelaire & Co.: Intertexts: Pascal, Franklin, Rousseau, Laclos, Stendhal, Poe, Marx, and Others.* Toronto: Editions du Gref, 2009.

Zola, Émile. *Germinal.* Paris: Charpentier, 1885.

_____. *Thérèse Raquin.* Nouvelle édition. Paris: Charpentier, 1886.

Biography of Charles Baudelaire_____

Tom Hubbard

Of nineteenth-century poets, it was Walt Whitman who most explicitly rejoiced in his "contradictions." It would be difficult, though, to name any major poet or creative artist in any form or period, who wasn't driven by his or her "contradictions." In the case of Charles Baudelaire, we have a man and an artist who often lived in bohemian squalor, but who insisted on appearing neat and dapper, aspiring to be the elegant man-about-town—the *flâneur,* the dandy. He took drugs (including hashish)—his "paradis artificiels"—but he would have scorned the unkempt, stoned hippies who formulated the counter-culture a hundred years after his death. He was the petulant rebel who was also a crusty conservative, his obsession with Satanism accompanying a staunch if unorthodox Catholicism. His poetry took as its subject-matter destitution, prostitution, the teeming urban *mélange* of disease and sex, about which "respectable" society would have preferred to remain in denial—and yet the whole was contained in severely disciplined, almost perfectly poised verse forms that many would associate with long literary tradition and "classical" restraint. Contradictions, yes—but the energies of art depend on contradictions for their creative release. A one-dimensional art is no art at all.

Charles Baudelaire was born in 1821 in a city, Paris, that would undergo drastic changes during his lifetime. During the reign (1852–70) of Napoléon III, Baron Haussmann would gut the city, demolishing its labyrinthine core and replacing it with grand boulevards. These new thoroughfares would serve the commercial and domestic needs of a prosperous bourgeoisie, as well as deter the barricade-building of a discontented proletariat which—if it became troublesome—could be further deterred by the line of fire, which such newly broad avenues could offer the armed guardians of the state.

Yet for much of his early and later life, Baudelaire did not actually live in the city which so fascinated and repelled him. In 1827, his father—his mother's senior by thirty-three years—died when Charles was not quite six years old. The next year, Caroline Baudelaire took a second husband, the army officer Jacques Aupick, who was posted to Lyon. There, in France's second city, Charles was sent to a boarding school, the Collège de Lyon. Tensions grew between the young boy and his strict if well-meaning (and not unkindly) stepfather. Charles assiduously read romantic poetry, and like so many literary aspirants of his time, was reluctant to contemplate any career other than that of writing. Not for him was the security of the legal or any other well-regarded profession.

Back in Paris in his late teens, he became a denizen of the Latin Quarter, and his wayward behaviour led to his expulsion from the Lycee Louis-le-Grand. In 1841, his family took drastic measures and sent him far from the temptations of the capital: accordingly, he was put on a ship bound for India. He never reached that country, preferring to linger on the islands of Mauritius and Réunion: unwittingly, his family had dispatched him in the direction of those loci which became the source of that store of Baudelaire's imagery best summed up as exotic-erotic.

The "voyage" would become a major theme of Baudelaire's poetry, most notably of the final poem in the later editions of his sole poetry collection, *Les Fleurs du mal*. There was an alternative, in his imagination, to the matter of Paris: the poet could deploy the urban scene when it suited him, but there was also the possibility of escape—in his art, if not in his life—to the unknown and the infinite.

By the early 1840s, Baudelaire was writing many of the poems that would later be collected in *Les Fleurs du mal*. In 1842, newly returned to Paris, he made important literary friendships and embarked on his relationship with Jeanne Duval, his "Black Venus", who was an actress of mixed race. Edouard Manet's portrait of her, draped sensuously and challengingly across an ample sofa, is one of the treasures of the Museum of Fine Arts in Budapest. Duval was the object of Baudelaire's most enduring (and enduringly tempestuous) *amour*.

By 1847, Baudelaire had begun to establish himself as a critic of the visual arts, displaying an especial affinity with the painter Eugène Delacroix; had made a failed suicide attempt; and had begun to bring out his translations of his transatlantic kindred spirit, Edgar Allan Poe. As someone who loathed his own stepfather, Baudelaire—in a gesture of solidarity—dropped the "Allan" (i.e., Poe's equally loathed stepfather) in all citations of the American writer's name. To this day, the French reading public know him as Edgar Poe. It is as if Baudelaire re-created his mentor for a literary culture very different from that of the United States, or as one critic has put it more drily: "*Edgarpo* is to the French almost another person than Edgar Allan Poe, as the English-speaking world knows him" (Cunliffe 71).

"The Imp of the Perverse" is one of the many Poe tales and sketches translated by Baudelaire. That "imp," that spirit of the perverse provokes us into certain actions "merely because we feel we should not." Such actions could even include standing on the edge of a precipice and following the urge to plunge into the abyss—the "gouffre", so to speak, which lurks darkly and invitingly through much of Baudelaire's poetry (Poe 532–3). In early 1847, Baudelaire, not normally a short-story writer like Poe, brought out his sole effort in the genre, the novella "La Fanfarlo." The protagonist of Baudelaire's tale is Samuel Cramer, an outrageous dandy whose actions it is difficult to judge as sincere or merely a pretense of sincerity. Cramer flirts more or less decorously with one woman and actively pursues another—the vulgar, sexy Fanfarlo, who is an actress and is clearly modelled on Jeanne Duval. Baudelaire subjects Cramer, and indeed himself, to a send-up. "La Fanfarlo" is in large part a self-mocking self-portrait.

The dandy, or to cite his even more sophisticated persona, the *flâneur*, is Baudelaire's gift to the great gallery of literary archetypes. The *flâneur* is akin to the Danish existentialist philosopher Søren Kierkegaard, who sat at a Copenhagen café, puffed on a cigar, observed the happy bourgeois gentlemen and ladies in the street, then resolved that his mission in life would be to create difficulties everywhere. At a slight remove, the *flâneur* can also be comparable to the "Superfluous Man," who pervades so much nineteenth-century

Russian literature, for example: Mikhail Lermontov's trouble-making-for-the-hell-of-it character, Pechorin; Alexander Pushkin's arrogant, cultivated Eugene Onegin; and the Westernized gentry, out of kilter with their backward, repressive homeland in the novels of Ivan Turgenev, the friend of Baudelaire's friend Flaubert. All these fellows just don't fit in with their society and its prevailing values (or, as they would see it, its lack of values).

At the shabbier end of a spectrum of exiles, aliens, members of self-perceived élites against the crowd, are Herman Melville's "isolatoes," such as the hapless clerk Bartleby in the story named after him; Dostoyevsky's "underground man" railing maliciously against the nineteenth-century god of material "Progress;" and George Gissing's down-at-heels cultured gentlemen (and ladies), forced to take on literary hackwork that is unworthy of their refined, classical tastes. Gissing explained the title of his 1884 novel *The Unclassed*: "Male and female, all the prominent persons of the story dwell in a limbo [Baudelaire's *Les Limbes*?—TH] external to society. They refuse the statistic badge—will not be 'classed and done with'" (Gissing i).

The *flâneur* and his multifarious cousins usher in the existentially-challenged outsiders *(étrangers)* of twentieth-century literature and life. An age of uncertainty followed one of naïve faith in "Progress." It cannot, therefore, be wondered why many in that later century, as distinct from his own, felt that Baudelaire was "their" poet.

Baudelaire's participation in the 1848 revolution gave way to disillusionment with politics, especially of the "progressive" sort. But he was far from becoming the turncoat reactionary of cliché, eagerly and totally embracing an establishment that was formerly despised. No: in 1857, *Les Fleurs du mal* appeared. Book and author were prosecuted for blasphemy and obscenity. Baudelaire was humiliated by his fine of three hundred francs and the suppression of a number of poems in the collection. True, Baudelaire comes across, embarrassingly, as something of a toady in his desperate attempts to court well-known literary figures such as Sainte-Beuve

The professed scorner of literary prizes and official honors made a failed bid to be elected a member of the Academy.

To counter this by saying that Baudelaire was never the model bourgeois citizen, contented and complacent, would be a massive understatement. At least two other women—Marie Daubrun (another actress) and the statuesquely beautiful Madame Apollonie Sabatier—were the objects of his pursuit. By the late 1850s, his health was in decline, the symptoms of syphilis becoming increasingly apparent.

Subsequent to the death of his tough-loving stepfather, General Aupick, that military man who could never understand the point of all that poetry-and-art nonsense, there came a reconciliation between Baudelaire and his mother, at whose home in the Norman coastal town of Honfleur he would stay. The relationship with Jeanne Duval was far from over, but Baudelaire's lover was also not in good health, and in 1861, she was hospitalized. By the early 1860s, Baudelaire's money problems worsened—in spite of his now varied output: his prose poems were appearing, as well as his enthusiastic essay on the composer Richard Wagner, another key influence—again from a non-literary art form—on Baudelaire's views on aesthetics. In 1862, Algernon Swinburne introduced Baudelaire's poetry to the English-speaking world.

On April 24, 1864, Baudelaire arrived in Brussels, seeking better fortune in France's northern French-speaking neighbor. However, he came to despise Belgium and the Belgians, and spat out his bile in a text variously titled *Pauvre Belgique* or *La Belgique déshabillée*, as well as in a number of scurrilous poems. Today, most people walk up and down the Rue de la Montagne in Brussels, incognizant of the fact that no. 28 was the site of the Hôtel du Grand Miroir, where Baudelaire lodged during his final years. The nearby Marché aux Herbes (Grassmarket), Galéries Hubert, and the famous La Grand-Place are stronger attractions for twentieth- and twenty-first-century revellers.

In his book *The Flâneur*, Edmund White describes Baudelaire's rooms in the Hôtel de Lauzun, back in the poet's native city and in his younger days:

His apartment in Paris was decorated with a glossy wallpaper covered with red and black branches and at the one big window were draperies of a heavy, ancient damask. Baudelaire had scratched the lower panes so that only the sky could be seen and the expensive river view was occluded. On the walls hung the series of Delacroix's *Hamlet* lithographs, unframed but protected by glass, and the same artist's painting of *The Women if Algiers*. The furniture—armchairs covered with grey slipcovers, divans and an oval table in walnut— was all immense, fashioned for a race of titans (White 129).

In stark contrast, we have the witness of Georges Barral, a young writer and secretary to Baudelaire's photographer friend Nadar. Barral spent five days with the poet in the Belgian capital, visiting him in his room at the Hôtel du Grand Miroir:

> Je suis impressionné péniblement par la médiocrité de l'ameublement: un lit en faux acajou avec édredon vert, une armoire, une commode, un canapé râpé, un fauteuil usé, deux chaises au cannage fatigué, une petite carpette. Nulle pendule sur la cheminée; à sa place, une lampe sous abat-jour (Barral 39–40).

Nevertheless, pathetically enough, that faded *flâneur* Baudelaire had made an effort to give this unpromising environment something of his old flair and cultivation:

> Une table couverte de papiers et de livres s'appuie au mur, et sur ce mur règne une tenture décolorée. Au milieu de la pièce, vivement éclairée par une fenêtre assez haute, un guéridon resplendit. Le couvert a été préparé avec élégance. La nappe: éblouissement de blancheur. Elle est d'une trame fine serrée, douce au toucher et à l'œil (Barral 39–40).

We sense in these last years in Belgium an aura of tragic dignity, even grandeur, belonging to Baudelaire. That earlier life, with its sillinesses, the posturings unworthy of the great poet that he was almost in spite of himself, now found a certain redemption.

In his chapter on Baudelaire in his highly entertaining book on nineteenth-century French writers, *Something to Declare*, the novelist Julian Barnes makes this observation: "I once knew a neighbourhood greengrocer who had suffered all his life from a disfiguring skin disease; his children knew his face only as a piece of gaudy patchwork. In his late fifties, he got cancer. The drugs he was given had the unexpected side effect of clearing up his skin complaint: so as he lay dying, his children were able to see their father's true face for the first time. Something like this happens with Baudelaire" (108–09). In March of 1866, Baudelaire suffered a stroke, which paralysed him: he lost the power of speech. When his coarse, crass photographer friend Nadar visited him "and argued against the immortality of the soul, the poet could only point his fists at the sun in impotent protest" (Barnes 110). Nadar gathered together his cronies for a visit to a Brussels brothel, but Baudelaire grabbed the young Barral and warned him against dishonoring himself. Barral was powerfully impressed by the older man's gravity: "Je m'endormis, ce soir-là, lentement, gardant l'impression très nette que Baudelaire venait de me preserver pour jamais des compromissions louches et des liaisons ignominieuses" (Barral 80). An act of gratuitous kindness by Baudelaire towards an elderly stranger is also recorded from the Brussels years: the old man was being mocked by a crowd during a religious procession. Baudelaire took his arm and gently led him to the church of Sainte-Gudule.

During his first months in Brussels, Baudelaire had given a series of lectures and readings in the city. Disaster struck when he announced to his audience that he was in the course of losing his virginity as a public speaker. The room was then emptied of a group of schoolgirls, ushered out of their seats by their indignant teachers. The hall was depleted further until only one staunch admirer of the poet was left to offer homage: this was Camille Lemonnier, who went on to write about Baudelaire and to become a major Belgian literary figure in his own right. As so often in Baudelaire's life, farce mingled with pathos. But, by 1866, the farce was over when Baudelaire had a fall while visiting the baroque church of Saint-Loup in the Belgian city of Namur: the end, as it were, was precipitated by a piously Catholic pilgrimage. The paralyzing stroke followed, and Baudelaire's mother arrived in Brussels to look after him. In July, the poet was brought back to Paris and died a year later, on August 31, 1867, in his mother's arms. He was buried in the cemetery in Montparnasse in his native city. So, at last, he ended his literary "voyages" in that Paris, which—as eloquently expressed by the cultural historian Andrew Hussey—was for Baudelaire "a city of fragments, intimate drama, old myths, displacement and exile" (272).

Works Cited

Barnes, Julian. *Something to Declare: Essays on France*. New York: Alfred A. Knopf, 2002.

Barral, Georges. *Cinq journées avec Charles Baudelaire à Bruxelles*. [Sens:] Obsidiane, 1995.

Cunliffe, Maurice. *The Literature of the United States*. 3rd. ed. Harmondsworth: Penguin, 1967.

Gissing, George. *The Unclassed*. New ed. London: Lawrence & Bullen, 1895.

Hussey, Andrew. *Paris: The Secret History*. London & New York: Penguin, 2007.

Poe, Edgar Allan. *The Works of Edgar Allan Poe*. Vol. 2. New York: A.C. Armstrong, [c. 1884].

CRITICAL
CONTEXTS

Celebrating the New: Baudelaire and His Times

Rosemary Lloyd

In 1845, Baudelaire, who had just turned twenty-four, concluded his account of the annual art exhibition with a rousing call to his contemporaries to look to the world in which they lived to find the subject matter for their works of art. It is this attitude of mind that makes his writing, whether creative or critical, speak so directly to today's readers. While many writers and artists of his time were harking back to a far-off past, either in antiquity or in an adventurous image of Richelieu's seventeenth century, or evoking tranquil, timeless pastoral paradises, this was not the stuff of which he believed great modern art should be made. "Au vent qui soufflera demain nul ne tend l'oreille; et pourtant l'héroïsme *de la vie moderne* nous entoure et nous presse" (Baudelaire, *Œuvres Complètes*, 2: 407), he insists, exhorting the painters and, by implication, the writers and musicians of his time to find novel ways of depicting this new heroism. Since our age, he continues, has no lack of subjects for a modern epic, what the true artist needs to do is reveal the heroic side of everyday, contemporary existence, and reveal, as he puts it, "combien nous sommes grands et poétiques dans nos cravates et nos bottes vernies." No costume dramas for Baudelaire, no lyres and togas, but rather a longing for "cette joie singulière de célébrer l'avènement du *neuf*!" (Baudelaire,*Œuvres Complètes*, 2: 407). Though Baudelaire could also value and evoke the intense power of nostalgia, this longing for the new would stay with him throughout his life, as his 1859 poem "Le Voyage" suggests, with its final cry: "Enfer ou Ciel, qu'importe / Au fond de l'inconnu pour trouver du *nouveau*!" (Baudelaire, *Œuvres Complètes*, 1: 134).

To appreciate the fervor with which Baudelaire upholds an art that is modern, and to understand what aspects of modernity he seeks to promote, we need to understand the historical and artistic context in which he is writing. There are two main aspects of that context to bear in mind here: the cultural and the political. They are, of course, closely intertwined. The world around him was in flux, physically and politically, as the monarchy gave way to a short-lived republic in 1848, and then, after Louis Napoléon's *coup d'état* in 1851, to the Second Empire. Both socially and physically, Paris, as Honoré de Balzac's novels make abundantly clear, had already started to change well before the 1850s, with the industrial revolution bringing large numbers of people from the provinces to the capital, but the city's transformation intensified as Louis Napoléon, now the Emperor Napoléon III, through his minister the Baron Haussmann, set about converting the city into a physical representation of his own power. Working-class dwellings in the city center were removed to make way for residences for the middle classes, with the proletariat being exiled to the city's fringes. The narrow streets, which had been so easy to barricade, thus hamstringing the forces of order, were razed and replaced by wide boulevards and open vistas. These wider streets in turn made it possible for vehicles to move more quickly, intensifying the impression of speed and noise that Baudelaire identifies as characteristic of a modern city. From the 1840s, the cathedral-like railway stations began to appear, the great boulevards were illuminated by gas from 1857, and the growing numbers of cafés and bars made it possible for the city-dweller to transform the street and its population into a constantly changing spectacle, by night as well as by day. Hardly surprising then, that as Baudelaire reveals in his essay on the artist Constantin Guys, "Le Peintre de la vie moderne," modernity for him is closely linked to the fleeting, the transient, the briefly glimpsed and the rapidly noted. It involved not just new ways of experiencing the world, but also innovative ways of depicting it.

What Baudelaire seeks in the true artist of modernity is the ability to convey the sense of movement. Where classical art seeks to promote timeless values through perfectly finished works of art, great modern artists, for him, reveal that the sketch may be just as great a work of art because it manages to convey more intensely the essence of a fleeting glimpse, a short-lived, but powerful, experience. This is also what Baudelaire attempts to do in some of his most powerful poems and prose poems. In sending his poem "Le Cygne" to Victor Hugo, for instance, he insists: "Ce qui était important pour moi, c'était de dire vite tout ce qu'un accident, une image, peut contenir de suggestions, et comment la vue d'un animal souffrant pousse l'esprit vers tous les êtres que nous aimons, qui sont absents et qui souffrent, vers tous ceux qui sont privés de quelque chose d'irretrouvable" (Baudelaire, *Correspondances* I 623).

The impassioned observation, combined with the ability to capture fleeting moments that Baudelaire admires in novelists like Balzac and such painters as Constantin Guys is also a hallmark of his own approach to the modern world. Strolling through the main thoroughfares, or sitting in an outdoor café, he drinks in the rapidly changing cityscape, together with the intellectual suggestions it inspires and transforms them into a work of art. "Mon rêve", he wrote to his mother in 1860, "est de fondre des *qualités littéraires* avec la *mise en scène tumultueuse* du boulevard" (Baudelaire, *Correspondances* II 98). This is what he does most obviously, perhaps, in his poem "A une passante," where the poet persona sits at an outdoor café, "crispé comme un extravagant," while the street howls all around him (Baudelaire, *Œuvres Complètes*, 1: 93). Watching a woman pass by, he imagines an intense love affair with her, in a vision all the more exciting, as he knows it to be unrealizable. The responsibilities and disillusionments of a sustained relationship are avoided by the multiplicity of possibilities offered by a world dominated by rapidly growing populations and ephemeral encounters.

Responding enthusiastically to the spectacle of the city is one thing: reacting to a political situation may be quite different. Although the 1851 *coup d'état* filled him with disgust after his elation during the 1848 revolution, when the monarchy was finally overthrown and replaced with a short-lived republic, Baudelaire found he could not entirely turn away from politics, like certain of his contemporaries, notably the poets Charles René Leconte de Lisle and Théophile Gautier. In March 1852, he could proclaim: "le 2 décembre [that is, the *coup d'état*] m'a physiquement dépolitiqué" (Baudelaire, *Correspondances* I 188), and yet, writing to his friend

Nadar in 1859, he confesses : "je me suis vingt fois persuadé que je ne m'intéressais plus à la politique, et à chaque question grave, je suis repris de curiosité et de passion" (Baudelaire, *Correspondances* I 578). While specific political questions rarely enter into his creative writing, those "grave" general questions—of material versus spiritual or cultural values, of the relationship between rich and poor, of the criteria by which governments and individuals are to be judged—are frequently reflected in his writing, and are part of the modernism he demands of others, too. Scientific inventions, part of this rapidly developing new world, can be brought in to illuminate these basic questions. Thus, new developments in the production of glass, enabling larger shop or café windows, together with increased use of gas lighting, inspired him, in his prose poem "Les Yeux des pauvres" for example, to show the poor family gazing in on the rich family eating in a café, spending more in a single sitting than the poor could earn in a week.

On the cultural side, moreover, many of his contemporaries seemed unaware of the artistic capital that could be made from the many changes going on all around them. Like the majority of men of his social class, Baudelaire had been steeped in the classics throughout his school years. Both the 1789 Revolution and even more so the Emperor Napoléon I had drawn much of their imagery of governance from the Romans, and for many artists and writers of the mid-nineteenth century, Greek and Roman antiquity was still the period to which they most often turned for inspiration. Yet many were finding that their classical education stood them in poor stead for the needs of an increasingly industrial world.[1] Others, like Baudelaire, saw the ridiculous side of a world undergoing intensely rapid social and physical change, but still harking back for its models to a civilization that had flourished nearly two thousand years ago. Honoré Daumier, in a hilarious series of caricatures titled *Histoire ancienne* (1841–1843), and Jacques Offenbach, in his parodic operetta, *Orphée aux enfers* (1858), for instance, reduced the noble heroes and gods of antiquity to their modern-day, bourgeois equivalents, complete with balding heads, beer guts, night caps, and all.[2] In an angry and comic outburst in his refutation of what he terms the Pagan School, Baudelaire exclaims:

> Est-ce que le dieu Crépitus qui vous fera de la tisane le lendemain de vos stupides cérémonies? Est-ce Vénus Aphrodite ou Vénus Mercenaire qui soulagera les maux qu'elle vous aura causés ? Toutes ces statues de marbre seront-elles des femmes dévouées au jour de l'agonie, au jour du remords, au jour de l'impuissance? Buvez-vous des bouillons d'ambroisie? mangez-vous des côtelettes de Paros? Combien prête-t-on sur une lyre au Mont-de-Piété? (*Œuvres Complètes*, 2: 46).

For Baudelaire, unlike many of his contemporaries, it was clear that the old traditions were no longer valid and that new ones had yet to be formed, a situation both exhilarating and bewildering. (Elsewhere he insists, more ferociously, that France is currently going through a phase of vulgarity, and that Paris is the center of universal stupidity [*Œuvres Complètes*, 1: 182], necessitating more than merely enabling the formation of something better.) But he contends that, like all civilizations, the current one has its own inherent poetry, that it is just a question of finding it, based on the certainty that all kinds of beauty contain both the eternal and the transitory. "La vie parisienne," he exhorts his fellow artists and writers, "est féconde en sujets poétiques et merveilleux. Le merveilleux nous enveloppe et nous abreuve comme l'atmosphère; mais nous ne le voyons pas" (*Œuvres Complètes*, 2: 496). And to prove his point, he turns to Balzac, a contemporary writer whose novels are firmly based in the France of his own lifetime. The heroes of Homer's *Iliad* don't even come up to the ankles of Balzac's protagonists, Baudelaire affirms. Although Balzac had initially wanted to emulate the highly popular historical novelist Walter Scott, he had rapidly realized that his true gifts lay in depicting the world of his own time, a world inhabited by bankers and businessmen, journalists and poets, doctors and soldiers, farmers and courtesans, a world driven not by Olympian gods and goddesses, but by the twin forces of money and pleasure,[3] In creating his human comedy, Balzac had become, in Baudelaire's eyes, more heroic and poetic than any of his characters, setting others an example of what truly modern writing could be.

For Baudelaire, according to his account of the art salon of 1846, it was the Romantic Movement that best responded to modernity: "Pour moi," he affirms, "le romantisme est l'expression la plus récente, la plus actuelle du beau" (*Œuvres Complètes*, 2: 420). And he goes on to offer this resounding definition: "Qui dit romantisme dit art moderne—c'est-à-dire intimité, spiritualité, couleur, aspiration vers l'infini, exprimées par tous les moyens que contiennent les arts" (Baudelaire, *Œuvres Complètes,* 2: 421). The finest example of this new art in Baudelaire's eyes is provided by Eugène Delacroix, an artist he would continue to admire throughout his life. What he emphasizes in exploring Delacroix's work is the ability to draw on the lessons and traditions of the past, while adding to that foundation a consummate mastery in the depiction of "la douleur, la passion, le geste" (Baudelaire, *Œuvres Complètes,* 2: 441), aspects vital to Baudelaire's own creative art. He illustrates this contention later in the same essay when he describes another artist's painting of the traditional clown, Pierrot, criticizing it for not radically transforming and modernizing this conventional image by basing it on the work of the contemporary actor Debureau, who, he asserts, is "le vrai pierrot actuel, le pierrot de l'histoire moderne" (Baudelaire, *Œuvres Complètes,* 2: 451). Modernism, in other words, is not so much a rejection of the past as a transformation of tradition into the images of the present. As this suggests, modernism is also closely connected to Baudelaire's insistence on the right to contradict himself, the fascination with exploring both sides of a question. "Je n'ai jamais eu la prétention de ne pas me contredire", he wrote to a young critic, Armand Fraisse, on August 12, 1860. He goes on to write:

> Le seul orgueil que je me permette, c'est de m'appliquer à exprimer avec beauté n'importe quoi. Une âme très sincèrement éprise de vérité, mais très sensible, peut être ballottée du catholicisme au mysticisme, du manichéisme au magisme, sans que le public, si sa pâture d'amusement lui est servie, ait le droit de s'en préoccuper! (Baudelaire, *Nouvelles Lettres* 67).

In his own writing, Baudelaire does not reject out of hand the rich trove of ancient myths and legends, but rather uses it as a spring board into the creation of contemporary images and metaphors. To give an example: Andromaque, the grieving widow living out a life of exile far from her native Troy, serves in "Le Cygne" as a template suggesting a wide range of exiles, including, for example, Africans now living in Europe, or those around whom the city was changing so fast that they felt in exile even at home, or those who were society's outcasts, the ragpickers and prostitutes who inhabit the streets without inhabiting the society.

As he explains in a much later essay, *Le Peintre de la vie moderne*, which was first published in 1863:

> Le passé est intéressant non seulement par la beauté qu'ont su en extraire les artistes pour qui il était le présent, mais aussi comme passé, pour sa valeur historique. Il en est de même du présent. Le plaisir que nous retirons de la représentation du présent tient non seulement à la beauté dont il peut être revêtu, mais aussi à sa qualité essentielle du présent (Baudelaire, *Œuvres Complètes*, 2: 684).

As with so many of his aesthetic statements, Baudelaire insists, therefore, on the duality of beauty, the way in which the pleasure it gives derives both from an element that is permanent and unchanging and from a component that is fleeting, valid only for the particular moment it represents. "Le beau", he insists, "est fait d'un élément éternel, invariable, dont la qualité est excessivement difficile à déterminer, et d'un élément relatif, circonstanciel" (Baudelaire, *Œuvres Complètes*, 2: 685). Only by bearing this truth in mind can the artist or writer transform the world in which he or she lives into great art, revealing the multiple levels of metaphor the modern city reveals. That recent innovation, prose poetry, he maintains in a letter to his friend, the writer Arsène Houssaye, is born from "la fréquentation des villes énormes," from the "croisement de leurs innombrables rapports" (Baudelaire, *Œuvres Complètes*, 1: 276). Modernism thus demands an art form capable of revealing those countless links, across time and space, as well as between concepts. Only then will it be truly representative of its time, inspired by the great modern cities and, at the same time, reflecting them in its themes and in its formal structures. This is why, in his Salon of 1859, he calls on contemporary artists to focus on:

> un genre que j'appellerais volontiers le paysage des grandes villes, c'est-à-dire la collection des beautés et grandeurs qui résultent d'une puissante agglomération d'hommes et de monuments, le charme profond et compliqué d'une capital âgée et vieillie dans les gloires et les tribulations de la vie (Baudelaire, *Œuvres Complètes*, 2: 666).

What is important here is that it is not just the most recent developments that are interesting for the artist or poet, but the modern city seen across time, as a product and a representation of the passage of time.

This question of the ways in which the contemporary world was to be transformed into art is crucial to Baudelaire's thinking throughout his adult life and shapes much of his criticism, as well as his creative writing. Fancioulle, in the prose poem "Une mort héroïque", provides an image of the artist as hero, continuing to produce perfect art under the threat of execution, but to show this, Baudelaire places him in a world that seems remote in both time and space to that of Baudelaire himself. His letters, as well as his literary and art criticism, show him confronting the question of how this heroism is to be depicted in forms of creative writing that will construct a world immediately familiar to the contemporary reader.

In doing so, he does not simply accept as valid all that is modern. Of course, there is much that Baudelaire detests in the modern world, attitudes of mind or even linguistic tics that he delights in excoriating. In a letter to his publisher, Auguste Poulet-Malassis, for instance, he says of Victor Hugo's latest publication, *La Légende des siècles*, that it "a décidément un meilleur air de livre que *Les Contemplations*, sauf encore quelques petites folies modernes" (*Correspondances* I 605). The most obvious of those modern follies would have been the belief in human progress expressed in Hugo's anthology, a belief Baudelaire derided. "Quoi de plus absurde que le Progrès"? he asks in *Fusées,* adding ferociously: "l'homme, comme cela est prouvé par le fait journalier, est toujours semblable et égal à l'homme, c'est-à-dire toujours à l'état sauvage" (Baudelaire *Œuvres Complètes*, 1: 663). Just as disturbing to him was the conviction that his contemporaries were rejecting art in favor of basely utilitarian values: in a letter to Hugo, he spoke of the age as "un temps où le monde s'éloigne de l'art avec [...] horreur, où les hommes se laissent abrutir par l'idée exclusive d'utilité" (*Correspondances* I 597).

Language, too, was changing and not always in ways that pleased him. Thus we find him fulminating against the word "chic," which he describes as a "mot affreux et bizarre et de moderne fabrique, dont j'ignore même l'orthographe, mais que je suis oblige d'employer, parce qu'il est consacré par les artistes pour exprimer une monstruosité moderne" (*Œuvres Complètes*, 2: 468). Equally, he despises the adjective *littéraire*, describing it as belonging to the awful slang of his age (Baudelaire, *Correspondances*, 1: 298). He himself, however, makes use of new words when it suits him: *modernité* itself is listed by the great dictionary compiler Emile Littré as a neologism. Théophile Gautier, the poet to whom Baudelaire dedicated his collection of poems, *Les Fleurs du mal*, used it a few years before *Le Peintre de la vie moderne* in newspaper articles which he subsequently collected in his volume *Les Beaux-Arts en Europe* published in 1855. Modernism, in other words, is not just a mindless acceptance of what is thought, written and done now, but a constantly questioning analysis of the contemporary, and Baudelaire makes use of it when it suits him, picking through modern concepts and slang as a rag picker might examine a city's trash to find potential treasure.

Central to his image of what is worth treasuring in the modern world is the sense that, for earlier ages, the primary aim of art, poetry and music had been to "enchanter l'esprit en lui présentant des tableaux de béatitude" (Baudelaire, *Œuvres Complètes* II 168), images in sharp contrast with the life of contention and struggle in which we actually live. Modern art, according to Baudelaire, seeks, on the contrary, to acknowledge and represent the reality of evil and suffering. Beethoven in music, Maturin in the novel, Poe in poetry and prose, and Byron in poetry have all shown the way, he insists, by using their different forms of art to project "des rayons splendides, éblouissantes, sur le Lucifer latent qui est installé dans tout cœur humain" (*Œuvres Complètes*, 2: 168). This is fundamental to Baudelaire's own artistic aims too: his desire to show the attraction of evil, "les fleurs du Mal."

In comparison with that of antiquity, modern suffering may often seem banal, Baudelaire concedes, but it is nonetheless real and powerful for that. In his review of Flaubert's novel, *Madame Bovary*, he acknowledges that Emma makes herself ridiculous by idealizing the philanderer Rodolphe and falling in love with a notary's clerk before finally finding herself reduced, as he puts it, to pursuing "l'idéal à travers les bastringues et les estaminets de la prefecture." But, he adds, using a classical allusion to underline Emma's modernity, "qu'importe? Disons-le, avouons-le, c'est un César à Carpentras: elle poursuit l'Idéal» (*Œuvres Complètes*, 2: 84). The point is that we cannot all be great heroes in great cities, but we can be loyal to our ideal even if, living in the provinces, those around us fall far short of the goals we set.

In another comment on *Madame Bovary*, Baudelaire emphasizes a further aspect of the novel that seems to him especially modern, typical of a world in which respect for spiritual qualities was rapidly being replaced by an overvaluation of the material. He refers to that episode "si remarquable, si plein de désolation, si véritablement *moderne*, où la future adultère […] va demander secours à l'Eglise, à la divine Mère, à celle qui n'a pas d'excuses pour n'être pas toujours prête." But when she seeks help from the local priest, he stupidly advises her: "Puisque vous êtes malade, madame, et puisque M. Bovary est médecin, *pourquoi n'allez-vous pas trouver votre mari*" (*Œuvres Complètes,* 2: 85). The incompetent priest, unprepared to help in such matters and unable to recognize that an illness can be spiritual rather than physical, strikes Baudelaire as not only quintessentially modern but also an intrinsic part of everyday experience.

The painful secret causing Emma's suffering (that she finds marriage boring in comparison with the image of passionate love she has drawn from her reading, both sacred and profane) is both essentially eternal, in that women down the ages have shared it, and treated here in a way that is fundamentally modern. Similarly, Baudelaire finds in Delacroix a series of depictions of women who suffer from "un secret douloureux, impossible à enfouir dans les profondeurs de la dissimulation" (*Œuvres Complètes,* 2: 594). Both physically and spiritually these women offer the finest image of "la femme moderne, surtout la femme moderne dans sa manifestation héroïque, dans le sense infernal ou divin" (*Œuvres Complètes,* 2: 594). Although they appear to represent historical or literary figures—Cleopatra or Ophelia for instance—it is Delacroix's modernity that enables these female figures both to encapsulate eternal truths and to represent contemporary experience. Once again, it is the idea of heroism that is associated with modernity, and what Baudelaire admires is Delacroix's ability to depict a contemporary form of heroism, while suggesting the timelessness of the human condition. Like the narrator in Baudelaire's poem "La Vie antérieure," the women in these paintings are distinguished by a "secret douloureux" (*Œuvres Complètes,* 1: 18). Incapable of hiding their suffering, however much they seek to disguise it, they suggest to the viewer the internal struggles they undergo:

> Qu'elles se distinguent par le charme du crime ou par l'odeur de la sainteté, que leurs gestes soient alanguis ou violents, ces femmes malades du cœur ou de l'esprit ont dans les yeux le plombé de la fièvre ou la nitescence anormale et bizarre de leur mal, dans le regard, l'intensité du surnaturalisme (*Œuvres Complètes,* 2: 594).

Baudelaire himself suggests the suffering of women in his poem "Les Petites Vieilles," as he watches old women wandering through what he suggestively terms "les plis sinueux des vieilles capitales" ("Les Petites Vieilles," *Œuvres Complètes,* 1: 89, line 1). Attempting, as he does in so many of his poems and prose poems, to read the story of other people's lives, he sees in them representatives of women hurt by their country, by their spouse, by their children, such that "Toutes auraient pu faire un fleuve avec leurs pleurs" ("Les Petites Vieilles," *Œuvres Complètes,* 1: 89, line 48).

In a companion piece to "Les Petites Vieilles," titled "Les Sept Vieillards," he focuses more on the sense of vertigo and loneliness induced by living in a metropolis, where the sheer numbers of people force the individual to realize how little he or she counts in the grand scheme of things. To convey such a sense of despair, Baudelaire felt he had to push poetry to the limits of what it could achieve, as he admits in a letter accompanying the poem (*Correspondances* 1: 583). Modern themes, he acknowledges, require a modern treatment that may force genres almost beyond the boundaries of the possible. Suffering, physical or mental, is for Baudelaire the mark of the outstanding modern individual, and by showing this suffering, instead of representing perfect beauty or health, by revealing anguish rather than calm, Delacroix becomes, for the poet, not just the ideal representative of modern art, but the model other artists, in whatever media they use, should follow.

Plunging into the abyss, exploring dingy alleyways, opening his mind to the creative works of other artists: in whatever way he could, Baudelaire set out to discover, explore, and analyze the new, and in so doing, created an image of what it means to be modern that continues to shape the writing of our own age.

Notes

1. For an outstanding contemporary example of this, see Jacques Vallès' novel *Le Bachelier*.
2. Cartoons from this series can be seen at http://expositions.bnf.fr/homere/feuille/04.htm
3. See Balzac's "Avant-propos" to *La Comédie humaine* in, for example, Balzac's *Écrits sur le roman*, 275–306.

Works Cited

Balzac, Honoré de. *Écrits sur le roman*. Paris: Livre de Poche, 2000.

Baudelaire, Charles. *Correspondances*. Vol. 1–2. Paris: Gallimard, 1973.

_____. *Nouvelles Lettres*. Paris: Fayard, 2000.

_____. *Œuvres Complètes*. Vol. 1–2. Paris: Gallimard, 1975.

Bibliothèque nationale de France. *Homère*. 2006. Web. 25 Sept. 2013. <http://expositions.bnf.fr/homere/feuille/04.htm>.

Lloyd, Rosemary. *Baudelaire's World*. Ithaca, NY: Cornell UP, 2002.

Lough, John & Muriel Lough. *An Introduction to Nineteenth-Century France*. London: Longman, 1978.

Nisbet, Robert A. *History of the Idea of Progress*. New York: Basic, 1980.

Vallès, Jules. *Le Bachelier*. Paris: Garnier-Flammarion, 1970.

The Critical Reception of Baudelaire's Poetry

Tom Hubbard

"We know no spectacle so ridiculous," wrote the historian and essayist Lord Macaulay, "as the British public in one of its fits of morality." In 1857, much the same could have been said about the French, or at least its established public bodies, such as the courts and the press. Gustave Flaubert's novel *Madame Bovary* had been prosecuted for offenses against religion and morality. The result was an acquittal. Later that year, Charles Baudelaire's sole poetry collection, *Les Fleurs du mal*, was accused of obscenity. This time, the author lost his case, and was fined three hundred francs. Just over a hundred years later, in 1960, the publisher Penguin Books was up before an English court for issuing a paperback edition of D. H. Lawrence's *Lady Chatterley's Lover*. That trial, notoriously, descended into farce, as is often the case when self-righteous, pompous authorities attempt to censor works of literature. Such events generate much work (and money) for newspaper editors and lawyers. It was said that the "Lady Chatterley trial" was the most expensive seminar ever given on the works of D. H. Lawrence. It's much cheaper to hire professors.

It was claimed that the French authorities, angry at Flaubert's acquittal, were determined that Baudelaire should not get off so lightly and that there was collusion between the press and the Ministry of the Interior to have the poet face the judges. Certainly, on the part of the press, there was no limit to the ferocity of Gustave Bourdin's review of *Les Fleurs du mal* in *Le Figaro* of July 5, 1857:

> Il y a des moments où l'on doute de l'état mental de M.Baudelaire [...] L'odieux y coudoie l'ignoble; - le repoussant s'y allie à l'infect [...] Ce livre est un hôpital ouvert à toutes les démences de l'esprit, à toutes les putridités du cœur [...] rien ne peut justifier un homme de plus de trente [ans] d'avoir donné la publicité du livre à de semblables monstruosités (Bandy 31–32).

Baudelaire's friends and colleagues rallied to his defense, some more bravely and outspokenly (and indeed more perceptively) than others. On July 15, the *Moniteur universel* carried a radiant critique by Edouard Thierry: "J'ai déjà rapproché de Mirabeau l'auteur des *Fleurs du mal*, je le rapproche de Dante, et je réponds que le vieux Florentin reconnaîtrait plus d'une fois dans le poète français sa fougue, sa parole effrayante, ses images implacables et la sonorité de son vers d'airain" (Bandy 33). Baudelaire, then, was up there with the very greatest. Could there be many examples, besides Dante, of the maximum spiritual and artistic power? It was as if *Les Fleurs du mal* was being claimed as the *Inferno* of the nineteenth century.

Thierry's article was one of several which were collected together to bolster Baudelaire's defense during the trial. Jules Barbey d'Aurevilly's contribution was especially striking: among the ingredients of Baudelaire's poetry, Barbey claimed, was "quelque chose du gothique fleuri ou de l'architecture morisque." He returns to that latter image in arguing for *"une architecture secrète"* of *Les Fleurs du mal*—that is, each poem is not only valuable in itself, but also as an essential part of the book as a carefully constructed unity. Such insistence on the integrity of *Les Fleurs du mal* has marked much discussion ever since, notably in the work of Randolph Paul Runyon, a contributor to the present volume. The conclusion of Barbey's essay is one of the most famous comments on Baudelaire's work: "Après les *Fleurs du mal*, il n'y a plus que deux parties à prendre pour le poète qui les fit éclore: ou se brûler la cervelle … ou se faire chrétien" (Bandy 169). It's a colorful (if indirect) articulation of the major point in Baudelaire's defense, that far from advocating sin and Satanism, he is in fact, as a good Catholic, warning against their allure. Barbey also follows Thierry in making favorable comparisons with the great Florentine, though the references to a Dante "d'une époque déchue […] du Dante athée et moderne, du Dante venu après Voltaire" (Bandy 168) may have raised a few eyebrows.

The influential critic Charles Sainte-Beuve was Baudelaire's senior by seventeen years, and the younger man looked up to him as a mentor, and indeed as an adopted "uncle." It was important for Baudelaire to keep Sainte-Beuve not only on side, but also supportive. However, as stressed by many, including Enid Starkie (*Baudelaire* 372–3), the older man offered ill-conceived advice regarding defense strategies for the trial; five years later, when Baudelaire sought Sainte-Beuve's testimonial in an application for membership of the Académie Française, the resulting text was not well-placed to secure Baudelaire's election. Sainte-Beuve was a somewhat reptilian creature and not to be trusted. His piece is excruciatingly patronizing, and seems more concerned to show off his imaginative prose style than to help his young protégé. It's curious that he sends off an almost Barbey-like account full of exotic, oriental architectural imagery, with added extras; one image in particular has become perhaps the most notorious early response to Baudelaire's work:

> M. Baudelaire a trouvé moyen de se bâtir, à l'extrèmité d'une langue de terre réputée inhabitable et par delà les confins du romantisme connu, un kiosque bizarre, fort orné, fort tourmenté, mais coquet et mystérieux […] Ce singulier kiosque, fait de marqueterie, d'une originalité concertée et composite, qui, depuis quelque temps, attire les regards de la pointe extrême du Kamtchatka romantique, j'appelle cela la folie Baudelaire (Bandy 58–9).

"Folie," in this context, means an architectural "folly," that is the kind of eccentric, ornamental small building to be found on the private land of aristocrats—but the word can still mean "folly" in the more usual sense. With help like that, Baudelaire may have wondered, who needs hindrance?

Baudelaire professed gratitude to Sainte-Beuve—he could hardly do otherwise—but it's not difficult to detect a slightly tart comment on his "uncle's" fantasia upon that large peninsula of the Russian Far East (relatively speaking, it's near Alaska): "Quant à ce que vous appelez mon *Kamschatka*," Baudelaire writes to Sainte-Beuve, "si je recevait souvent des encouragements aussi vigoureux que celui-ci, je croie que j'aurais la force d'en faire une immense *Sibérie*, mais une chaude et peuplée" (Baudelaire, *Correspondances* II 219).

It is refreshing to encounter a critic, in September of 1857, who does not parade his own ego while discussing *Les Fleurs du mal* and instead homes in on specific poems with a view to close and sensitive readings. This was the relatively unknown Armand Fraisse, who was based in Lyon and was, therefore, at some distance from the hothouse atmosphere of the capital. Back in November of 1855, one of the earliest responses to Baudelaire as a poet came in the obtuse piece by Louis Goudall in (again!) *Le Figaro*. Attacking what he called "cette poésie de charnier et d'abattoir," he objected in particular to instances of Baudelaire's use of "l'adjectif-cheville." in "Au lecteur," for example *"plaisants* dessins," "canevas *banal,"* *"piteux* destins" (Bandy 20–22, Guyaux 145). Two years later, Armand Fraisse made an effort to understand where Goudall could only rush to condemn. An adjective, far from being "cheville" seems, for Fraisse, to signal a definite poetic strategy, even an uncanny inventiveness on Baudelaire's part, creating startling antitheses. Fraisse writes:

> Les procédés de M. Baudelaire pour arriver à certain effets sont un peu uniformes. Il emploie très souvent le contraste et les oppositions brusques d'images et de mots; il aime à charger les substantifs d'épithètes inattendues et quelquefois inexplicables. C'est ainsi que les mots *charmant* et *aimable* foisonnent dans son livre, placés avec une incohérence étudiée (25).

He quotes, as does Goudall, the poem "Au lecteur," and draws attention to "amiable pestilence," "aimables remords" (an expression loathed by a later hostile critic, Ferdinand Brunetière, in terms that echo Goudall [Brunetière, "Charles Baudelaire" 69–70]). If Fraisse, though, sounds bemused by Baudelaire's "épithètes inattendues," he is not exactly trashing them, and he goes on to appreciate "Une Charogne" as the most thorough example of Baudelaire's "excentricités systématiques," and makes a point of quoting the last three stanzas as "la conclusion de cette délicieuse description" (26–27).

In fact, Fraisse's article is often celebrated for its sympathetically probing analysis, in stark contrast to the usual superficialities to which *Les Fleurs du mal* was subjected in the wake of its first appearance. Maria C. Scott (203) has highlighted Fraisse's suggestion that Baudelaire may be enjoying a grim jest at his complacent readers' expense: "L'auteur est-il sérieux? Son livre sort-il d'une imagination bizarre mais consciencieuse, ou n'est-iL qu'une mystification colossale? [...] Si M. Baudelaire abordait la satire, il y obtendrait, sans nul doute, de grands succès" (Fraisse 24, 30). Fraisse concludes his article in a manner that leaves us in no doubt that he is a rare critic of an even rarer poet and at such an early stage of the latter's reputation: "J'aime mieux la plus informe ébauche pétrie par une vraie main d'homme, une main vivante, une main créatrice, que toutes les choses correctes, limes, grattées, polies, sortant d'un moule ou d'une machine [...] C'est pourquoi j'ai parlé si longuement de M. Baudelaire" (32–33).

More private responses from Baudelaire's contemporaries came in the form of correspondence. Early in 1859, the good-natured, ever-dependable Charles Asselineau went further then most who praised, if they did not blame: in congratulating his friend on producing such a "diamant" as "L'Albatros" he suggested that Baudelaire provide an extra stanza between the second and the last, in order to show more strongly the awkwardness of the great bird on the ship's deck (Pichois 18). Baudelaire duly complied, with such vivid details as the sailor who mockingly sticks a pipe in the albatross' beak. If we wanted to be solemn about this, we might call this creative dialogue between Asselineau and Baudelaire an example of "interactive reception," but we already have more than enough literary-critical jargon in circulation.

Elsewhere among the letters sent to Baudelaire by his confrères, there is unintended comedy in the encomiums offered by Gustave Flaubert and Victor Hugo. Flaubert, that earlier target of the forces of justice, exceeded his eloquence in finding a fellow-fighter against the hypocritical bourgeois establishment; more significantly, he sees in Baudelaire an exemplar of his own doctrine of impersonality, whereby the artist does not intrude himself into his creations. This is also a time of growing insistence, by Flaubert and writers who followed him (such as Henry James), that literature should be regarded, above all, on a par with music and the visual arts, rather than being just another commercial, utilitarian profession loyal to the vulgar status quo. True, Baudelaire would have broadly agreed with that, but one still has the feeling that Flaubert has his own, rather than Baudelaire's, practice in mind: "En résumé," writes Flaubert in July 1857, "ce qui me plait avant tout dans votre livre, c'est que l'art y prédomine. Et puis vous chantez la chair sans l'aimer, d'une façon triste et détachée qui m'est sympathique. Vous êtes resistant comme la marbre et pénétrant comme un brouillard d'Angleterre" (Pichois 150). Claude Pichois comments drily: "Reste que Baudelaire semble avoir mieux compris Flaubert que Flaubert, Baudelaire" (149).

In October 1859, Victor Hugo famously commended Baudelaire for having created "un frisson nouveau," but though he mentioned the poem "Les Sept vieillards" and "Les Petites vieilles," he did not go into detail about the causes of that "frisson" (Pichois 188). He was anxious to assert to Baudelaire that the cause of art was also the cause of social progress, but the latter was anathema to the younger poet who loftily disdained anything that reeked of sentimental humanitarianism. (When reading Baudelaire, it's advisable to adopt a willing suspension of political correctness.)

As a major poet older than Baudelaire by ten years, and surviving him by five, Théophile Gautier was well-placed to offer a reading of Baudelaire that bridged the Romanticism of the early nineteenth century with the emerging modernism of the 1870s/1880s and beyond. Among Gautier's several essays on Baudelaire, we encounter a comparison which is of especial interest to American readers: not with Edgar Allan Poe—which we might have expected, given Baudelaire's commitment to him as translator and interpreter of his work for the French—but with Nathaniel Hawthorne. "Rappaccini's Daughter," the Hawthorne story which is the focus of Gautier's argument, concerns a young woman whose mad-scientist father has raised her in seclusion and who walks in his garden of poisonous flowers, which spell dubious promise for any would-be suitor. Flowers of "mal." (= evil / suffering / illness / premature death) indeed. Referring Baudelaire's deadly plants back to Hawthorne's, Gautier writes "elles ont ces couleurs sombre et métalliques, ces frondaisons vert-de-grisées, et ces odeurs qui portent à la tête. Sa muse ressemble à la fille du docteur qu'aucun poison ne saurait atteindre, mais dont le teint, par sa matité exsangue, trahit l'influence du milieu qu'elle habite" (Bandy 174). To a Baudelaire-Hawthorne connection we shall return, in the context of an essay by Henry James.

The foregoing concerns reception by Baudelaire's contemporaries. From the 1880s onwards, we enter a new phase, around which cluster such concepts as synesthesia (the influence of Swedenborg's "correspondances," as mediated by Baudelaire, between sounds, colors, scents, tastes etc.), "l'art pour l'art." (on which Baudelaire held views more nuanced than those of his professed disciples near the century's end), decadence and Symbolism (of which tendencies, not altogether identical with each other, Baudelaire was held to be the leading progenitor). Central to these vexed questions is Baudelaire's *influence* on self-proclaimed acolytes, over which a dead or even a living poet can have no control, as distinct from *reception*, where those who are critics, but not necessarily poets, engage discursively with Baudelaire's œuvre. It must be granted that one cannot—and perhaps should not—try to demarcate too clearly between influence and reception: the one slips only too easily into the other.

Joris-Karl Huysmans' novel *A Rebours* (1884) centers on Des Esseintes, a well-off aesthete who leads a hermit-like existence in his Paris home, devoted to the cultivation of his senses, aloof from the vulgar realities beyond his walls. The book is well-known for its send-up of "correspondances," the interrelationships of "les parfums, les couleurs et les sons" to quote Baudelaire's eponymous sonnet. Des Esseintes possesses a "liqueur organ," which he "plays" by selectively imbibing the contents of the little glasses of sundry liqueurs, which are arranged systematically, like the equivalent of a keyboard. The varying tastes of the drinks "correspond" to instruments of the orchestra, so he can play a symphony in his head as, with virtuoso skill, he takes sip after sip of curaçao, kümmel, and kirsch, with gin, whiskey, and brandy also at hand whenever the masterpiece requires further "orchestral" effects.

Beyond this synesthetic fantasia, however, Huysmans also offers more serious analysis of Baudelaire—albeit this is offered in the course of, not a critical monograph, but a novel! He is alert to the structural felicities of such as "L'Irréparable" and "Le Balcon," "où le dernier strophe est l'écho du premier et revient, ainsi qu'un refrain, noyer l'âme dans des infinis de mélancholie et de langueur" (Huysmans 199). There is anticipation, as it were, of Freudian and post-Freudian perspectives in this summary of Baudelaire's profundities: "il était descendu jusqu'au fond de l'inépuisable mine, s'était engagé à travers des galleries abandonées ou inconnues, avait abouti à ces districts de l'âme où se ramifient les végétations monstrueuses de la pensée" (231ff).

According to Huysmans, writing through the mind of his character Des Esseintes, Baudelaire had gone further than any previous authors in exploring those dark places of the unconscious self. Dreams, all that is hauntingly atmospheric, the "voyage" to the exotic and "oriental," "correspondances," and synesthesia—there was certainly much in Baudelaire that would appeal to the Symbolists, who regarded him as their precursor. "*Nommer* un objet," declared Stéphane Mallarmé, the arch-Symbolist poet, "c'est supprimer les trois quarts de la jouissance du poème qui est faite de deviner peu à peu: le *suggérer*, voilà le rêve" (Huret 60). However, the Symbolists were not the first to exaggerate Baudelaire's "orientalism"—contrary to assumptions, he had never reached India! Moreover, any morbid, nightmarish atmospherics came from further back, via Edgar Allan Poe (who was admittedly introduced to France by Baudelaire), as was also the case with the theory of "correspondances," which, as indicated above, Baudelaire had not in fact initiated, having adopted it from the philosopher Swedenborg. Suggestiveness—yes, but that implies a certain vagueness, and there is a critical consensus that Baudelaire's poetry deploys very precise images; is finely chiselled; is closer, in other words, to the impersonal, objective, *sculptural* quality of the Parnassians than to the highly subjective and non-referential *musical* tendencies of the Symbolists. Michael Hamburger has contrasted Baudelaire's rejection of out and out "l'art pour l'art" as a "puérile utopie" with the extreme aestheticism of Mallarmé's escapist dismissal of external reality as "le mirage brutale, la cité, ses gouvernements, le code" (Hamburger, ch.1; Baudelaire, *L'Art romantique* 125; and Mallarmé, "La musique" 309). "La cité!" Baudelaire, rather, was the pioneering poet of just that, the city. Mallarmé took over Baudelaire's image of the swan (in his sonnet beginning "Le Vièrge, le vivace, et le bel aujourd'hui") but transports the bird from the Parisian Seine of Baudelaire's "Le Cygne" to a "lac dur oublié" of the Symbolist never-neverland (Mallarmé, *Œuvres completes* 36).

One would have thought that there was more purchase, for the Symbolists and their contemporaries, in Baudelaire's notion of the poet as "exilé" like his albatross and his swan (it's arguable that the "exil inutile" [*Œuvres completes* 37] of Mallarmé's swan is less urgent, less tragic). The poet's preoccupations cannot be appreciated by "les vulgaires profanes" (Baudelaire, *Œuvres complètes,* 1: 191). In the "Prologue" to his *Poèmes saturniens* (1866), his first collection and published just within the lifetime of Baudelaire, whom he admired, Paul Verlaine wrote defiantly of the poet's plight: "Le monde, que troublait parole profonde / Les exile. À leur tour, ils exilent le monde" (60). To this keyword "exil" we can add the related concepts of 'l'élite' against "la foule." These all converge in the writings of the Belgian Symbolist Georges Rodenbach, one of Mallarmé's protégés but very much his own man: his contribution to post-Baudelairean discourse is so unique as to be unignorable.

Rodenbach is best-known for his novel *Bruges-la-morte* (1892), a tale of dank canals, a male protagonist's brooding sexual obsessions, the premature deaths of two young and beautiful women, who are each other's double. If this is Rodenbach's most Poe-like production, an earlier novel, *L'Art en exil* (1889)—as its title alone would suggest—is his most Baudelairean. (In many ways, it's a more subtly Baudelairean novel than Huysmans' *A Rebours*). *L'Art en exil* tells of Jean Rembrandt, a thus artistically-named poet, living his internal "exil" in his native Flemish town (which is loosely based on Rodenbach's own home town of Ghent). He toils doggedly at his poetry to which the surrounding provincials are woefully indifferent. His wife, a pious, conventional girl, turns out not to be the ideal soulmate for a struggling literary man: he reads Hugo and (of course) Baudelaire to her, to no avail, and as regards his own poetry, she is interested only in how much money he'll earn from it. So far, so coolly, is the whole thing narrated: Rodenbach, like Baudelaire, is too sophisticated to identify totally with his alienated aesthetes. However, it is when the couple take a short holiday in a coastal village that they experience something of an epiphany; at this point, Rodenbach's prose has echoes of both the Hugo of *Les Travailleurs de la mer* and of the Baudelaire of the "voyage" poems and the prose passages (in *Mon cœur mis a nu*) on the sea's suggestion of the idea of infinity: "'Si l'océan est si triste,'" muses Jean to his wife, "'ne crois-tu pas que c'est parce qu'il est seul? Il est le dépareillé, celui de l'irrémédiable célibat ....'" The sight of ships' sails suggests "des nostalgies de départ [...] Heure bien faite pour aimer, pour être deux, où l'on rêvait d'émigrer vers des archipels fabuleux et quelque île de légende où ce serait le paradis reconquis de ne plus vivre qu'ensemble comme un unique couple initial ...." (Rodenbach, *L'Art en exil* 79, 82). Alas, quotidian reality doesn't measure up to such aspirations.

Ten years on, Rodenbach included an essay on Baudelaire in a collection of pieces on a number of luminaries in literature and the visual arts: the book, not surprisingly, is entitled *L'Elite*. He distinguishes Baudelaire from previous French poets, Hugo and the others, who would "épouser la foule"; Baudelaire could never bring himself to do that. However, Rodenbach does not so much accommodate Baudelaire to the wilfully esoteric, sexily-macabre Symbolist agenda of his "continuateurs." as align him to a more traditional system: "Il apparaît ce qu'il est essentiellement: un POÈTE CATHOLIQUE [...] Parmi les vices modernes et la corruption effrénée dont il subit la contagion, il continue à être le depositaire du dogme, le dénonciateur du péché." Baudelaire is not a Satanist: in the poet's work, Satan's presence is not different from his place in Catholicism. After all, Rodenbach points out, the demons depicted as gargoyles on Notre-Dame do not prevent that building being a cathedral, a Catholic High Church: similarly, Baudelaire's gargoyles hardly preclude him from being a devout

Catholic (Rodenbach, *L'Elite* 4–5, 7). In effect, Rodenbach draws on points raised in defense of Baudelaire at the time of his trial, and in turn signals twentieth-century interpretations of Baudelaire as an essentially religious, and Christian, poet. Such views, as we shall see, will not go unchallenged in that new and more secularly-minded century.

As Baudelaire's reputation steadily grew beyond France, the responses of critics and poets in other countries highlighted the differences in cultural preoccupations across Europe and North America. In England, the first notable article on Baudelaire appeared in 1862, five years before his death. This piece was by Algernon Swinburne, who was gaining notoriety for his louche, sensuous poetry. In English and in French, Baudelaire seemed to call forth a rich prose style from those who ventured to write about him. Swinburne allowed his teeming imagination to give Baudelaire's poetry a memorable welcome to the English-speaking world:

> It has the languid lurid beauty of close and threatening weather – a heavy heated temperature, with dangerous hothouse scents in it; thick shadow of cloud about it, and fire of molten light. It is quite clear of all whining and windy lamentation; there is nothing of the blubbering and shrieking style long since exploded (29).

At times, Swinburne, otherwise not averse to being outrageous, is at pains to assure his respectable British readers that, really, Baudelaire is not the shameful creature they might think he is. Of "Une Charogne." he writes: "[…] even of the loathsomest bodily putrescence and decay he can make some noble use"; while denying that it's an artist's job "to warn against evil," he maintains that "those who will look for them will find moralities in plenty behind every poem of M. Baudelaire's; […] Like a medieval preacher, when he has drawn the heathen love, he puts sin on its right hand and death on its left" (32).

Baudelaire thanked his English confrère warmly for the article, but was moved to assert his avoidance of any simplistic standpoint. "Permettez-moi cependant," he wrote to Swinburne in October 1863, "de vous dire que vous avez poussé un peu loin ma défense. Je ne suis pas si *moraliste* que vous feignez obligeamment de le croire. Je crois simplement (comme vous, sans doute) que tout poème, tout objet d'art *bien fait* suggérer naturellement et forcément une *morale*. C'est l'affaire du lecteur. J'ai meme une haîne très décidée contre toute *intention* morale exclusive dans un poème." (Baudelaire, *Correspondances* II 325).

We owe Swinburne a debt for drawing forth Baudelaire's very nuanced statement on the relationship between art and morality. Swinburne himself is not so subtle as regards the "languid lurid beauty" of his own poetry, which in its desire to shock for shocking's sake, possesses merely the superficial trappings of Baudelairean influence. Later in life Swinburne would admit that he did not really have much in common with Baudelaire. The contrast between the two poets was well summed up in 1891 by the Belgian poet Emile Verhaeren: "L'un est latin, non seulement dans la forme parfait et équilibrée, mais dans la netteté et la directe traduction de l'idée: l'autre, au contraire, est bouillonant et erratique, volutant et embroussaillé" (Verhaeren 114).

In 1875, there appeared an essay on Baudelaire by the critic George Saintsbury; it is a more sober account than that of Swinburne thirteen years earlier. Saintsbury is more aware of the complexities of Baudelaire's position on "l'art pour l'art." In particular, he quotes this important statement by Baudelaire from an article of 1852: "Le goût immodéré de la forme pousse à des désordres monstrueux et inconnus [...] La passion frénétique de l'art est un chancre qui dévore le reste; et comme l'absence nette du juste et du vrai dans l'art équivant à l'absence d'art, l'homme entire s'évanouit; la spécialisation excessive d'une faculté aboutit au néant" (Baudelaire, *L'Art romantique* 296; Saintsbury 13). Saintsbury's choice of this passage accords with the contemporary British /English bias towards the moral rather than the aesthetic and to a belief that to become a whole person, one must marshal all aspects of one's development— aesthetic, moral, spiritual, economic, etc.—without allowing one to predominate to the exclusion of the others. At the same time, Saintsbury reminds his English readers that the French, including Baudelaire, have taught us to treat literature in its own terms, with the implication that in Britain it has been subservient to commercial and/or moral agendas:

> We have had in England authors in every kind not to be surpassed in genius, but we have always lacked more or less the class of *écrivains artistes*—writers who have recognised the fact that writing is an art, and who have applied themselves with the patient energy of sculptors, painters and musicians to the discovery of its secrets (Saintsbury 26–27).

This is well-balanced criticism at a time when Swinburne and later poets were over-eager to find in Baudelaire encouragement to pose as naughty boys intent on infuriating bourgeois philistine daddy and his peers. Invariably, after a period of self-consciously shocking behavior, they would return, like sheepish prodigal sons, to the homely conservative values they had professed to mock and despise. Robert Louis Stevenson, as the author of *Strange Case of Dr. Jekyll and Mr. Hyde* (1886) would seem, on the face of it, to be a likely disciple of Baudelaire at his most macabre and demoniacal. He claimed that, in his youth, he was an imitator of the Frenchman: "I have thus played the sedulous ape to [...] Baudelaire" (Stevenson, *Memories and Portraits* 29)—but this is part of a fairly long list of literary mentors and, to be fair, the mature Stevenson is aware of the superficiality of his early enthusiasm. In fact, like the pious Victorian Scottish Presbyterian that he was, he objected to Baudelaire allowing himself to translate into French Poe's story "Hop-Frog," "that pointless farrago of horrors" (Stevenson, *Essays Literary and Critical* 179). It is true that Stevenson was more of a "voyageur." in literal fact than was Baudelaire, with a final home in Samoa, but the Scotsman's "to travel hopefully is a better thing than to arrive" sounds pretty tame after Baudelaire's "les vrais voyageurs sont ceux-là qui partent / Pour partir" (Stevenson, *Virginibus Puerisque* 85; Baudelaire, *Œuvres complètes,* 1: 130, lines 17–18). Stevenson's sympathies for the hunchbacks, hobos, and prostitutes of Edinburgh's dingier precincts are weak and patronizing beside Baudelaire's "Ainsi qu'un débauché pauvre qui baise et mange / Le sein martyrisé d'une antique catin." (*Œuvres complètes,* 1: 5, lines 17–18). Unlike Baudelaire, Stevenson was a good man, but Baudelaire was by far the greater artist.

The British (and the Scots) could be ridiculous—to echo Lord Macaulay—in their periodic fits of *im*morality. After Stevenson, the even naughtier English poets of the "Naughty 'Nineties," parading their "Frenchness" before stodgier, more conventional Anglo-Saxons, translated a good deal of Baudelaire into English. The results are mixed: there is no shortage of pallid imitations, but the most haunting attempts include those by Lord Alfred Douglas, the sometime lover of Oscar Wilde. Another Baudelaire translator of the time was Arthur Symons, who was also a critic. In allying Baudelaire with the Symbolists, he may have been treading on dubious ground, but, in general, he had a fine understanding of French literature, and he has left us this moving summing-up of our poet: "Baudelaire lived and died solitary, secret, a confessor of sins who has never told the whole truth, le *mauvais moine* of his own sonnet, an ascetic of passion, a hermit of the brothel" (Symons 115).

In the United States, the first important essay on Baudelaire was by Eugene Benson and was published anonymously in the *Atlantic Monthly* of February 1869. Seven years later, in *The Nation*, the novelist Henry James weighed in with an essay that denounces Baudelaire for an essential triviality, for giving us the superficial, disgusting trappings of evil ("stinking corpses" etc.) rather than a profound insight into the moral universe. In other words, Baudelaire has been too caught up with his beloved Poe, for whom James has no time; he prefers to compare Baudelaire—adversely—with a fellow American more worthy of attention. Here is an interesting observation to set beside Gautier's more mutually favorable remarks on the "fleurs du mal" in "Rappaccini's Daughter": "A good way to embrace Baudelaire at a glance," writes James, "is to say that he was, in his treatment of evil, exactly what Hawthorne was not—Hawthorne, who felt the thing at its source, deep in the human consciousness. Baudelaire's infinitely slighter volume of genius apart, he was a sort of Hawthorne reversed" (James 56). Henry James, not unlike his close friend Stevenson, possessed a Protestant-Puritan sensibility that would be ill-disposed to appreciate Baudelaire, and it has been said, moreover, that as a novelist, James was not best-placed to judge a poet.

In Russia, the aging Leo Tolstoy renounced his earlier works, including the novels *War and Peace* and *Anna Karenina*, which are regarded as world masterpieces, in order to devote himself to championing the poor and the dispossessed of his country. He evolved an uncomplicated Christianity based on ethics and eschewing the supernatural and ritual preoccupations of the official church. In the last phase of his literary work, he concentrated on writing parables which resembled the folk tales of the Russian peasants, and which preached a message of human compassion and the simple life shorn of aristocratic luxury. In his *What Is Art?* (1898), he denounced what he called "counterfeit art" and attacked the poetry of Baudelaire, which he lumped in with the Symbolists and Decadents *en masse*: their work, according to Tolstoy, was incomprehensible, artificial, and irrelevant if not even injurious to the cause of social justice. Baudelaire's "Je t'adore à l'égal de la voûte nocturne" and "Duellum" come in for particular condemnation on the grounds of their obscurity: it's not worth the trouble trying to understand them, as the emotions they convey are, in Tolstoy's view, utterly vile (Tolstoy 160–1).

In Germany, the philosopher Nietzsche also denounced "decadence," but for different reasons. To him, decadence in art was characterized by neurosis, whereas the modern age (the 1880s onwards) required the strength and will-power of exceptional men. God was dead, according to Nietzsche, and all forms of weakness, including the submissive "slave" morality of Christianity, must be rejected. However, it has been argued, specifically in Jacques Le Rider's 1992 article "Nietzsche et Baudelaire," that Nietzsche came to adopt a love-hate attitude to Baudelaire, for he saw in the poet someone who keenly perceived the temper of his time, and whose work was of European significance. Indeed, Nietzsche echoes Baudelaire's insistence that the grotesque and the sublime can co-exist, that no subject-matter is off-limits to artistic treatment. Nietzsche maintained that "there is an art of the ugly soul side-by-side with the art of the beautiful soul, and the mightiest effects of art, the crushing of souls, moving of stones, and humanizing of beasts, have perhaps been best achieved precisely by that art" (Nietzsche 517). Both Baudelaire and Nietzsche perfectly sum up a leading feature of the arts in what we call the age of modernity. One of the greatest German-language poets of that age, Rainer Maria Rilke, lived in Paris where he encountered the squalor so vividly represented in Baudelaire's poetry. For especial praise he singled out "Une Charogne"; to Rilke, Baudelaire had been the pioneer of "objective expression," had opened up "artistic observation [...] far enough to see even in the horrific and apparently merely repulsive that which is and which, with everything else that is, *is valid*" (Rilke 314–15).

As for the Spanish-speaking countries, the Mexican poet Octavio Paz has remarked that the challenging French poetry initiated by Baudelaire was first received warmly in Hispanic America, which later passed it on to Spain (Paz 198–9). The implication is that Spain, being more aesthetically conservative, was slower to catch on.

As the twentieth century progressed, articles and books on Baudelaire became legion. The present essay has concentrated on the period since 1857 up to the First World War: criticism during this period created those areas of argument that would be developed and reshaped thereafter. Most major French writers since the 1920s have had their say on our poet: Paul Valéry declared that, in 1924, Baudelaire was "au comble de la gloire." (Valéry 598), and Marcel Proust praised *Les Fleurs du mal* as "ce livre sublime et grimaçant, où la débauche fait le signe de la croix, où le soin d'enseigner la plus profonde théologie est confié à Satan" (Proust 641)—which is hardly a new insight, but which neatly summarizes a consensus on Baudelaire and signals that he has "arrived." A young François Mauriac, in 1920, wrote on Baudelaire the Catholic, in effect building on Rodenbach's thesis twenty years earlier. T. S. Eliot also stressed Baudelaire as a religious poet, comparing him to Dante and suggesting that, for the Frenchman, "damnation itself is an immediate form of salvation—of salvation from the ennui of modern life, because it at least gives some significance to living" (Eliot 181). The young left-wing Scottish poet and Baudelaire translator Alan

Bold, in 1966, was repelled by Eliot's presentation of Baudelaire as "some kind of stiff-necked cleric" and expressed his preference for the analysis of "Le Voyage" by the Marxist critic Ernst Fischer (Baudelaire, *The Voyage* 9; Fischer 175–80).

Indeed, much Baudelaire criticism throughout the twentieth century could be said to fall into two antagonistic groupings: (1) the religious, transcending "this" world, concerned with individual salvation rather than social solidarity; (2) the secular, even atheistic, for which "this" world is the only one we know, when not God, but we as human beings may (or may not) make a choice to be socially committed, *engagé/es*. In a sense, this harks back to Tolstoy's anti-decadent social conscience, albeit without his roots in Christianity. Bold/Fischer clearly belong to this second tendency and are favorably disposed towards Baudelaire. The existentialist (and idiosyncratically Marxist) Jean-Paul Sartre also belongs to this group—but only up to a point: his 1946 book on Baudelaire is emphatically hostile to the poet. As a man of intense philosophical and political commitment, Sartre has no respect for "cette légereté métaphysique du monde baudelairien." The poet is a narcissist: the rest of us see a tree or a house and are too absorbed in this to be aware of ourselves: Baudelaire is more concerned to look at himself looking at the tree or the house. This arrested adolescent is, in effect, playing with fire: he claims to be both the victim and the executioner in the poem "L'Héautontimorouménos," but this is to avoid responsibility for his position in the moral universe. As an existentialist, Sartre believes that we have to make choices and deal with their consequences; as an active member of the Resistance against the Nazi occupation of France, he would be naturally ill-disposed towards a poet who loses himself in (to Sartre) facile abstractions. Baudelaire is guilty of "mauvaise foi." Sartre mocks Baudelaire's poses, the "dandyisme," the passive acceptance that he "n'est plus qu'un pantin dont on tire les ficelles" (Sartre 220, 26, 31, 104, 203). In his article "The De-demonization of evil," Ulrich Baer has made an invaluable comparison of Sartre's *Baudelaire* with Hannah Arendt's *Eichmann in Jerusalem*. Arendt saw and heard the Nazi mass-murderer in the dock and concluded that here was not some monster, but someone who was more akin to, say, a small-town functionary: here was "the banality of evil." Evil was not some phenomenon that we could conveniently externalize and fetishize as a devil with horns, it was latent in the unthinking, mechanical conduct of everyday bureaucratic procedures. Like Arendt, Sartre was demystifying evil, asserting that it was rather a question of specific acts, which we either choose or choose not to commit, to which we are acquiescent or otherwise. Baudelaire failed the test.

As with the case of Henry James on Baudelaire, Sartre has been criticized for being a non-poet who himself failed to address the actual poetry. Sartre's *Baudelaire* was highly controversial: critics, such as Georges Bataille and Georges Blin, have joined in the fray. For a detailed study, consult Susan Blood's *Baudelaire and the Aesthetics of Bad Faith* (1997).

To the second "grouping" described above belongs Walter Benjamin, more favorably disposed than Sartre to Baudelaire. The posthumously-supplied subtitle of his book *Charles Baudelaire: A Lyric Poet in the Era of High Capitalism* (1969) ably summarizes his Marxist-infused perspective. Of the poem "A une passante," Benjamin observed that "love itself is recognized as being stigmatized by the big city" (Benjamin 46). In the present volume, Beryl F. Schlossman examines Benjamin's Baudelaire in extensive detail.

Other French or Francophone writers who have contributed to the canon of Baudelaire criticism include Yves Bonnefoy, who praises the poet for confronting in his work the reality of death (a kind of reclamation of Baudelaire for existentialism, one might think—see also Edward K. Kaplan's essay in the present volume), Michel Foucault (comparison of the poet with the philosopher Kant), Jean Starobinski, and Bernard-Henri Lévy, who concentrates on Baudelaire's last years and "exil" in Belgium. Outside France, contributors to the present volume have been at the forefront of the bolder explorations of the poet. Beyond this eminent company, Clive Scott, author of *Translating Baudelaire* (2000), is the leading authority on Baudelaire in translation. Developments in critical theory have made their inevitable impact. For example, among those who have offered a feminist take on Baudelaire are such scholars as Elissa Marder, author of *Dead Time* (2001). We have come a long way since Christopher Isherwood's preface to his 1933 translation of Baudelaire's *Intimate Journals*: "Shy men of extreme sensibility are the born victims of the prostitute" (Baudelaire, *Intimate Journals* 10). In our time, a critic who wished to be taken seriously would not venture to write in that vein.

Works Cited

Baer, Ulrich. "The De-demonization of evil." *Cabinet Magazine* 5 (Winter 2001/02). Web. Sept. 13, 2013. <http://cabinetmagazine.org/issues/5/dedemonization.php>.

Bandy, W. T., ed. *Baudelaire Judged by His Contemporaries (1845-1867)*. New York: Institute of French Studies at Columbia University, 1933.

Baudelaire, Charles. *Correspondances*. 2 vols. Eds. Claude Pichois & Jean Ziegler. Paris: Gallimard, 1973.

_____. *Intimate Journals*. Trans. Christopher Isherwood, with an introduction by W. H. Auden. London: Panther, 1969.

_____. *Œuvres complètes*. 2 vols. Ed. Claude Pichois. Paris: Gallimard, 1975–76.

_____. *Œuvres complètes. L'Art romantique*. Ed. Jacques Crépet. Paris: Conard, 1925.

_____. *The Voyage: A translation by Alan Bold from Baudelaire's French*. Edinburgh: M. Macdonald, 1966.

Benjamin, Walter. *Charles Baudelaire: A Lyric Poet in the Era of High Capitalism*. Trans. Harry Zohn. New York: Verso, 1983.

Brunetière, Ferdinand. "Charles Baudelaire." *Revue des deux mondes* 81 (1887): 69–70.

Eliot, T. S. *Selected Prose*. Ed. John Hayward. Harmondsworth: Penguin, 1963.

Fischer, Ernst. *The Necessity of Art: A Marxist Approach*. Trans. Anna Bostock. Harmondsworth: Penguin, 1963.

Fraisse, Armand. *Armand Fraisse sur Baudelaire 1857–1869*. Gembloux: Duculot, 1973.

Guyaux, André, ed. *Baudelaire: un demi-siècle de lectures des* Fleurs du mal *(1855–1905)*. Paris: Presses universitaires de Paris-Sorbonne, 2007.

Hamburger, Michael. *The Truth of Poetry: Tensions in Modern Poetry from Baudelaire to the 1960s*. Harmondsworth: Penguin, 1972.

Huret, Jules. *Enquête sur l'évolution littéraire: conversations avec [...] Stéphane Mallarmé [et a[]*. Paris: Charpentier, 1891.

Huysmans, Joris-Karl. *A rebours*. Paris: 10/18, 1975.

James, Henry. *Selected Literary Criticism*. Ed. Morris Shapira. Harmondsworth: Penguin, 1968.

Le Rider, Jacques. "Nietzsche et Baudelaire." *Littérature* 86 (1992): 85–101.

Mallarmé, Stéphane. "La musique et les lettres." *La revue blanche* 6:30 (1894): 297–309.

_____. *Œuvres completes*. Ed. Bertrand Marchal. Paris: Gallimard, 1998.

Marder, Elissa. *Dead Time: Temporal Disorders in the Wake of Modernity (Baudelaire and Flaubert)*. Stanford, CA: Stanford UP, 2001.

Nietzsche, Friedrich. *The Philosophy of Nietzsche*. Ed. Geoffrey Clive. New York: New American Library, 1965.

Paz, Octavio. *Convergences: Essays on Art and Literature*. Trans. Helen Lane. London: Bloomsbury, 1990.

Pichois, Claude, ed. *Lettres à Baudelaire*. Neuchâtel: Etudes Baudelairiennes 1V–V, 1973.

Proust, Marcel. "A propos de Charles Baudelaire." *La nouvelle revue française* 93 (1921): 641–663.

Rilke, Rainer Maria. *Letters of Rainer Maria Rilke 1892–1910*. Trans. Jane Bannard Greene & M. D. Herter Norton. New York: The Norton Library, 1969.

Rodenbach, Georges. *L'Art en exil*. Paris: Librairie Moderne, 1889.

_____. *L'Elite*. Paris: Charpentier, 1899.

Saintsbury, George. *The Collected Essays and Papers [...] 1875–1923*. Vol. 4. New York: Dutton, 1924.

Sartre, Jean-Paul. *Baudelaire*. Reprint. Paris: Gallimard, 1970.

Scott, Clive. *Translating Baudelaire*. Exeter: U of Exeter P, 2000.

Scott, Maria C. *Baudelaire's "Le Spleen de Paris": Shifting Perspectives.* Farnham, England: Ashgate, 2005.

Starkie, Enid. *Baudelaire.* Harmondsworth: Penguin, 1971.

_____. *From Gautier to Eliot: the Influence of France on English Literature 1851–1939.* London: Hutchinson, 1960.

Stevenson, Robert Louis. *Essays Literary and Critical.* Tusitala Edition. London: Heinemaan, 1923.

_____. *Memories and Portraits.* Tusitala Edition. London: Heinemann, 1924.

_____. *Virginibus Puerisque.* Tusitala Edition. London: Heinemann, 1924.

Swinburne, Algernon. *Swinburne as Critic.* Ed. Clyde K. Hyder. Boston: Routledge, 1972.

Symons, Arthur. *The Symbolist Movement in Literature.* New York: Dutton, 1919.

Temple, Ruth Zabriskie. *The Critic's Alchemy: A Study of the Introduction of French Symbolism into England.* New York: Twayne, 1953.

Tolstoy, Leo. *What Is Art?* Trans. Aylmer Maude. Reprint. London: Oxford UP, 1969.

Turquet-Milnes, Gladys. *The Influence of Baudelaire in France and England.* London: Constable, 1913.

Valéry, Paul. *Œuvres.* Ed. Jean Hytier. Vol. 1. Paris: Gallimard, 1957.

Verhaeren, Emile. *Hugo et le romantisme.* Brussels: Editions Complexe, 2002.

Verlaine, Paul. *Œuvres poétiques complètes.* Eds. Y. G. Le Dantec & Jacques Borel. Paris: Gallimard, 1962.

in the modern world. In several languages and in many forms, literature is at the center of Benjamin's thought on culture; poetry, translations, and a hybrid memoir shape the innovative writings on and around Baudelaire, capitalist culture, capital cities, and the arcades that correspond to the cityscapes of modernity, just as the shapes of Baudelaire's poems correspond to the conscious project of inscribing literature with history.

Beyond the illustration or poetic expression of historical phenomena in literature, Benjamin presents Baudelaire as the vector of history. I would suggest that the poetry of Baudelaire is the foundation for the monumental book project known as *The Arcades Project*. In addition to this large, unfinished project, Benjamin planned to complete *Charles Baudelaire: A Lyric Poet in the Period of High Capitalism*, a book on Baudelaire. The book-length essay titled *Paris in the Second Empire in Baudelaire* and "On Some Motifs in Baudelaire" were conceived as sections of the book. Two other sections, one on Baudelaire's allegory and another on the commodity, were projected, but have not been found in Benjamin's papers.

Baudelaire intrigues and moves Benjamin, and it is his poetry in particular that prompts and shapes Benjamin's theoretical exploration of the city in modern European history. Baudelaire as a subject of study is unique in Benjamin's writings, or perhaps one could say that Baudelaire is omnipresent, in correspondence with Benjamin's other topics. Baudelaire's poetry echoes through the range of Benjamin's interests and fields of inquiry. Like the French poet's figures of revenants and bohemian types, the image of Baudelaire breaks into Benjamin's thought. He reigns; he never leaves. Benjamin never forgets him. What I am calling Baudelaire-Ville is the city in poetry, the place where the poet embroiders his canvases of art and love, allegory and history.

Benjamin's early encounter with Baudelaire shaped a sustained interest in the poet, an exploration of translation, and several major theoretical topics concerning modern art, literature, and media, as well as urban culture. Benjamin's major works concerning the French poet are written during the years of the critic's exile in Paris.

A Une Passante: Walter Benjamin in Baudelaire–Ville

Beryl F. Schlossman

A Une Passante

La rue assourdissante autour de moi hurlait.
Longue, mince, en grand deuil, douleur majestueuse,
Une femme passa, d'une main fastueuse
Soulevant, balançant le feston et l'ourlet;

Agile et noble, avec sa jambe de statue.
Moi, je buvais, crispé comme un extravagant,
Dans son œil, ciel livide où germe l'ouragan,
La douceur qui fascine et le plaisir qui tue.

Un éclair... Puis la nuit! — Fugitive beauté,
Dont le regard m'a fait soudainement renaître,
Ne te verrai-je plus que dans l'éternité?

Ailleurs, bien loin d'ici! trop tard! jamais, peut-être!
Car j'ignore où tu fuis, tu ne sais où je vais,
O toi que j'eusse aimée, ô toi qui le savais!

To a Woman Passing By

Around me howled the deafening street.
Tall, slender, dressed in mourning, majestic grief,
A woman passed by, with ceremonious hand
lifting, swaying her festoon and hem;

Agile and noble, with the leg of a statue.
Clenched and extravagant, I drank
from her eye, a livid sky where hurricanes
take seed, sweet fascination and fatal pleasure.

The first important remarks about Baudelaire in the context of the research project appear in a brief descriptive sketch, written in 1935. In this short essay, Benjamin gave the revealing title of "Baudelaire or the Streets of Paris" to the section that evokes the major topics of his ambitious project on Paris as the ultimate capital of the nineteenth century, the city of modernity.

Several unconventional texts begin to give form to the aphorisms and citations that shape the unfinished monumental work, especially "Central Park." In 1938, Benjamin completed his major essay, "The Paris of the Second Empire in Baudelaire," and in 1939, he wrote another essay, "On Some Motifs in Baudelaire." Other parts of the project were not written. The monumental work intended to include Benjamin's Baudelaire essays, *The Arcades Project*, was unfinished at the time of Benjamin's death. Benjamin's essays are suggestive of the dimensions that the author intended to reflect in his creation (or a creatively-transformed construction), through literature, of a city, a life, and a poetics. The essays in the book were intended to move, through literature and through the dimension of time, toward a cultural archeology of modernity.

The constellation of early twentieth-century modernity pointed Benjamin toward Paris. The work of shaping the Baudelaire book and *The Arcades Project* about Paris and modern urban culture sustained the author through a decade of exile, poverty, hardship, uncertainty, and isolation. His unfinished work-in-progress about "the capital of the nineteenth century" continues to dazzle us today with its bold design, its powerful use of voice and citation, its intimate vision of a city caught up in modernity, and of the poet who gave that city its voices, images, portraits, impressions, landscapes and seascapes, urban snapshots, and cityscape.

Benjamin's work on Baudelaire is important for an understanding of the Second Empire as the moment of transformation. The Baudelaire essays focus on the preoccupations that dominate Benjamin's corpus; they allow readers to explore the intellectual parameters of the wildly modern virtual city of *The Arcades Project*. Like the Baudelaire essays, this unfinished monumental work deeply frightened some of Benjamin's closest friends with the boldness of its conceptualization. Benjamin's innovative approach to criticism is grounded in an attentive reading of the consequences of Baudelaire's work. Benjamin's reading and writing of modernity unfold at precisely the moment when Baudelaire's literary impact resonates across the avant-garde movements of dada and surrealism, and when Freud's psychoanalytic discovery and exploration of the unconscious and the traumatic experiences of modern life indirectly confirm Baudelaire's intuitions about art and life. Cultural perspective shapes literature—and the study of literature—across encounters of waking thought with the dreamlike fragments that emerge from the unconscious.

What does it mean to say that Benjamin reads Baudelaire as a vector of history? Benjamin seeks to understand the impact of Baudelaire's literary works as evidence of the historical testimony that Baudelaire observes around him. The deeply historical nature of Baudelaire's writing is uniquely conscious: Baudelaire the writer seeks to preserve the imprint of history and to write literary works that present and reflect history. Baudelaire's poetry in particular gives evidence of the impact of history on the lonely subjects of modernity. Recognized or subterranean, conscious or unconscious, history enters the lives of Baudelaire's emblematic and allegorical subjects in their experiences of time and memory.

The three chapters of Benjamin's *The Paris of the Second Empire in Baudelaire* elaborate two conceptual strands. First, Benjamin shapes his critique in the form of a portrait; he evokes photographs, paintings, and images of Baudelaire at work in allegorical roles and representations within his poetry. Baudelaire's anonymous narrators are sometimes evoked as the Poet, but frequently indicated only as an observant narrator or a man on the run, surrounded by the streets and the crowd. The poet invents new heroes—the disengaged dandy, the nonchalant flâneur, and the anonymous artist. Like the prostitute, these birds of prey sift through the crowd, looking for the evidence of desire even as the crowd consumes them. They prefer the vacant streets at the outskirts of town, the arcades, and the moody skies of autumn in Paris. Above all, the night world is their preferred ground.

The figures who inhabit Baudelaire's world are artists, flâneurs, dandies, and women, especially prostitutes. He sees the latter—'girls of the street' (naïvely named) or 'whores' (brutally named)—as Baudelaire's consorts and companions, more than any other people. In any case, women take the emotional heat in Baudelaire's world. In his poetry, women are vilified and adored, admired or pitied, followed or abandoned, worshipped or, occasionally, sacrificed. Baudelaire's figures act out their scripts, like actors on an asphalt stage, among the crowd. Their perceptions and experience seem to set them apart from their "semblances [semblables]," people who appear to be like them. They are, ambiguously, brothers or sisters to the figure of the Poet, who frequently plays the parts of Baudelaire's narrators.

Second, Benjamin's essays engage in the pursuit of motifs, lines of verse and prose, literary images and citations that emblematize Baudelaire's perceptions of modernity. The crowded cityscapes of Paris are shaped by the vicissitudes of capital; commerce orients the transformations of value that permeate culture. Benjamin points out that the solitary artist takes up the role of flâneur, the walker in the city, in search of the bizarre consolations of the crowd but also in search of a buyer. The magic of the crowd that Baudelaire frequently invokes veils the relationship between seller and buyer. The streets are the background for the crowd that intoxicates the poet and allows objects to appear in the disguise of anonymity. Baudelaire's complicity with women is related to his understanding that art has become a commodity, figured by the self-offering of the girl on the street. La bohème, in Benjamin's view, connects Baudelaire's pursuit of art with the proletarian world pushed to the edges of the Second Empire. For the flâneur, the harsh realities of love in the big city, like the melancholy mood of the artist, are masked by the veil of the crowd. Modernity is the context for the renewal of art, staged in the constellations of city life that Baudelaire translates into a work of lyric poetry that allows contemporary life to reshape the poetic images of antiquity. His use of allegory plunges into the past to revive the present, the "now."

Benjamin's theoretical writing on early modernity explores the writer's contemporary moment in Paris—the second and third decades of the twentieth century—in connection with the Second Empire and the late nineteenth century. He writes at a time when poetry had already projected itself into other genres, perhaps in tacit recognition of its compromised status in the modern world. In several languages and in many forms, literature is at the center of Benjamin's thought on culture; poetry, translations, and a hybrid memoir shape the innovative writings on and around Baudelaire, capitalist culture and capital cities, and the arcades that correspond to the cityscapes of modernity as the shapes of Baudelaire's poems correspond to the conscious project of inscribing literature with history.

Benjamin's study of Baudelaire in Second-Empire Paris explores the role of the city as a concentrated center of wealth, the "capital" that interested city-dwellers, ranging from Haussmann to the observers Marx and Engels, but also as a center of political repression, revolutionary activity, commodification, proletarian hardships, and the distractions of the poor that are portrayed in Baudelaire's writing. Benjamin wrote "On Some Motifs in Baudelaire," his last and perhaps his most powerful essay on Baudelaire, in a different intellectual context. The essay explores the capital city in literary and cultural terms, the heart of Paris, its life and color. In this essay, Baudelaire's poetics of the subject offers Benjamin the key to modernity: the new Paris, an allegorical entity alive to its subjects, thus puts an end to lyric poetry as it existed before the publication of *The Flowers of Evil*. Benjamin articulates a shift from Baudelaire, seen as an individual subject, a biographical entity, to Baudelaire as the literary corpus and the subjectivity of Paris.

Benjamin's essays and notes on Baudelaire's elaboration of Parisian modernity frequently refer to a passage in the poet's dedication of *Le Spleen de Paris* to Arsène Houssaye. In a careful digression on literary style, Baudelaire presents his second major poetic enterprise in words that evoke the "Tableaux Parisiens" as much as the prose poems:

Quel est celui de nous qui n'a pas... rêvé le miracle d'une prose poétique, musicale sans rythme et sans rime, assez souple et assez heurtée pour s'adapter aux mouvements lyriques de l'âme, aux ondulations de la rêverie, aux soubresauts de la conscience? [Who among us has not... dreamed the miracle of a poetic prose that would be musical without rhythm or rhyme, flexible enough and sufficiently abrupt to adapt to the lyrical movements of the heart, the undulations of daydreaming, the shocks of consciousness?]

Paris Spleen, also called *Les Petits poèmes en prose*, is a product of the effects of a vast collective creature that is latent, almost invisible, hidden among Baudelaire's fragments and poetic figures: the crowd. Benjamin considers the crowd as Baudelaire's most important motif. In the constellation of the poet's favorite rhetorical figures and visual images—words and things—many of them are related to the motif of the crowd. Baudelaire's strategic meditation is unusually candid about the impact of the city and its masses: "C'est surtout de la fréquentation des villes énormes, c'est du croisement de leurs innombrables rapports, que naît cet idéal obsédant [Above all, it is the experience of enormous cities, the intersecting of their innumerable connections, that gives birth to this obsessive ideal]." Loosely constructed, the book seeks "la description de la vie moderne, ou plutôt d'*une* vie moderne [to describe modern life, or rather *one* life that is modern]." That life is filled with melancholy and ennui, or spleen. The ideal of its depiction echoes the same strategic opposition of the first section of *Les Fleurs du mal*. This passage points toward the creation of "A une passante," a love-poem addressed to an unknown woman, who appears against the background of the street at nightfall. The narrator's experience of the shocks of city life shapes the encounter between the subject and the crowd.

A Woman in the Crowd

"Baudelaire leaves no doubt that *he* looked deep into the woman's eyes."

— Walter Benjamin

"A une passante" was first published on October 15, 1860 in *L'Artiste*, and appeared in the second and third editions of *Les Fleurs du mal*, within the section, titled "Tableaux Parisiens." The sonnet is filled with the narrator's passion; the arresting image of the passerby draws him into a storm of emptiness and plenitude, love, and desire. The unknown woman is not presented as a virgin on a pedestal, a figure of motherhood, an entertainer, or a prostitute. These non-identifications distinguish her from many of Baudelaire's figures of women, although there are images that connect her to several of Baudelaire's favorite feminine roles. We might see her, with Benjamin, as the incarnation of the urban crossroads experience that revitalizes the narrator of the poem, and as the allegory of woman who appears in a montage with the city and with death in Baudelaire's poetry. Benjamin sees the encounter between the poet and an unknown stranger in mourning as an allegorical event. Desire leads the narrator to an anticipation of death and the Night of Eternity (according to Baudelaire's use of capital letters). The woman's flight sharpens his longing for her love even as her disappearance marks the narrator's sensibility with the power of allegory: in "Baudelaire or the Streets of Paris," Benjamin writes: "It is the unique property of Baudelaire's poetry that the image of Woman and the image of Death are combined with a third image, the City" (4). This comment already points toward the reading of "A une passante." Later, Benjamin points out that the crowd is not named in the poem (5). The character of the encounter leads the narrator beyond the limitations of the woman's lack of identity. She remains an image produced by the crowd.

The sonnet's stately formal language is characterized by the flowing quality of the alexandrines and Baudelaire's skillful use of rhythm, rhyme, and dramatic tension. In one of Baudelaire's stylistic trademarks, however, it also introduces several abrupt, suspenseful breaks and ellipses. The combination of the melodic and lyric qualities with moments of violence—the evocation of noise, the ellipses of silence and disappearance—give the poem its extraordinary evocative power. The first line, with its urban scene, is permeated with the violence of sound, and the first break occurs immediately. In the next lines, the woman and her effects on the narrator are described. These include the musical rhythm of her movement, the fashion she wears, her gesture of lifting her skirts clear of the street. They lead into the evocation of the narrator's emotional and physical response to seeing her.

The first two stanzas of the sonnet portray the narrator's sudden violent passion as the effects of seeing the woman. At first he is shocked and sexually revitalized; the narrator beautifully and hyperbolically evokes the slowed rhythm of her dancelike movements. The description of his erotic rebirth includes elements of death: he is stopped in his tracks, and her leg resembles the idealized form of a statue. The exchange of glances takes on hyperbolic qualities: the narrator evokes looking deep into the woman's eyes as drinking nectar and poison, fascination and death. The last words of the second stanza shape the constellation of death, the city, and woman that Benjamin reads in Baudelaire's inscription of the Parisian crowds in his poetry (6).

After invoking the dangerous pleasure of love, the extravagant lover following this woman—or perhaps still frozen to the spot— immediately witnesses her flight and disappearance. The break occurs between the first eight lines and the final six lines, at the point of transformation that is typical of sonnet construction. The tone changes after the division between octet and sestet. A violent break occurs at the beginning of line nine, in the flash of lightning and the fall of night, underscored with the capital letter of allegory. Several breaks follow that point, as the narrator's sexualized response expands into a declaration of love and an accusation of the woman. The narrator imagines that she has already betrayed him and left him, even though, he claims, she knew that he loved her.

We ay follow Benjamin's analysis to interpret this nameless woman produced by the crowd as Baudelaire's invention. She is the allegorical figure or emblem of the crowd that enchants the poet with its powers of imagination and subjectivity. The narrator's desire for her is proportional to her unknown qualities. He will never see her again, and on this basis, she has become the urban object of desire. The narrator suffers, she brands him with the stigmata of city love, and only eternity—the infinity of time after death—will bring them together again in a ghostly echo of the city where they first saw each other.

Like the woman passing by, the city itself, and the crowd, nature remains anonymous. The effects of the crowd are perceived in the first line, and the effects of nature—light, lightning, and nightfall—appear at the second major break, at line nine. The appearance of the woman suspends the noise of the crowd and the sky of her eyes evokes nature as the mourning she wears evokes nightfall. She moves out of his sight, and he, "crispé comme un extravagant" in line six, cannot follow her path even as he is losing his own way.

Benjamin's analysis of the effects of the crowd on Baudelaire's figure of the erotician—the narrator in search of pleasure—can be understood in the context of some brief annotations in "Central Park" about the poet's suffering: the experience turns into one of the narrator's stations on the Via Dolorosa, as Benjamin names it (7). The narrator's passion is love at last sight rather than love at first sight, and he is spared the fulfillment of it (8).

These harsh remarks about the narrator's encounter deserve some explanation. The narrator's lament seems to ring false for Benjamin, since he sees the impact of the encounter in the stigmata of love, the visual mark of the poet's passion. His comments about "stigmatization" and "the stigmata" of love in the crowd are not metaphoric, but rather, allegorical: like the stigmata of Saint Francis, the marks of the narrator's passion are wounds that result from the vision of an apparition. Benjamin refers to the optical impact, the vision of the passerby, which Baudelaire evokes as an exchange of gazes. In the context of Baudelaire's passion for images—the source, in Benjamin's view, of Baudelaire's penchant for allegory—"A une passante" can be read in two ways: first, as a modern love poem shaped by the crowd, and second, as the evidence of the loss of traces of personal identity that Baudelaire transforms into a miniature baroque tragedy. Benjamin hints that the poetic shift toward the afterlife in the tercets gives evidence that the narrator, consumed with his loss, has had a close call with a woman who wears the black dress and the veils that Baudelaire associates with allegories of Death. The woman's disappearance allows for the final magic of the poem, as the poet turns his narrator's desire into love.

Note
The author gratefully acknowledges research support from the University of California, Irvine.

Works Cited
Baudelaire, Charles. *Œuvres complètes.* Paris: Gallimard, 1975–1976.

Benjamin, Walter. *The Writer of Modern Life: Essays on Charles Baudelaire.* Ed. Michael W. Jennings. Trans. Howard Eiland, Edmund Jephcott, Rodney Livingston, & Harry Zohn. Cambridge and London: The Belknap Press of Harvard University Press, 2006.

Coming to Terms: Baudelaire and Flaubert_____

Kathryn Oliver Mills

Charles Baudelaire and Gustave Flaubert were born in 1821. In 1857, the Second Empire prosecuted Flaubert's *Madame Bovary* as well as Baudelaire's *Les Fleurs du mal* for outraging public morals. The works of both authors are distinctive for how they combine romanticism with realism and subvert artistic as well as cultural expectations with irony. Finally, each man was a seismograph for his age as well as a model for ours: Elissa Marder has observed that Baudelaire and Flaubert are "the two authors from the nineteenth century that the twentieth century can't live without" (4). Given these common chronological, biographical, and literary landmarks, it's surprising that these men did not have more to say to one another; Flaubert's correspondence with Baudelaire amounts to only half a page in the Pléiade index of his correspondence, compared with four pages for that with Hugo. It's also surprising that relatively few critical works are devoted to a concomitant study of Baudelaire and Flaubert. Moreover, none of those few critical works develops several salient points that their œuvres share and that particularly illuminate each author's significance to modernity: both writers thought that art should respond to a changing period; both thought the literary conventions at their disposal were not adequate to the task; both sought to forge a form of literature that would—literally—come to terms with their era; and for both men, this form involved permutations of prose and poetry.[1] These are the four points this essay will address.

In 1863, with *Le Peintre de la vie moderne*, Baudelaire declared that, in the future, art had to represent the realities of an emergent, modern world: "Il s'agit, pour lui, de dégager de la mode ce qu'elle peut contenir de poétique dans l'historique, de tirer l'éternel du transitoire" (*Curiosités esthétiques* 466). Flaubert, too, emphasized the reciprocity he perceived between art and world: "Donc cherchons à voir les choses *comme elles sont* [italics mine] et ne voulons pas avoir plus d'esprit que le bon Dieu....habituons-nous à considérer le monde comme une œuvre d'art dont il faut reproduire les procédés dans nos œuvres" (*Correspondances* II 284). In Baudelaire's and Flaubert's time, "les choses comme elles sont" involved change. Writing about the emergence of the electric telegraph, Flaubert noted that "Nous aurons fait ce qu'il y a de plus difficile et de moins glorieux: la transition...l'avenir nous tourmente et le passé nous retient..." (*Correspondances* I 730). Despite a certain degree of private contempt for the "banalité" resulting from modern society, and reputations in some quarters as "disciples of pure art," Flaubert and Baudelaire believed that art and its context had to reflect each other. Thus, in a drastically changing era, art had to take a new direction.

Although for many critics, Baudelaire's *Les Fleurs du mal* and Flaubert's *Madame Bovary* and *L'Education sentimentale* define the modernity of these two authors, in fact, those well-known books principally exploit traditional forms of literature to undermine them, which is why the legal arbiters for contemporary social norms condemned Baudelaire's and Flaubert's first works.[2] *Les Fleurs du mal* works both with and against romanticism as well as classicism. In 1802, Chateaubriand, who knew whereof he spoke, defined the romantic soul and its *mal du siècle* thus: "Dégoûtées par leur siècle, effrayées par leur religion, elles [ces âmes ardentes] sont restées dans le monde sans se livrer au monde." Baudelaire wrote his poems some fifty years later, but Chateaubriand's romantic model clearly describes the speaker of *Les Fleurs du mal*. Like the romantic hero, the poet of *Les Fleurs du mal* is unable to function in the "real world": "ses ailes de géant l'empêchent de marcher" ("L'Albatros," *Oc* 9–10, line 16). "Le Cygne" elaborates on the existential dilemma depicted throughout Baudelaire's verse: as the speaker walks around Paris, newly redesigned for the modern era by Haussmann, he is caught between worlds that no longer exist (the classical Antiquity of "Andromaque" as well as the way Paris used to be) and one that does exist (Paris in the 1850s), but which he cannot embrace: "Paris change! mais rien dans ma mélancolie/N'a bougé!" (*Œuvres complètes* 86, lines 29–30).

Melancholy is romantic, but the solipsism of Baudelaire's verse goes beyond even that of the French romantic poets, who could at least often find an analogue for their emotions in nature. In the face of realities that he cannot accept, the speaker of "Le Cygne" and of *Les Fleurs du mal* retreats into a world of literary figures: "Tout pout moi devient allégorie" (Line 31). Poetic form contributes to the poet's sense of alienation from daily life as well. Like "Le Cygne," "Le Soleil" is included in "Tableaux Parisiens," a section ostensibly devoted to Parisian scenes and is about taking a walk in the city. However, "Le Soleil" is one of many poems in *Les Fleurs du mal* that self-consciously replaces the urban landscape with rimes and verse:

> Je vais m'exercer seul à ma fantasque escrime,
> Flairant dans tous les coins les hasards de la rime,
> Trébuchant sur les mots comme sur les pavés
> Heurtant parfois des vers depuis longtemps rêvés
>
> (*Œuvres complètes* 83, lines 5–8).

While city streets metamorphose gently into classical form in "Le Soleil," Baudelaire's recurrent play on the two meanings of *vers* in French ("verse" and "worms") indicates a more destructive relationship between the form of verse and actuality. *Vers* as worms devour the cadaver in "Une charogne," and *vers* as verse maintain the "forme et essence divine" of the poet's "amours décomposés" (*Œuvres complètes* 32, lines 47–8). "Essence divine" sounds exalted, but the "vermine" that surround it and the decomposing loves that constitute it, are not. Furthermore, both forms of "vers" efface the physical world that the speaker, as an inhabitant, needs to accommodate. In Baudelaire's poetic universe, "vers" break matter down, and "vers" transform elemental matter into art.

There is a sense in which this alchemizing procedure is inherent in verse. In his work on semiology, Laurent Jenny suggested that metrical principles establish a disjunction between idealized form and the vagaries of reality; the ideal dominates such that the real world falls away, to be replaced by artistic form.[3] Whether or not this is generally true of metrical poetry—and I think it is not—it is true of *Les Fleurs du mal.* Baudelaire's verse is consistently and painfully left to contemplate itself and its own creations rather than the daily life and even the natural world that surround it. Walter Benjamin observed that lyric poetry had lost its "aura" in Baudelaire's time because of the collection's particularly marked and seminal disjunction between word and world (192). Indeed, the intensity of this introversion ultimately inverts the structures that inform it. Baudelaire frequently takes romantic or classical topoi and turns them inside out: pastoral strolls become city walks that, in their turn, become abstractions; "Une charogne" invokes Ronsard's "Mignonne, allons voir si la rose," while substituting a rotting corpse for a fading rose and by urging his beloved into the arms of the waiting "ver/mine" rather than into his own. On the cusp of a new era, *Les Fleurs du mal* invokes certain literary conventions at the same time that it shows those conventions to be void of their original significance.

If the inability of Baudelaire's speaker to accept current realities in verse is slightly neurotic and distinctly tragic, the same incapacity in Flaubert's longer works of prose is ignominious. Flaubert himself researched and presented the historical background of *Madame Bovary* and *L'Education sentimentale* with the rigor of an investigative journalist; in both novels, for example, he meticulously surveys the emerging economy founded on banks, credit, and industry.[4] However, the protagonists of those novels are blithely and disastrously oblivious to the facts of their economic situations. Emma and Frédéric aspire to a class higher than their own by spending freely and relying on credit; in the end, debt pushes Emma to suicide, and Frédéric's ultimate status as a *petit bourgeois* epitomizes the shipwreck of his dreams.

The primary failings of Emma and Frédéric, though, are sentimental, and they contribute decisively to their instigators' fatal ends. Emma engages in a series of adulterous affairs before her death; Frédéric fails to make anything of his passion for Madame Arnoux. These downfalls, too, occur because these characters ignore reality, in this case, by relying too heavily on a literary mode that does not address what they are living. Frédéric pursues Mme Arnoux because she "ressemblait aux femmes des livres romantiques" (53). Indeed, for him she becomes a romantic literary construct, Charlotte to his Werther (618), separate from the real world of experience. In place of the long-awaited kiss, Frédéric makes the following declaration to Mme Arnoux at the end of novel: "…et les délices de la chair étaient contenues pour moi dans votre nom que je me répétais, en tâchant de le baiser sur mes lèvres" (69). While in some contexts—in Goethe's authentically romantic work, for example—this statement of love could legitimately represent the power of words in human affairs, in *L'Education sentimentale* Frédéric's romantic words function as affectations and fall flat, along with the rest of his vain statements.

In *Madame Bovary*, it is Emma who casts herself as a romantic novel's heroine. She is formed by the "Lamartinian" tales an old maid told her at the convent, and one result is that she enchants Léon as "l'amoureuse de tous les romans, l'héroïne de tous les drames, le vague *elle* de tous les volumes de vers" (289).[5] Another result is that her love life, like Frédéric's, becomes a matter of romantic formulations, vapid because they lack actual referents. "Emma cherchait à savoir ce que l'on entendait au juste dans la vie par les mots de 'félicité,' de 'passion,' et 'd'ivresse,' qui lui avaient paru si beaux dans les livres" (69). Again, one could imagine contexts in which those words might have real power. Not so for Emma, however. In Flaubert's novels, unfortunately, the phrases of romanticism are effective only when they are cynically exploited by the likes of Rodolphe, Emma's manipulative lover. Peter Brooks has pointed out that Flaubert's characters invoke traditional genres—that of the "great love story," for example—only to see those genres invalidated, "both through the refusal of story, and through an implicit demonstration that the socio-historical conditions of 'love' have changed since the era of the great Romantic novelists" (188–9). There are key moments when Flaubert empathizes with romantic aspirations for love, the ideal, the infinite, either on behalf of his characters or as narrator. However, he does so hopelessly. In the novels that work within traditional forms, "La parole humaine est comme un chaudron fêlé où nous battons des mélodies à faire danser les ours, quand on voudrait attendrir les étoiles" (*Madame Bovary* 219). The sad ends of Emma and Frédéric indicate that—however enticing its promises—in *Madame Bovary* and *L'Education sentimentale* conventional language is a "cracked cauldron" with an illusory hold on reality, a limited capacity to reach beyond it, and a propensity to fall into clichés.

Flaubert characterized the historical period of transition he was experiencing as "crépuscule" (*Correspondances* I 679), a word that means both "dusk" and "dawn." Baudelaire's verse and Flaubert's first and longer novels represent the corruption and end of the romantic mode and era, as the Second Empire's condemnation confirms. Flaubert's *Trois contes* and Baudelaire's *Le Spleen de Paris,* on the other hand, announce the beginning of a modern literary age and sensibility.

When *Trois contes* was first published, in 1877, contemporary critics praised it for its realism.[6] Due to the constraints of time and space, this essay will use "Un Coeur simple" to represent Flaubert's tales. Félicité's daily routine is rigorous: she starts her day at dawn with mass and works until evening, without interruption (11). Despite her virtue, senseless misery batters Félicité's life from start to finish. She is fired from her first job for a theft she did not commit; her first and only lover jilts her; she catches a cold that makes her deaf; and she loses all that is dear to her: Victor, her precious nephew, her beloved charge Virginie, and her parrot Loulou. While their stories lack the contemporary setting of "Un Coeur simple," the other two "contes"—"Saint Julien de l'Hospitalier" and "Hérodias"—are comparably grim. Saint Julien slaughters quantities of beautiful animals, and even his parents, before he meets his apotheosis by embracing a leper. In "Hérodias," Iaokanann's head is chopped off, and "comme elle était très lourde," the story concludes somewhat ingloriously as three men take turns hauling it off.

Le Spleen de Paris is similarly gritty in its details, although Baudelaire practices his own insistence on contemporaneity more consistently. "Perte d'auréole" (*Œuvres complètes* 352) functions as the new form's *ars poetica*, and the history of this prose poem's composition demonstrates Baudelaire's evolution as a modern artist. In "Perte d'auréole," the poet unwittingly drops his halo in one of Haussmann's new *boulevards*. In an early version, the poet picks his halo up, as if to embrace the hallowed traditions of poetry once again;[7] in the text's final version, the poet-speaker decides to leave the halo in the mud, for "some bad poet." From the thematic and formal pedestal imposed by the classical and romantic traditions, poetry has literally fallen into prose and the street.

What Barbara Johnson called "la banalisation" of poetry (54) is carried out in the themes of Baudelaire's prose poems. Two poems with the same title, one in verse, the other in prose, illustrate this change. "L'Invitation au voyage" in verse (*Œuvres complètes* 53–4) leaves the speaker in his dream with the poem's concluding refrain: "Là, tout n'est qu'ordre et beauté,/Luxe, calme et volupté" (lines 41–2). In contrast, "L'Invitation au voyage" in prose takes the narrator from "there" to "here" with his thoughts returning from the "Infini" to the woman he is addressing at the poem's end. The "Infinite" prose poetry's invitation to a voyage represents, moreover, includes—of all things—pots and pans. Indeed, although there are a few fantastical works, typical subjects of Baudelaire's prose poetry are for the most part life's ordinary moments—sunsets, workdays, a journey's end—rather than the obsession with beauty and art that dominates *Les Fleurs du mal.* Furthermore, the reality of poverty is featured in such prose poems as "Assommons les pauvres," "Les Yeux des pauvres," "Le Joujou du pauvre," and while there are certainly beggars and so on in *Les Fleurs du mal*, the two collections treat the subject very differently. In *Les Fleurs du mal,* poor people are in a sense commodified as art. "À Une mendiante rousse," for example, presents the beggar girl by relating her to the Renaissance writers Ronsard and Belleau. *Le Spleen de Paris*, on the other hand, very rarely uses explicit artistic terms—references to artists or to literary figures, such as "allégorie," for instance—to represent the poor.

In fact, the themes of *Le Spleen de Paris* are not only quotidian, they verge on journalistic reporting both in content and in style: published in newspapers, the paragraphs and subjects of prose poetry resemble that contemporary medium. Jonathan Monroe made this connection (24),[8] and in *Rules of Art*, the sociologist Pierre Bourdieu notes that the emergence of prose poetry related directly to changes in the market and publishing economy brought about by the popular press (140). Newspaper circulation increased four thousand percent between 1830 and 1860 (Terdiman 47): Baudelaire's disapprobation of newspapers is on record—he labeled them a "dégoûtant apéritif" (*Œuvres complètes* 706)—but he could not have been immune to such sociological pressures. Baudelaire called Guys' sketches for the *Illustrated London News* "les archives précieuses de la vie civilisée," and the same could be said about his own prose poetry.

The introduction of prose into poetry allowed Baudelaire to take on modern life. However, for Baudelaire as well as for Flaubert, "painting modern life" in words involved poetry in addition to prose. Flaubert wrote about his literary goal of giving "à la prose le rythme du vers (en la laissant prose et très prose)" (*Correspondances* II 287) in order to describe ordinary life. Echoing Flaubert's formal preoccupations almost perfectly, and in roughly the same time frame, in "À Arsène Houssaye" (Baudelaire's preface to *Le Spleen de Paris)*, Baudelaire proposed to put into practice his ideas about modern art with "le miracle d'une prose poétique," a form that he also called "petits poèmes en prose" in his correspondence. This formal conjunction facilitated both authors' quests to discover the "poétique dans l'historique, de tirer l'éternel du transitoire" (*Curiosités esthétiques* 466).

Flaubert's prose is generally "poetic"; it is well known that he worried over questions of rhythm and sonority in all of his novels. There is good reason, though, to view *Trois contes* as the most complete embodiment of his aim to merge prose with poetry. The use of imagery to signify in the three tales—with the parrot "Loulou" in "Un Coeur simple," with Saint Julien's stained-glass window, and with Saint John's severed head in "Hérodias"— invokes the "figure" which Tzvetan Todorov called the root of poetic language (14). Further, the *Trois contes* achieve a relative degree of compression, one of the formal criteria that Suzanne Bernard had defined in her seminal discussion of prose poetry, *Le Poème en prose de Baudelaire jusqu'à nos jours* (763–73). Other aspects of *Trois contes*—the lyric rhythm of its prose, with its frequent groups of three; the tight *enchaînements* between chapters; the space created between the lines for Félicité's emotions—only emphasize the link between lyricism and Flaubert's last published work. And it is the poetry of "Un Coeur simple" that allows Félicité to surmount the grim circumstances laid out in Flaubert's prose.

Initially Félicité's problems appear to be of a specifically linguistic order: she can't argue her case against the unjustified accusation of theft; she doesn't say a word to her would-be lover throughout courtship and abandonment; she can't locate her nephew, Victor, on the map; she can't read the letter announcing Victor's death; she can't understand the catechism; and the meaning of her existence is reduced to three clichéd phrases that she exchanges with a parrot standing in for the Holy Ghost. Some of these events are outside her power to modulate—Victor's death, for example—but Félicité seems unable to navigate these situations because of her limited verbal ability.

This illiterate servant girl, however, crafts a language that goes beyond both prosaic and romantic words. Félicité's instinctual sense of honor as well as her body language (crying out, responding to her lover's indistinct flow of words with "Ah," and lowering her head, running away) triumph over the seducer's standard patter, a verbosity that reveals the potential meaninglessness of words as it semi-dissolves into ineffectual clichés. Her instinct for depth of meaning also protects her from Bourais' condescension when he explains where Félicité's nephew is on a map, "allegoriz[ing] the separation between figures of desire and its referents," as Nathaniel Wing wrote about how Emma used the map of Paris (54). In contrast, the referents and figures of desire of both Félicité and Flaubert's poetic prose are tightly linked: cigars give Félicité a distinct picture of Victor circulating in a "cloud of tobacco smoke" in Havana, a far more vivid image than Bourais' discussion of latitude and longitude (18).[9] Furthermore, when she uses words (another kind of "referent"), they are limited, but full of heart to an extent that elevates the banality of her circumstances. Her main interlocutor is Loulou, a parrot. Félicité responds to Loulou's mechanical, repetitive phrases "par des mots sans suite" (46). But Félicité's heart "s'épanchait" in her disjointed words, and Loulou helps her understand the mystery of the Holy Ghost, something that sustains her in her many acts of kindness. Flaubert underlines the tight, paradoxical, and tricky relationship between the sacred and the profane in language by inserting babbling and *logos* within Loulou's very name.[10] On the one hand, the moniker is a meaningless repetition of two syllables; on the other hand, Flaubert's nickname for his much beloved niece Caroline was Loulou. Félicité does not contemplate the meaning of such words as "félicité," "passion," or "ivresse," like Emma, nor does she speak in romantic jargon. However, this humble woman's grotesquely limited and highly imaginative grasp of language allows her to surpass the limitations of both traditional verbal structures and conventional, limited modes of understanding.[11] By extension, Flaubert, too, has found a vehicle that—by transfiguring standard forms—addresses his requirements for modern art.

Like Flaubert, the narrator of Baudelaire's prose poetry transcends the ordinary elements that its prose represents—workdays, criminals, sunsets—through poetry. As Robert Kopp has pointed out, in *Le Spleen de Paris* Baudelaire attempts "not only to run away from the world, but also to run towards the *heart* [italics mine] of the world, into the crowds, the street fairs, the life of everyday" (xxvii). When the speaker of the aforementioned "Invitation au Voyage" in prose returns to reality at the poem's conclusion, his "pensées" are "enrichies" by their dreaming excursions. Two other poems with the same title, one in verse and one in prose poetry, also allow a focused sense of what's at issue in the traditional form, on the one hand, and in the revolutionary one on the other. In the verse version of "Crépuscule du Soir" (*Œuvres complètes* 94–5), dusk brings out the dispossessed—demons, robbers, prostitutes likened to the "ver" (worm/verse) that "robs man of his nourishment" (line 20)—and this poem concludes with the dark of night, and unhappiness. In the prose version of "Crépuscule du Soir," the quotidian dusk's transparent clouds, sunset colors, and emerging stars thread through the prose, in the style of poetry, to become the dancer's dress. And that concluding image lyrically symbolizes the heart of man as well as the "fires of fantasy" that both depend on, and illuminate, the "mourning of the night" (*Œuvres complètes* 312). In the same spirit of discovering the sublime within the pedestrian (Kierkegaard's phrase to describe the reconciliation of the transcendent with the everyday) in "Une mort héroïque," Fancioulle's art is composed of simple gestures—"Ce bouffon allait, venait, riait, pleurait, se convulsait"—but from those elements arises "le mystère de la vie" and "une indéstructible auréole" (*Œuvres complètes* 321).

Indeed: the "auréole" that fell into the mud with prose poetry (in "Perte d'Auréole," notably) is reborn from that mud, that is to say, from the prose of life's ordinary moments. When Benjamin argued that poetry had lost its "aura" in the era of high capitalism, he defined "aura" as the perception that "The person we look at, or who feels he is being looked at, looks at us in turn" (188). Benjamin uses that definition to argue that lyric poetry was no longer possible in "the era of high capitalism." At the same time, Benjamin's discussion of poetry's aura also unwittingly indicates that prose poetry was—for Baudelaire, anyway—the lyric's new form.

In contrast with the eyes of *Les Fleurs du mal*, often represented as cold, inanimate jewels, or as deflecting, reversing mirrors, the vision of *Le Spleen de Paris* is generally characterized in terms of depth, perception, and responsiveness. "Les Yeux des pauvres" is an especially striking example of prose poetry's world-view (*Œuvres complètes* 317–19). The narrator of this prose poem describes a poor family in terms of their eyes' wistful response to the luxury of a new *boulevard* café ("Les yeux du père disaient…" "Les yeux du petit garçon…" "Quant aux yeux du plus petit…"). He himself is touched by this sight ("j'étais attendri par cette famille d'yeux…"). Then he rejects what he would have adored in *Les Fleurs du mal*—the beautiful, green, and "impermeable" eyes of his beloved—because they deflect the beggar-family's plight as effectively as the eyes of Beauty deflected the suffering lover in *Les Fleurs du mal,* notably in "La Beauté." From *Les Fleurs du mal* to *Le Spleen de Paris*, the *Weltanschauung* of Baudelaire's poetry changed from "eyes of which one is inclined to say that they have lost their ability to look" (Benjamin 189) to eyes invested "with the ability to look at us in return" (Benjamin 188), the *sine qua non* not only of humanity, but of haloes (auras), which in their turn—by virtue of their vital connection with life—are the "well-spring of poetry" (Benjamin 200). For Flaubert, prose was reborn with poetry; for Baudelaire, poetry was reinvigorated by prose; *Trois contes* and *Le Spleen de Paris,* these authors' last published works, combine not only those two ends of the formal spectrum, but also the poles of quotidian and transcendent experience. In doing so, *Trois contes* and *Le Spleen de Paris* answer these two authors' shared criteria for "painting modern life."

In 1848, France deposed its last reigning king; from 1853 to 1858 Baron Haussmann undertook the public works that turned Paris into a modern capital; between 1858 and 1870, the four major French banks were founded, creating the economic basis for commercial expansion; in 1855, the Bessemer converter for steel was invented, one of many technological inventions that fostered industrial development; in 1869, the first transatlantic cable was put into service, changing the nature of communication. Bourdieu wrote: "Form is the most profound 'reality effect'" (107). The writer unconsciously reveals profound social structures "inaccessible to ordinary intuition" in form, as an "anamnesis (*sic*) of all that ordinarily remains buried" (110). Baudelaire and Flaubert knew this. Flaubert wrote of form as "la chair même de la pensée" (*Correspondances* II 286) and Baudelaire's dream of poetic prose in "À Arsène Houssaye" sprang from the "croisements" and "innombrables rapports" of enormous cities. By capitalizing on the stylistic properties of prose and by revolutionizing traditional formal categories with the introduction of poetry into prose, Baudelaire and Flaubert gave expression to a new era, and—in Bourdieu's terms— "made the real rise up" in the 1850s and 1860s (108). That formal revolution launched the kind of stylistic experimentation that would allow literature to start both addressing and coming to terms with the modern age.

Notes

1. There are notable exceptions, but as Carrie Noland pointed out, literary studies, particularly within French literature, have generally neglected socio-historical factors. See Carrie Noland, *Poetry at*

Stake: Lyric Aesthetics and the Challenge of Technology (Princeton: Princeton UP, 1999) 11. Pierre Bourdieu makes the same observation in *The Rules of Art: Genesis and Structure of the Literary Field* (Stanford UP, 1995). In the second edition of his invaluable work, *The Uses of Uncertainty* (Cornell UP, 1985, 2006), Jonathan Culler remarks that his own critical work was lacking in cultural context (242). In *Dead Time: Temporal Disorders in the Wake of Modernity (Baudelaire and Flaubert)* (Stanford UP, 2001), Elissa Marder adds some degree of historical context to the French literary tradition and specifically to the study of Baudelaire together with Flaubert; the temporal structures she considers are generally psychological rather than conventionally historical, however.

2.　Dominick LaCapra considers *Madame Bovary* as social criticism in *Madame Bovary on Trial* (Cornell UP, 1982, 1986).

3.　Verse confronts the "idéal, et revient ainsi à lui-même, fût ce dans la concordance syntaxico-métrique." Laurent Jenny, *La Parole singulière* (Editions Blin, 1990), 121.

4.　*L'Education sentimentale* starts with a date, "15 septembre 1840." The novel spans the years 1840–1867. And within that period, the events of 1848 are dealt with in great detail. Gilbert Guisan explored Flaubert's debt to Daniel Stein's *L'Histoire de Révolution de 1848* for the major tableaux of the uprising, and Stratton Buck took the issue of Flaubert's historical authenticity even further by poring over newspapers and reviews of the day to point out that the most mundane of subjects is soundly researched. Stratton Buck, "Sources historiques et techniques romanesques dans *L'Éducation sentimentale,*" *Revue d'Histoire Littéraire de la France* 65 (1963): 619–34. Guilbert Guisan, "Flaubert et la Révolution de 1848," *Revue d'Histoire Littéraire de la France* 58, (1958): 18–204.

5.　In *The Limits of Narrative* (Cambridge: Cambridge UP, 1986), Nathaniel Wing has beautifully expanded on how Emma's reality is defined by fiction that has no impact on the real world (41).

6.　Hans Peter Lund, *Gustave Flaubert: Trois contes* (Presses Universitaires de France, 1994), 97.

7.　Charles Baudelaire, *Fusées, Œuvres complètes,* ed. Claude Pichois (Paris: Gallimard, 1975–1976) 659. See also Claude Pichois' comment on the connection between this fragment and the later version of "Perte d'Auréole," *Œuvres complètes,* 1347.

8. Monroe also writes that Baudelaire's prose "comes to represent something like the intractable medium of what Jameson calls history" in *A Poverty of Objects* (Cornell UP, 1987), 24. And Richard Terdiman characterizes *Le Spleen de Paris* as the "site of class struggles" in *Discourse Counter/Discourse* (Cornell UP, 1985), 47.

9. Timothy Unwin, too, notices that, in contrast with *Madame Bovary*, where Flaubert's irony accentuates the "décalage entre la réalité objective et le monde intérieur de son héroïne," the "monde intérieur" and a "réalité objective" coexist in *Trois contes. Flaubert et Baudelaire: Affinités spirituelles et esthétiques* (Paris: Nizet, 1982), 46.

10. Eugenio Donato, *The Script of Decadence* (Oxford UP, 1993), 108.

11. Ann Murphy also develops the sacred of Félicité's discourse in "The Order of Speech in Flaubert's *Trois contes,*" in *The French Review* 65.3 (February 1992): 402–14. Her focus, though, is on the function of repetition.

Works Cited

Baudelaire, Charles. *Correspondances.* Ed. Claude Pichois. 2 Vols. Paris: Gallimard, 1966, 1973.

_____. *Œuvres complètes.* Edited by Claude Pichois. Paris: Gallimard, 1975–76.

_____. *Curiosités esthétiques L'Art romantique.* Ed. Henri Lemaître. Paris, Garnier, 1962, 1986.

Benjamin, Walter. *Illuminations.* Ed. Hannah Arendt. Trans. Harry Zohn. New York: Schocken Books, 1969.

Bernard, Suzanne. *Le Poème en prose de Baudelaire jusqu'à nos jours.* Paris: Nizet, 1959.

Bourdieu, Pierre. *The Rules of Art Genesis and Structure of the Literary Field.* Stanford, CA: Stanford UP, 1995.

Brooks, Peter. *Reading for the Plot: Design and Intention in Narrative.* New York: Vintage Books, 1984.

Buck, Stratton. "Sources historiques et techniques romanesques dans *L'Éducation sentimentale.*" *Revue d'Histoire Littéraire de la France* 65 (1963): 619–34.

Culler, Jonathan. *The Uses of Uncertainty.* Ithaca, NY: Cornell UP, 1985, 2006.

Donato, Eugenio. *The Script of Decadence*. Oxford, UK: Oxford UP, 1993.

Flaubert, Gustave. *Correspondances*. Ed. Jean Bruneau. 4 Vols. Paris: Gallimard, 1973.

_____. *L'Éducation sentimentale*. Ed. Pierre Marc de Biaisi. Paris: Librairie Générale Française, 2002.

_____. *Madame Bovary*. Ed. Jacques Suffel. Paris: Garnier Flammarion, 1966.

_____. *Trois contes*. Paris: Gallimard, 2003.

Guisan, Guilbert. "Flaubert et la Révolution de 1848." *Revue d'Histoire Littéraire de la France* 58, 1958. 18–204.

Jenny, Laurent. *La Parole singulière*. Paris: Editions Blin, 1990.

Johnson, Barbara. *Défigurations du langage poétique*. Paris: Flammarion: 1979.

LaCapra, Dominick. *Madame Bovary on Trial*. Ithaca: Cornell UP, 1982, 1986.

Lund, Hans Peter. *Gustave Flaubert: Trois contes*. Paris: Presses Universitaires de France, 1994.

Marder, Elissa. *Dead Time: Temporal Disorders in the Wake of Modernity (Baudelaire and Flaubert)*. Palo Alto: Stanford UP, 2001.

Monroe, Jonathan. *A Poverty of Objects*. Ithaca: Cornell UP, 1987.

Murphy, Ann. "The Order of Speech in Flaubert's *Trois contes*." *The French Review* 65.3 (February 1992): 402–14.

Noland, Carrie. *Poetry at Stake: Lyric Aesthetics and the Challenge of Technology*. Princeton, NJ: Princeton UP, 1999.

Terdiman, Richard. *Discourse Counter/Discourse*. Ithaca, NY: Cornell UP, 1985.

Todorov, Tzvetan. "Synecdoques." *Sémantique de la Poésie*. Paris: Seuil, 1979. 7–26.

Unwin, Timothy. *Flaubert et Baudelaire: Affinités spirituelles et esthétiques*. Paris: Nizet, 1982.

Wing, Nathaniel. *The Limits of Narrative*. Cambridge, UK: Cambridge UP, 1986.

CRITICAL
READINGS

Baudelaire and Poe

Lois Davis Vines

Baudelaire's obsession with Edgar Allan Poe (1809–1849) is unique in literary history. Baudelaire discovered in the American writer his personal and artistic soul mate. When he was in his mid-twenties, Baudelaire read by chance some tales by Poe published in French newspapers and began his search to find out all he could about this unknown writer. He described his excitement in a letter dated 1860, saying: "In 1846 or '47 I came across a few fragments by Edgar Poe. I experienced a singular shock" (Lloyd 148). He then describes how he made contact with Americans living in Paris in an effort to learn more about Poe and to read everything available he had written. Baudelaire goes on to say in his letter: "And then—believe me if you will—I found poems and short stories that I had thought of, but in a vague, confused, and disorderly way and that Poe had been able to bring together to perfection. It was that that lay behind my enthusiasm and my long years of patience" (Lloyd 148). These few lines offer intriguing clues to explore, in order to understand this legendary case of influence.

Baudelaire scholars have done extensive research to discover Poe's texts published in France that had such a profound effect on Baudelaire. W. T. Bandy is convinced that Baudelaire read a French translation of "The Black Cat" in the newspaper *La Démocratie pacifique* on January 26, 1847 (xiv–xv). A year earlier, a twenty-page article about Poe by the French journalist E. D. Forgues came out in the prestigious *Revue des deux Mondes*, in which Forgues praised the American writer's captivating tales and his "peculiar lucidity of intellect" (Alexander 79–96). Through his contacts with Americans, Baudelaire obtained an obituary after Poe's death in 1849, describing the poignant details of his sad life.

As Baudelaire learned about Poe's struggle in America to be recognized as a talented poet, short-story writer, and literary critic, he felt a close affinity with him as a person and as an artist. Both poets attempted to earn a living through writing, a profession that most often left them impoverished. They had both been brought up in non-traditional, middle-class families, Baudelaire by his mother and a step-father endowed with a strict military personality, and Poe by his foster parents, the Allans, whose high expectations he was never able to meet. Both Poe and Baudelaire struggled with addictions, Poe with alcohol and Baudelaire with drugs, especially hashish, and their creative endeavors were considered to be outside the mainstream. Poe's tales and poems were looked down upon by the New England transcendentalists. His contemporary Ralph Waldo Emerson (1803–1882) referred to Poe as "the jingle man," and James Russell Lowell (1819–1891) remarked sarcastically in *A Fable for Critics*: "Here comes Poe with his raven like Barnaby Rudge/ Three-fifths of him genius and two-fifths sheer fudge" (58). Charles Dickens wrote a novel entitled *Barnaby Rudge*, in which there is a talking raven, thus in addition to insulting Poe, Lowell is suggesting that the idea was not original. Baudelaire's humiliation came when his collection of poems, *Les Fleurs du mal,* was officially declared a "crime of outrage against public morality" by a French court upon publication in 1857. Copies of the edition were confiscated, and Baudelaire was fined 300 francs (*Œuvres complètes*, 1: xl). Six of his poems were judged obscene and banned from any future publication. One of the condemned poems, bearing the innocent title *"Les Bijoux,"* introduces sensuality in the first two lines: *"La très-chère était nue, et, connaissant mon coeur/ Elle n'avait gardé que ses bijoux sonores"* (*Œuvres complètes* 158). The other five forbidden poems include *"Lesbos," "Les Femmes damnées," "Le Léthé," "A celle qui est trop gaie,"* and *"Les Métamorphoses du vampire"* (*Œuvres complètes* 150–159). A second edition of *Les Fleurs du mal* was published in 1861, with thirty-one new poems replacing those that had been condemned, and a third edition, with additional new poems, came out posthumously in 1868. In spite of these negative receptions, Poe's poem "The Raven" brought him public acclaim, and *Les Fleurs du mal,* recognized as innovative, was appreciated by other poets and the public.

Inspiration, Influence, and Imitation

Poe and Baudelaire were faced with a similar artistic dilemma. In America, Henry Wadsworth Longfellow (1807–1882) was greatly admired during the time Poe was submitting his work for publication. In France, Victor Hugo (1802–1885) dominated the literary scene. For poets coming of age in both countries, the options were to follow in the steps of these eminent poets and their contemporaries (and probably be judged inferior to them) or venture in a new direction at the risk of being rejected by critics and the public. In his 1852 essay on Poe's life and work, Baudelaire portrays the American poet as having been born with *"pas de chance"* tattooed on his forehead in a culture that had neither pity nor time for *"un poète que la douleur et l'isolement pouvaient rendre fou"* (*Œuvres en prose* 1001, 1003). He praises Poe for rejecting *"l'idée d'utilité directe"* in poetry, which must have no other purpose than the creation of beauty: *"[La poésie] s'adresse au sens du beau et non à un autre"* (*Oeuvres en prose* 1011). Baudelaire saw in Poe a martyr willing to sacrifice comfort in his life and recognition in his literary endeavors in order to remain true to his poetic principles. Baudelaire's 1852 essay and a similar one, also devoted to Poe and published in 1856, express qualities that inspired the French poet to pursue his own vision of poetic creation. Baudelaire's poem *"L'Albatros"* can be read as a homage to Poe and to all poets whose works are ridiculed. The beautiful bird that flies high over the seas is brought down by the ship's crew, who make fun of the albatross as it lies limp and ugly on the deck. The last four lines of the poem express the analogy:

> Le Poëte est semblable au prince des nuées
> Qui hante la tempête et se rit de l'archer;
> Exilé sur le sol au milieu des huées,
> Ses ailes de géant l'empêchent de marcher
>
> (*Œuvres complètes*, 1: 9–10).

Two of Poe's literary essays translated by Baudelaire had a major influence on the French poet. "The Philosophy of Composition," in which Poe describes step-by-step how he created "The Raven" is entitled *La Genèse d'un poème* in Baudelaire's translation, which begins with a prose version in French of "The Raven" (*Œuvres en prose* 979–997). In his essay, Poe expresses his belief that a poem is not created in a frenzy of inspiration, but rather by a calculated mental process that leads to the desired effect, the elevation of the soul to the realm of Beauty, its unique purpose. He reveals that the creation of his poem "The Raven" began with the last line, "Nevermore," and that the raven would symbolize the two most moving themes in poetry, death and Beauty, thus the death of a beautiful woman. He then explains how he used mood contrast, sound, and meaning to achieve the desired effect (*Œuvres en prose* 991). Baudelaire was impressed by Poe's description of poetic creation and by his belief that a poem, by its very nature, must be short in order to maintain the desired effect.

Baudelaire's translation of "The Poetic Principle" is an interesting example of his thoughts completely merging with Poe's. His French text of "The Poetic Principle" is found embedded in the 1857 preface to a collection of Poe's tales, "Notes nouvelles sur Edgar Poe" (*Œuvres en prose* 1059–1062). Baudelaire uses quotation marks around one sentence taken from "The Poetic Principle," then continues expressing ideas about poetry that come verbatim from Poe's essay (*Œuvres en prose* 1059). If the reader has the impression that this is a case of plagiarism, the thought is confirmed in Baudelaire's essay on Théophile Gautier, in which he states: "Il est permis quelquefois, je présume, de se citer soi-même, surtout pour éviter de se paraphraser" (*Œuvres complètes*, 2: 112). Poe's text in French then follows without any indication that the ideas expressed are other than Baudelaire's. In a paragraph introducing "The Poetic Principle," Baudelaire praises Poe for having "soumis l'inspiration à la méthode, à l'analyse la plus sévère" and for adapting the rhythm, rime, and refrain to evoke the desired feeling. (*Œuvres en prose* 1058). Baudelaire uses the word "correspondance," although the term is not found in the English version of "The Poetic Principle." His description of the poetic ideal expresses the meaning of poetry for the Symbolist poets:

C'est cet admirable, cet immortel instinct du Beau qui nous fait considérer la Terre et ses spectacles comme un aperçu, comme une correspondance du ciel. La soif insatiable de tout ce qui est au-delà, et que révèle la vie, est la preuve la plus évidente de notre immortalité. C'est à la fois par la poésie et à travers la poésie, par et à travers la musique que l'âme entrevoit les splendeurs situées derrière le tombeau (*Œuvres en Prose* 1060).

In his poem *"Correspondances,"* Baudelaire evokes a supernal beauty that man can only glimpse through *"des forêts de symboles"* and which can be transmitted through colors, odors, and sounds. It is the poet who serves as translator between the real world and this mystical beauty.

Baudelaire's Poetry and Poe

Baudelaire translated only four of Poe's poems: "The Raven," rendered in French prose in his version of "The Philosophy of Composition," "To My Mother," a sonnet serving as a dedication to *Histoires extraordinaires,* "The Conqueror Worm," included in the tale *Ligeia*, and "The Haunted Palace," in his translation of *The Fall of the House of Usher.* Baudelaire's familiarity with other poems by Poe is evident in his "Sabatier Cycle," in which he expresses his love for the ideal woman and uses themes, words, and phrases that are found in some of Poe's poems. Madame Sabatier was a Paris demimondaine, the mistress of a rich gentleman, who supported her lifestyle with an apartment and other high-class amenities. Although of humble birth, she was beautiful, intelligent, sophisticated, and sensitive to the endeavors of writers, artists, and musicians. On Sunday evenings, she hosted dinners for her entourage of talented friends from the artistic milieus of Paris. Baudelaire was first introduced to this intimate circle in 1846 by his friend Théophile Gautier and was immediately fascinated by Madame Sabatier. Four years later, he began sending her anonymous letters and poems, one of which was published in *la Revue de Paris* in 1855 and recognized by Madame Sabatier, thus revealing his identity (Moss 11–13). Supremely flattered by such idealistic devotion, she offered herself to Baudelaire in August 1857, but he declined, saying that he wanted to keep her as a *"déesse"* and not reduce her to a woman.

He continued to frequent her soirées as a friend and enjoyed the company of Flaubert and other lesser-known writers.

Peter Wetherill's detailed study of poems by Baudelaire and Poe led him to the conclusion that by the tone and details, Baudelaire's "Sabatier Cycle" seems to be an imitation of Poe. Among Wetherill's numerous examples, his analysis of Baudelaire's "*Le Flambeau vivant*" and Poe's "To Helen" offers convincing evidence. The theme of the beloved's eyes is found in both poems, in which eight lines bear a close resemblance; two examples from the poems follow:

> "To Helen" line 10 "...they lead me through the years."
> "*Le Flambeau vivant*." Line 1: "*Ils marchent devant moi, ces Yeux pleins de lumières*"
> "To Helen" line 11: "They are my ministers—yet I their slave."
> "*Le Flambeau vivant*" line 7: "*Ils sont mes serviteurs et je suis leur esclave;*"
>
> (Wetherill 136).

After similarities between some of his poems and Poe's were pointed out, Baudelaire defended the originality of his work in a letter written in 1865: "I lost a great deal of time in translating Edgar Poe and the great benefit it brought me was to make some kindly souls say I'd borrowed *my* poems from Poe—poems I'd written ten years before I knew Poe's works" (Lloyd 221). Charles Asselineau, Poe's friend and biographer, was certain that Baudelaire completed the poems in question before 1856. Another contemporary, Ernest Prarond, recalled that Baudelaire constantly rewrote and corrected his poems, thus allowing the possibility of including lines translated from Poe (Lemonnier 18–26).

Baudelaire as Translator

Considering Baudelaire's relatively short life (46 years), his literary accomplishments are all the more impressive. The two volumes of his *Œuvres complètes*, which include his poetry, essays, and other miscellaneous writings, total 1,843 pages. His Poe translations are collected in a separate volume, *Edgar Allan Poe, Œuvres en prose*, with 1,136 pages. Between 1848, shortly after Baudelaire discovered

Poe and published his first translation, Poe's tale "Mesmeric Revelation," and his death in 1867, he produced five volumes of Poe's work that includes forty-five tales; Poe's only novel, *The Adventures of Arthur Gordon Pym*; several essays; "Eureka;" and Baudelaire's own prefaces and biographical articles about Poe. Baudelaire's knowledge of English was very limited when he began to translate Poe. His mother was born in England and spent most of her childhood there, but his practice with her was on a very elementary level. He studied English in school without acquiring the knowledge he would need to understand a skilled writer of American English. His enthusiasm for Poe was so intense that he learned English as he translated, thus making the time-consuming art of rendering the texts into French all the more tedious. He managed to find dictionaries of American English and was constantly in search of Americans visiting or living in Paris who could elucidate certain expressions that still left him puzzled. The inevitable question arises as to the quality of Baudelaire's translations. American scholar Patrick Quinn set out to put the question to rest by comparing Baudelaire's versions to the originals (4–5). His meticulous study shows that in particular cases, Baudelaire's French improved or even corrected Poe's faulty syntax and vocabulary; other examples indicate that Baudelaire misunderstood certain expressions that were difficult for a non-Anglophone. Quinn concludes that "this or that detail may have been overlooked or improved, or weakened in translation. But there is no full-scale transmutation. Baudelaire did not melt down these stories, remove their dross, and recast them in the pure gold of his French" (134).

Nevertheless, Baudelaire's translations of Poe's tales are considered the "gold standard" for translators, who rarely produce another French version of those stories. In 2006, François Gallix published a collection of Poe's stories entitled *Autres Histoires non traduites par Baudelaire*, indicating that the interest in translating Poe's tales has never waned. After examining the tales Baudelaire selected for translation and the ones left behind, Quinn remarked that Baudelaire's experience as a literary critic paid off in his selection of forty-five tales considered the best out of the seventy-one Poe published (Quinn 135). Baudelaire also had a sense of marketing. In a letter to the literary critic Sainte-Beuve, he mentions that he organized the stories into two volumes, the first of which "was designed as bait for the public: tricks, divination, leg-pulls, etc. . . the second volume is of a loftier kind of fantastic: hallucinations, mental illness, pure grotesque, supernaturalism, etc" (Lloyd 84). Baudelaire's translations and essays about Poe would contribute to Poe's renown and influence in France, throughout Europe, and, eventually, throughout the world.

The French poet and essayist Paul Valéry (1871–1945) remarked that "Baudelaire and Edgar Allan Poe exchanged values" (*Collected Works* VIII 204), meaning that Baudelaire's literary destiny was strongly influenced by Poe and that Baudelaire in turn played a major role in establishing Poe as a great writer, whose literary endeavors were appreciated far beyond his own country. Thanks to Baudelaire's translations and essays about Poe's life and work, two of France's greatest Symbolist poets, Stéphane Mallarmé and Paul Valéry, continued to write about him and translate his work.

Works Cited

Alexander, Jean. *Affidavits of Genius: Edgar Allan Poe and the French Critics*. Port Washington, NY: Kennikat Press, 1971.

Baudelaire, Charles. *Œuvres complètes*. Ed. Claude Pichois. 2 vols. Paris: Gallimard, 1975–6.

Gallix, François. *Autres Histoires non traduites par Baudelaire* in *Edgar Allan Poe. Histoires, Essais et poèmes*. Ed. Jean-Pierre Naugrette. Paris: La Pochothèque, 2006.

Lemonnier, Léon. *Edgar Poe et la critique française*. Paris: P.U.F., 1928.

Lloyd, Rosemary. *Selected Letters of Baudelaire, The Conquest of Solitude*. Chicago: U of Chicago P, 1986.

Lowell, James Russell. *A Fable for Critics*. Boston: Tecknor & Fields, 1856.

Moss, Armand. *Baudelaire et Madame Sabatier*. Paris: Nizet, 1975.

Poe, Edgar Allan. *Œuvres en prose*. Trans. Charles Baudelaire. Paris: Gallimard (Bibliothèque de la Pléiade), 1951.

Quinn, Patrick. *The French Face of Edgar Poe*. Carbondale, IL: Southern Illinois UP, 1957.

Valéry, Paul. *The Collected Works of Paul Valéry*. Ed. Jackson Mathews. 15 vols. Princeton NJ: Princeton UP, 1956–75. Bollingen Ser.

Wetherill, Peter M. *Charles Baudelaire et la poésie d'Edgar Allan Poe*. Paris: Nizet, 1962.

"Le Cygne"—Paris Downstream

Beryl F. Schlossman

Even among the "Tableaux Parisiens," the late series of poems that includes some of Baudelaire's masterpieces of modernity, "Le Cygne" is sensational. This extraordinary poem continues to resonate in a contemporary (late modernist and post-modern) sensibility. It is considered one of the greatest French poems as well as an example of Baudelaire's evocative magic. The poem shapes a two-fold invisible drama, in which the modern city is confronted with classical antiquity, and classical figures cry out to a solitary witness of modern life. Filled with lamentation, "Le Cygne" is provocative, simultaneously enigmatic and tender. Its focus is on the upheaval of nineteenth-century Paris, but it also explicitly invokes the outmoded baroque figures of melancholy and allegory. The poem reveals the core of Baudelaire's aesthetic, the poetic evocation of chance encounters in crowded city streets, and the capturing of that experience in art.

Formal aspects of "Le Cygne" include a mirrored, two-part structure, in which evocations of characters from antiquity and modernity appear in an irregular sequence, as if they were figures glimpsed in the crowd. The mirroring effects, however, rely on symmetry and regular prosody. The poem's two parts include six stanzas each (with an extra stanza in part one), the verse form is the alexandrine, the rhyme scheme is Baudelaire's preferred pattern of alternating feminine and masculine rhymes throughout the poem. The symmetries of characters and allusions to antiquity occur within the thoughts and emotions of a narrator walking through the city streets, and in particular, in a renovated area near the Louvre, close to the Seine river.

"Le Cygne" dramatizes the effects of exile, mourning, and melancholy on four suggestive figures. Each of them plays an allegorical role. The captive Swan and the black woman follow the initial evocation of Andromache by the Poet walking in Paris;

the two male speakers of poetic lament, the narrator-poet and the Swan, are accompanied in the poem by two silent female figures, Andromache and the African woman. The Swan and Hector's widow are summoned from the antiquity of Latin literature; the ancient city of Rome is the mid-point on a trajectory of identifications leading from Troy to Paris. Like the Swan, the narrator-poet and the anonymous woman are caught up in the paths of Parisian modernity, and they yearn for what has been lost. The silent melancholy of the two women occupies the thoughts of the Narrator-flâneur; the Swan is the only character who speaks. The strangeness of the talking bird indicates the allegorical strategy at work in the poem. Derived from Ovid and Virgil, the Swan connects antiquity to the modern city. Captive and alone in the dust, the Swan has "le cœur plein [a heart filled with his beautiful native lake]." His words from the heart discretely inscribe love within a staged landscape of emptiness, mourning, and melancholy that underscores the silence of the other characters.

Andromache is named in an exclamation at the beginning of the poem: "Andromache, I think of you!" She will reappear later, like the Swan who is evoked after her. The sequence is inversed in the second part of the poem, which evokes the Swan before Andromache. Like the feminine and masculine rhymes, the figures in the poem alternate. But in between these symmetries, the expression of emotions swings between exclamations and whispers, and the figures of exaggeration (hyperbole) and understatement (litote). These oppositions continue the patterns of mirrored images.

The city appears in unexpected, surprising shapes, and takes many forms—dusty and sunny, foggy and cold, dark and threatening—while the narrator's complaints bring back the distant past and appear to disregard the present: he sees the swan and the menagerie where only half-constructed buildings fill an unfinished space. The ancient swan works as an emblem, the poetic image of exile, brought into the present tense of the "new" Paris—the source of the narrator's melancholy.

Baroque iconography frequently portrays Melancholy as a woman. Baudelaire was familiar with the iconographic tradition that produced Albrecht Dürer's famous allegory of Melancholy. Like Gérard de Nerval, who explicitly evokes her figure in *Les Filles du feu* and other works, Baudelaire alludes to the feminine personification of Melancholy in many of his poets, jugglers, and mimes. He highlights the feminine counterparts of his figures of the artist. Several feminine figures appear in the time-space of "Le Cygne." Baudelaire places a woman on the stage of allegory: the poet's Narrators—flâneurs, lovers, artists, and poets—speak in her name. She appears in poetic images and visible figures, painted or sculpted in the verbal art of ekphrasis. She puts in an appearance as goddess, ghost, or flower: evocations of beauty and death turn her into marble statues, fetishes, and fragments of the object of desire. The poet gathers her spiritual and sensual qualities into an "idée fixe," an obsession that gives erotic form to an aesthetic ideal. Her melancholy permeates Baudelaire's representations of love and art.

In Book Three of Virgil's *Aeneid*, Aeneas sees Andromache absorbed in ritual to honor Hector at her replicated altar before she sees him: she has not yet begun her lament. Her ecstasy in Baudelaire's poem might refer to her cult of the dead or to the terror that turns her pale when she sees Aeneas and his followers. Like her, the modern Narrator of Baudelaire's poem elaborates his lyric lament without a sound, but the reader enters his thoughts. The African woman exiled in Paris shares the silence of Andromache: the reader has no access to their thoughts. Silence characterizes the absorption of the melancholic.

The common trait that connects these figures is their gaze of estrangement and longing. In part one, the tragic lament of the allegorical Swan is linked to Andromache's silent mourning, and part two alludes to her lengthy speech to Aeneas. A gaze or a look, a reflection, and a silenced voice transform the writing of antiquity into intimately familiar memories. These elements take the swan out of French romanticism and into Baudelaire's modern Parisian representation of Latin allegory. Baudelaire restores some of the resonances that Latin literature borrowed from Greek tragedy. In the poem, the swan shares Andromache's classical origin, the African woman's loss of a distant homeland, and the Narrator's lament. Like the Swan, gasping for water, both women appear close to death; the African is losing the breath of life through consumption, and Andromache swoons over her altar to Hector. They appear to dwell among the poet's "Parisian things" [choses parisiennes]," the objects and commodities of the city. The black woman moves through the streets, imprisoned by a white ground of fog; like the swan, she longs for her lost homeland. He gesticulates in the dust; she moves through the streets, thinking of the trees of Africa.

The contrasts take the form of whiteness on a dark ground, and blackness on a pale ground; the interplay of tones, black on white and white on black, points toward the colors of melancholy and the paleness associated with libertine women; with colonial violence; and finally, with graphic art and writing itself. The white swan's sky is a screen of light, empty of the black storm he implores to come: the black woman's sky is a white screen of fog. Each languishes for what is behind the screen, for something that has been reduced to an image, a vision, an illusion. The pale orphans wilt like flowers, and the ghost-like Narrator, like the self-torturing "Héautontimorouménos," has a heart filled with ironic reflection, the black poison of melancholy. Exile and mourning set up the correspondences among these four characters. The Swan's exile is presented in modern terms of loss and longing. He speaks for Andromache, bent in a melancholic ecstasy over her artificial altar; for the African woman, a dying victim of colonial violence, who is forced to walk the streets; and for the melancholic narrator who conjures their images out of thin air, but who describes his memories as heavy petrifying thoughts. Andromache is almost an image of that petrification: she has no object left to receive her gaze weighted down with memory, now that her son has been taken like Hector to the Underworld. Even her altar is fake, and the cenotaph does not contain a physical trace of the beloved Hector to connect the dead to the living.

In Baudelaire's tableau, the Swan combines masculine seduction and virility with the perfect feminine beauty that Latin antiquity found idealized in Greek aesthetics. Baudelaire's Swan connects modernity with the Orient of the classical world, and with the other (supernatural) world of Greek and Roman gods. He bears the magical illusion of antiquity, distanced in place and time from the modern city of the poem. The mythical metamorphoses of the gods shape classical prehistory, Ovid's subject in the *Metamorphoses.* Zeus took the form of a swan to seduce a mortal, Leda. The mythical love affair returns, with its ideals of virility and beauty, in Renaissance and baroque art.

In the poem, the name of Helenus recalls the name of Helen, the most beautiful woman in the world, and the daughter of Zeus in the form of a swan and the mortal Leda. Helen's prestige and value are maintained until twentieth-century modernism puts the value of art and beauty into question. Helen's beauty remains unique in Greek and Trojan memory. The source of the desire that led Paris to take her from Menelaus, her beauty is seen as the cause of the Trojan war. In Euripides' *Helen*, she says that she wants to wash her beauty off like paint. *Agalma*, the word for beauty, is the same word that is used in the play to describe the empty phantom (Segal). *Agalma* also connotes ornament, jewel, and a precious object contained inside something else, but beauty in general, and the beauty of Helen, are treated ambiguously in the play (Segal). *Kallos* is an empty illusion, a source of destruction, and a curse for Helen, but its magic shapes the object of desire.

In the war, Achilles kills Hector and defiles his body; Achilles' son Pyrrhus takes Andromache as his slave and his wife. Later, he leaves her for Hermione, Helen's sister and a daughter of Leda. The *Aeneid* portrays Andromache at the moment when Aeneas meets her, as he leads the exiled Trojans in search of the site of their new city.

Helen's beauty is fatal for Troy, and her memory haunts the destiny of Andromache. After the war, Hector's death, the loss of Astyanax, and exile, Andromache falls to a third husband, Helenus, when Pyrrhus leaves her for Hermione. This context suggests Andromache's equivalence with the Swan as an animal in part two of "Le Cygne." When Troy is defeated, Hector's widow loses her elevated status. Andromache is forced to take a new husband, and to produce children. Baudelaire's narrator points out her animal-like sexual captivity with a hint of sadism that underscores his tenderness for her.

Baudelaire's poem does not mention Helen, but her unnatural beauty and divine origin are knotted in the ruin of Troy. The relation linking Zeus' desire for Leda, his metamorphosis into a swan, and the beauty of the god-swan's human daughter remains enigmatic, but the fascination of swans for French romantic writers seems to cover for something more than their identification with ancient Greeks. The swan seems to conceal something else beneath its whiteness and cold perfection, or as the father of unsurpassed and immortal beauty; attributed to Helen, ideal beauty itself might be a screen. In Horace and Ronsard, the virile and divine swan becomes a figure of the poet. Nerval recalls the poets in the wild swans of "Sylvie," and Flaubert's "Dictionnaire des idées reçues" laboriously composed by Bouvard and Pécuchet displays the image of Virgil the swan of Mantova, and Plato's swan singing before its death. In Baudelaire's "La Beauté," the figure of the poet is threatened by the swan-white figure of ideal Beauty: her eyes are mirrors for his reflection, and she threatens him with eternal silence. Her figure is suggestive of Gautier's snow goddesses and alabaster creatures from antiquity, but the impact of the feminine on Baudelaire's poetics leads from the swanlike muse's eyes to the poet-figures of the Parisian Tableaux. Mirror images and melancholic reflections combine the swans of antiquity with the dark women of modernity.

Identified with the figure of the romantic artist, the swan recalls Helen's extraordinary beauty as well as the supernatural powers of Zeus. The classical and Renaissance personification of the swan suspends the poet between masculine and feminine identity, and confronts the artist with the threat of petrification, a dream of stone. Beautiful form brings the desiring viewer closer to death. The poet as swan is faced with the eroticism of art and the enigma of identity. Helen's desire to wash away her beauty like an image recalls these knots of art and being.

Colored in black and white in the Narrator's thoughts, Andromache, the swan, and the African woman evoke exile in a Parisian context. Against the background of Baudelaire's screens—

the cottony sky, the crowd, the blackness of night, or the walls around solitude—memories, landscapes of architecture, and ghostly figures show themselves in pictures that stop time and movement. The decorative swan appears displaced in the industrial and urban landscape of the modern world, where the violence of desire takes on other emblematic forms. The idyllic and pastoral modes are too remote to be reclaimed for modernity; Mallarmé's swan, the ghost of itself, is witness to this one-way street leading from antiquity to modern life.

Baudelaire is aware of the swan's decorative role in romanticism, and the structure of "Le Cygne" includes several precautions against potential misreadings. The narrator summons Andromache from the shades in the poem's first line, and uses her image, curved like Narcissus over her meager substitute for the river Simoïs, to set the tone for the introduction of the swan. Baudelaire follows the classical and Renaissance tradition that takes Narcissus seriously and shows him fatally imprisoned by his own unrecognized (and beautiful) image. He cannot give Echo the love for which she yearns, but neither can she save him from giving up his human life to become the silent image of a flower reflected in a watery surface. In love with an unknown other, he is a figure of insatiable desire, alienation, and estrangement. In Freud's enigmatic concept of narcissism, the mythical Narcissus is caught forever in the troubling magic spell of the image. He is in the power of an unidentified mysterious obstacle to desiring (loving?) the other.

Jean Starobinski compares Baudelaire's image of Andromache to the Narcissus-pose of Melancholia in the iconographic tradition of allegory (Starobinski). In the narrator's reflection, Andromache's curved figure swoons over a possible reflected image of herself, but her thoughts are directed toward the empty monument. An elegiac and solemn tone allows Baudelaire to maintain the poem's dramatic tension in spite of its length and its abrupt thematic and syntactic breaks. Characters, or allegorical figures, enter and disappear; scenes change. There is very little action or speech in the poem, with the exception of the swan's brief moment of lamentation in part one. The high style and the tone that dominate the poem provide an example of the Racinian echoes that Claudel recognized in the *Fleurs du mal*.

Baudelaire evokes the language of Virgil and Ovid as well as Racine. The tender voice characterizing the Narrator's conjuring of Andromache recalls the uncanny familiarity of Aeneas and Andromache in Virgil's text. The layering of present and past time that suggests an analogy between Parisian modernity and Trojan mourning recapitulates the temporality as well as the tone of Book Three of *The Aeneid*, when Andromache's melancholic narrative constructs the layers of present and past according to the Trojan war and its aftermath. "Le Cygne" sets up the intersection of antiquity and modernity through temporal transfers, layers of correspondences that draw these characters together through allegory and analogy, the poet's constructions, indicated in the Narrator's thoughts. The Narrator-flâneur and the black woman, forced like him to walk the streets, are lost in their longing and isolated by the anonymity of modern life. Andromache is a thought, almost a Shade; the Narrator invokes her as the mourning widow who turns her back on a possible future. Implicit in Baudelaire's interpretation of her is Racine's "Andromaque," a play that follows the suggestions of classical tragedy to portray the magical attraction that she holds for Pyrrhus and her renunciation of love. Her melancholy form connects her with the object of the narrator's extravagant desire in "A une passante." Mourning and the renunciation of love shape the experience of the modern figure of the poet as well as his figures of women. Baudelaire takes up Virgil's depiction of Andromache with the implicit parallel between his fictive narrator and the dispossessed Aeneas.

The poet boldly shifts the emblematic qualities of the wandering exile from Aeneas to the Swan, an anthropomorphic creature speaking in elegiac lines. Baudelaire's Swan recalls earlier talking animals in literature, from Aesop to La Fontaine, but within the modern urban setting of the poem—and in light of the silence of its other figures—the Swan is supernatural, even surreal.

He incarnates the estrangement that characterizes Allegory's relation to the people and things that it represents. When Virgil's Andromache tells Aeneas that her husband and captor treats her like an object or a possession, she evokes a form of estrangement that Baudelaire's poem extends to prostitution, exile, and colonial violence.

Baudelaire's allusions to Ovid's exile and to Ovid's verse about man, mentioned in *Fusées* 3, set up a correspondence between the despairing, lamenting Swan and the Narrator's complaint that the city changes more quickly than a mortal's heart. Melancholy and allegory are the rhyme words of this plaintive remark: it occurs in the context of a fragment of the cityscape that, for poetic and personal reasons, is particularly intimate and painful for Baudelaire. The poem implicitly provides this spot, the *Place du Carrousel*, with a history, a layered temporality, and with its own echo of the false Simoïs river. In the final stanzas of Part II, the expanded presence of the water and the replication of the rive recall the mythological alliance of Neptune and Troy evoked in the texts of Virgil and Ovid. Like Aeneas, the wandering Narrator pulls out to sea.

The poem intertwines the gaze of the desiring subject with the heavy thought of the melancholy subject. The initial evocation of Andromache sets up a chain of corresponding allegories that sustain the poem until the end, when the horn blows full-blast in answer to the Swan's lament and the exile's heart filled with images. This full breath of music is paired with the final moment, when the speaker's breath dies out in "bien d'autres encor!" The dry streams have become a vast ocean. From stream and native lake, the poem reaches across to India and Africa and the water expands into an ocean that threatens to submerge the islands of marooned sailors at the end of the poem. In contrast to the swan, exiled on land, they are prisoners of the sea. A second set of contrasting images allows Baudelaire's figures to reflect each other as doubles and as opposites. The sailors are paired with orphans drying out like flowers, and with all those who drink from the breast of the she-wolf, La Douleur. At the end of the poem, the four principal figures are drawn into a sea of exiles and mourners.

Images of water point to the sea god Neptune, who supports Troy against Greece. Baudelaire's allusions to Ovid anchor the Platonic and Christian images of the poet's wings in an implicit comparison of modern Paris to antiquity and disappearance of Troy. Paternal figures are absent, but the sea god is implicitly invoked in the Swan's call for rain, in the fullness and fertility of stream (and memory), and in the Swan's longing for his lake. Neptune is father to the beautiful Cycnus, who is killed by Achilles as he defends Troy. The body of Cycnus is invulnerable to attack; Achilles knocks him over, strangles him, and chokes Cycnus to death. In his death, perhaps Baudelaire saw an analogy with the death of Gérard de Nerval, found hanging on a streetlight of the rue de la Vieille Lanterne. Like Baudelaire's politically astute dedication to Hugo, the evocation of Ovid's Cycnus is a screen for mourning. The poem's setting points to a hidden evocation of the poet and friend lost to madness and death. The Seine too is hidden, absent from the poem but vividly present at the Carrousel bridge, and the Place du Carrousel between the Tuileries and the Louvre. The vanished Doyenné quarter where Nerval lived is the site of the Narrator's memories in the poem. Baudelaire's grief and horror at Nerval's apparent suicide enter the poem through hidden figures. The world of "Le Cygne" is dark and sleepless, and the daylight is shadowed with mourning.

The Swan's captivity occurs in nineteenth-century Paris, but Baudelaire borrows his uplifted gaze from two lines of Ovid's *Metamorphoses*: "Os homini sublime dedit, coelumque tueri/ Jussit, et erectos ad sidera tollere vultus [the creator lifted man's face, ordered him to contemplate the skies and to fix his gaze on the stars]" (I 84–86). Baudelaire transforms the quotation in *Fusées* when he alludes to "le visage humain, qu'Ovide croyait façonné pour refléter les astres [the human face, that Ovid thought was shaped to reflect the stars]" (*Œuvres complètes*, 1: 651). In the last stanza of Part One, the Swan is like Ovid's nameless man: the human gaze turns into a mirror for the stars, like the man observed by the forest of symbols in "Correspondances." The Swan's longing gaze into the cruel sky shapes the set of visions at work in the poem.

Baudelaire's dedication of the poem to the exiled Victor Hugo underlines the Second Empire political context of "Le Cygne," but the poem explores the destinies of exiles who have little in common with the authoritative figure of Hugo, the bard and visionary patriarch. The Narrator and the other anonymous figures at the end of the poem find themselves in a sea filled with exiles described by Tacitus, and the she-wolf of Pain recalls the founding of Rome. The poem suggests a parallel between the Swan and the poet Ovid exiled to the end of the empire: Baudelaire's borrowing from Virgil introduces Aeneas and the widowed mother, Andromache, into this constellation of mourning and the fate of wanderers and exiles.

The poem is filled with the allusions to fertility and plenitude of breath—air, poetic inspiration, and music; the absence of air, the lack of breath, is doubled in the poem with references to water. The body of the dead Cycnus is not found, unlike the bodies of Hector and Nerval, the classical and the modern heroes implicit in the poem's double set of poetic references. The father is not the sun of "Je n'ai pas oublié..." or the sun-god of the narrator's childhood in *Aurélia*, but Neptune, who transforms his dead son's body into a swan. Other Cycnus characters of antiquity also die violent deaths; their swan-shape is evocative of mourning (perhaps because of Melancolia's leaning pose) and with beauty. When a Cycnus who was king of Liguria plunged into violent mourning for his friend Phaethon, he was transformed into a swan. In an earlier version, Cycnus, a son of Neptune, was abandoned at birth on the shore and raised by a swan. A third Cycnus, a son of Apollo, was handsome and vain, and after driving his last lover to suicide, he jumped from a cliff into the lake where his lover had drowned. Apollo pities him and turns him (and his mother) into swans.

These swan-contexts resonate in the contexts of art, beauty, and suffering. The allegorical wolf of Pain near the end of the poem connects the Narrator's grief to the other figures who are poetically connected to him. Beyond the figures in the poem, Andromache, the African woman, and the Swan, anonymous orphans and sailors cover for the personal connections, especially between the Swan and Nerval, between the black woman and the women in Baudelaire's life who are connected with the West Indies—the nameless Malabar slave seen in Mauritius, Dorothée the prostitute Baudelaire saw in Réunion, and the only woman other than his mother with whom

Baudelaire lived for an extended period, Jeanne Duval. Although their relationship was marked by Baudelaire's constant complaints of incompatibility and later by resignation and a sense of duty toward his former lover, he mourned her loss long after their final break-up, according to his letters. "La Douleur" often appears in Baudelaire's letters when he speaks of Jeanne.

The allegorical process of "Le Cygne" is anchored in two conceptual correspondences: first, modernity and antiquity portrayed in cities (Paris and Troy/Rome) and in captive women (the dying African and the mourning Trojan); second, modern and classical figures wandering in exile, the Narrator and Ovid. Baudelaire's anonymous Narrator walks in search of a solution to exile, and the disguised figure of Ovid, exiled and allegorized as the Swan, utters the poem's single articulated lament. Allegory reshapes time in a series of correspondences or encounters. On the stage of memory and in the city, its visual counterpart filled with images of old and new, the cross-sections of Time interpenetrate and overlap each other in montage or collage. Memory is the only terrain (or faculty) that Baudelaire's Swan poem Narrator describes as fertile.

Baudelaire uses the fiction of the melancholy Narrator to shape the poem according to the cross-section of time that appears as the obsessional *idée fixe*. The Narrator invokes several shades from the Underworld. They are connected to the walker in the modern city through the thoughts of mourning and melancholy that he shares with them: exile, flight, wandering, and the death-like states of ecstasy afflict them. The imprisoned Swan appears following the first summoning of Andromache: the Swan 'translates' her experience and longing into the animal terms of her descent into slavery and the humiliations of her womanly life as the wife of Pyrrhus and Helenus. Her debasement seems to intensify the Narrator's tender love for her.

Baudelaire's Narrator remains more discrete about the anonymous African woman, whom his contemporaries might have compared to Jeanne Duval, known in the later years of her life as Baudelaire's mistress, the title of her portrait painted by Manet. The poem entitled "A une malabaraise" explicitly evokes the fate of women of color in Paris: "Comme tu pleurerais tes loisirs... si [...] il te fallait glaner ton souper dans nos fanges/ Et vendre le parfum de tes charmes étranges [how you would lament your lost pastime... if you had to glean your supper in our mud/ and sell the perfume of your strange charms]." These lines are followed by an image of the woman walking in the fog and imaginatively seeing the phantoms of palm trees that Baudelaire reshapes for the elliptical evocation of the African woman's plight in "Le Cygne." "A une malabaraise" clearly tells her story in the terms of colonialism. The later poem renders this story as a sketch of the figure, her suffering, and the image of the absent trees looming out of the fog.

Echoed in "Le Cygne," the lines about the woman's fate in urban exile erase her Indian origin in the earlier poem and prevent the reader from connecting her with Jeanne Duval, whose mother had come to France from the Antilles. The Malabaraise was a slave; Dorothée was a prostitute, struggling (according to Baudelaire) to buy the freedom of a young sister. In April 1859, Jeanne was hospitalized for serious illness, a possible effect of Baudelaire's long-term syphilis. Charity, grief, and guilt are the feelings that Baudelaire preserves for Jeanne Duval. The two poems are not about her, nor were they written for her, but Jeanne is a hidden figure in their reflections of slavery, prostitution, and fatal illness. Her invisible presence can be felt in other texts about the erotic charms of women from the colonies. In "Le Cygne," the Narrator intimately knows the black woman's life, but without the erotic impact inscribed in "A une passante."

Unlike Virgil's Aeneas, the Narrator does not appear to Andromache or interact with her in the melancholy scene that he stages. The poem recalls the moment when Aeneas' sea voyage brings him before her. Engaged in the ritual offering of gifts and food to Hector, Andromache kneels before the altars that have been imitated within the reconstructed replica of Troy. The arrival of Aeneas and his men interrupts her cult of the dead: she appears to him swooning in fear. Baudelaire's poetic representation allows pre-Haussmannized Paris and Andromache's exile to shine through the sketch of contemporary Paris in 1859.

In Baudelaire's Parisian picture, the cityscape is in metamorphosis. Like Constantin Guys and the Impressionists, the poet captures atmospheric effects through suggestion and quick sketches. Baudelaire's "tableau" appears only in the Narrator's memory. It is constructed in alternating emptiness and overflow, the earth dry as a desert and the too blue sky, the little artificial river and the swell of the ocean around lost sailors on tiny islands. These hyperboles of baroque tragedy are evoked as backdrops in Baudelaire's portraits of cityscapes; even the replicated Simoïs, mentioned by the Narrator, is an aesthetic construction that takes on a new life as an aesthetic element of the Parisian cityscape in "Le Cygne." The exiled Swan's native land also appears as a tableau, a fixed image that rises in the Parisian setting of his lament. Through the poem's evocatively corresponding images of the Narrator, Andromache, the Swan, and the African woman, Baudelaire almost imperceptibly melts classical antiquity into modernity.

Baudelaire's poem brings the shade of Andromache into the Swan's dusty animal-show of desire and melancholy. The narrator walks and thinks her into the present. There is a replica of an altar, a cenotaph, and an imitation of the Simoïs river, a fake rivulet watered by the tears of a woman in black, who bends in the pose of Melancholia, but remains young and beautiful, as she is for Racine's Pyrrhus, who falls in love with her and prefers her to Hermione. In Baudelaire's poem, she appears alone, without her husbands or children, in an ecstasy of mourning. The narrator seizes her image tenderly, and thinks himself into her mourning. She takes him back to the secret of Gérard, the man in black, who could not forget his lost mother. All his life, in clarity and in hallucinations, Gérard searches for traces of his vanished mother. He looks for her in the returning objects of desire, the daughters of flaming passion he calls "les filles du feu." Nerval's figures of the feminine are authentic only after death, when they belong to his cult of the Night and the Black Virgin.

The Poet takes the widow Andromache as his mask; her tears for Hector hide his own tears at the site of memory and the cityscape that has swallowed that memory. The mask is the Simois, a name

that almost echoes the "similia" of Analogy. It is false and true, like the widow who remarries, Nerval's mother Gertrude or Baudelaire's mother, Caroline Dufayis, loved by her son most tenderly in the days of her widowed solitude.

Death takes possession of the beauty of the Other. Its threats remain part of the Devil's arsenal, but the consolations of the beyond have shrunk to Baudelaire's notion of "hygiene." At the edge of the Seine, Baudelaire pulls back. He reshapes Andromache's replica of Troy into a small theater of painted cardboard, near the menagerie that alludes to her downfall. She leans into her grief, and he hides behind her, anonymous, looking at streets that have disappeared. Imprisoned by dust and captivity, the Swan who cannot fly away is the poet's friend, whose corpse hung from a streetlight. Like Plato's winged souls or Nerval's fantastic visions of himself in *Aurelia*, each of Ovid's swans flies away when a man falls to his death. Baudelaire sets a scene of breathless suffocation at the end of "Le Cygne."

Baudelaire subtracts the altar from Andromache's curve of melancholy. In his representation of her; she lives on but is displaced. He finds her among the Shades. Ecstasy is the name that he gives to her displacement or exile, outside herself, absorbed in the thought of Hector. The Poet mirrors her grief and silence, but only the Swan utters a lamentation. In Virgil, Seneca, and Racine, Andromache never stops talking, but here, she is silent, and the Poet knows her story as if it belonged to him.

The Narrator conjures up the Swan's poetic lamentation to thunder and rain. The Swan's strangeness dissolves the present sketch of Paris at the Place du Carrousel, near the little Arc of Triumph and the entrance to the Louvre, the palace of kings and their art. In between, is the vanished impasse du Doyenné. Nerval is latent in the evocations of the plenitude of breath or spirit that inspires the poet, but also in the thirst, dryness, and breathlessness that afflict the crowd at the end. In the final surrender to melancholy, the horn sounds in the forest, but the Narrator's voice dies away breathlessly in "bien d'autres encor"; in the final flood of the Narrator's thoughts, Andromache's dry stream fills with tears that hyperbole transforms into a great ocean. The poem's prosodic and

semantic contradictions shape the correspondence of antiquity and modernity that, for Benjamin, turns the poem into art glass—brittle but translucent, covered with reflections and hidden figures.

Baudelaire's image of Andromache in mourning fits traditional representations of Melancholia. The question of her status as melancholic or mourner depends, ultimately, on her relationship to her loss and to language. Following the destruction of Troy, she is in mourning for all possible objects: she has lost her husband and son, her family and country, and ultimately, her social, personal, and sexual identity. The Greeks use her as a symbolically resonant commodity, enslaved in marriage and child-bearing. In Virgil's text, Andromache's estrangement is limited by her awareness of the present: her lamentation to Aeneas breaks the melancholy silence with a precise account of her losses. In Baudelaire's poem, silence shifts her bereavement toward the estrangement and emptiness of melancholy, in which the self succumbs to the shadow of the beloved objects of loss.

Walter Benjamin's writing on Baudelaire explores estrangement in modern life through the forms of commodification that Baudelaire's poetry exposes in erotic and historical contexts and, through allegory, as a literary mode of representing "Parisian things." "Baudelaire, or the streets of Paris" is the title of chapter five of Walter Benjamin's theoretical preface to his unfinished book on the Parisian arcades. It evokes the allegorical quality of Baudelaire's art, and describes his 'genius' as melancholy. Baudelaire's poetry is grounded in Paris, and requires the crowd as the veil of its fantasmagoria. Benjamin writes: "The unique quality of Baudelaire's poetry is that the images of Woman and Death are steeped in a third, the image of Paris."

The Parisian Tableaux (Pictures) draw on the artifices of painting, diorama, theater, and sculpture to portray the intimate figures of exile in modern life. Benjamin sees them as the centerpiece of Baudelaire's writing of the capital of modernity. The nineteenth century popularized "tableaux" (a parlor-game of imitating paintings) related to a theatrical praxis that is still common. As the curtain rises or falls, characters and walk-ons stand motionless on the stage. This cross-section of time is a typical element of Baudelaire's art. For

Benjamin, Baudelaire is the passerby as flâneur, voyeur, loiterer, and homeless vagabond. He inscribes the uproar of modernity in the secrets of allegory. His wandering and his poetically engaged figures and narrators anticipate Benjamin's exile.

In the context of his completed book on the lyric poet in high capitalism, the essay "On Some Motifs in Baudelaire," and the unfinished Arcades work, Benjamin's brief commentary on the poem opens a theoretical frame for reading allegory and modernity. In a fragment about Paris, Benjamin extends his reading of "The Swan" to his own experience of modern life. Theory reaches out to poetry: Benjamin's Parisian fragment potentially adds him to the exiles of "Le Cygne" and virtually extends Baudelaire's evocation of colonialism into the twentieth century.

In "Le Cygne," Benjamin reads the intersections of history through one of the highest points of Baudelaire's poetic art: "Baudelaire's aesthetic reflections cannot present modernity's interpenetration with antiquity as clearly as certain poems of the *Fleurs du mal*. 'Le Cygne' is at the top of the list of these poems. Not by chance is it an allegorical poem. The city, conceived in continual movement, becomes petrified. It becomes as brittle as glass, but as transparent as glass—it allows its meaning to show through. "(La forme d'une ville/ Change plus vite, hélas! que le coeur d'un mortel)." This comment draws together many of Benjamin's comments on allegory, and adds the dimension of visual transparence, as if one could see, in Baudelaire's evocations of the city, all the way through time and space to the Paris of Baudelaire's youth. Beyond it, allegory evokes Ovid's longing in exile and to Virgil's underworld.

The past flees toward the night of Time. In Baudelaire's poetry, exile and memory have become inseparable from the poetics of modernity. Baudelaire turns them into Parisian things, tableaux, or frozen pictures. His new modernist aesthetic of baroque darkness revives the allegorical tradition that produced the figures of Melancholy, but he recreates these figures in modern dress, gesture, and allusion. The monumentalized figure of mourning is a debased widow who has fallen yet again; her debasement equals her

poignancy in Baudelaire's poem, closer to Virgil than to Racine. Her miniaturized monument to her husband is also a monument to the lost city of Troy. The little river that is named as a double (Simois like similia) flows only with her tears. Andromache's reconstructed Troy is almost like a toy city for the dead Astyanax.

She draws Aeneas into her world of similes and images, lost origins and doubles. When they part, she speaks to Ascanius and gives him extra gifts because, she says, he is like her own son, Hector's heir, her only hope. Thrown down from a cliff, Astyanax enters the company of men who die and are turned into swans. Baudelaire's Swan is related to the poetic bird of "L'Albatros" and perhaps to Coleridge's "Rime of the Ancient Mariner": the mariner, with his albatross has "a strange power of speech." Baudelaire's Swan poem takes the scene of exile in "La Bénédiction" and "L'Albatros" beyond romantic parables; the poem uses allegory to render antiquity and modernity in scenes, sketches, and intimate thoughts. Like "Icare" among "souvenirs de soleils [memories of suns]," who says "Je sens mon aile qui se casse [I feel my wing breaking]" the Swan speaks for the Poet (Œuvres complètes, 1: 143). The kaleidoscopic images of the sun are dazzlingly multiplied in the final vision of the dying Icarus, but Ovid's swan rises again from death and mourning, to sing the intimate transports of lyric and mortal life.

The secret complicity between the swans of antiquity and the curved posture of Melancholy is also the secret horror of Helen's mythical beauty, inseparable from death. Baudelaire's anonymous thinking Narrator in the city takes the aesthetic of evil and suffering into the Underworld; through memory and reflection, exile also represents a plenitude of intense pleasure, sexuality, and the relics of love. The physical immediacy of the Swan's lament to rain and thunder and the passerby of "A une passante," who compares the woman dressed in mourning with a flash of lightning, resonate in Baudelaire's coded language as moments of near-orgasmic pleasure.

The passage of Baudelaire's Narrator through memory and reflection is perceived or registered as a sectioning of Time; each character and site is evoked in a specific moment or temporal cross-section. Articulated as moments of shock, instants when time stops, this fiction of time anticipates the cinema's adaptation of "modern" time—its abrupt cuts, fade-outs, and flashbacks—as well as cinema's theatrical use of correspondence in montage. Baudelaire's construction of time in "Le Cygne" makes the past visible and allows the present to fade away; it recalls antiquity in the estrangement or ecstasy of mourning and in the exile's suffering at being torn out of a homeland, a way of life, and a temporal frame. The resulting confrontation melts the future into the past at a moment that opens the present as a kind of abyss. Several historical periods intersect in the Narrator's thought; several points in space intersect. The city street is confronted with an intimate interior space; the city also encounters exotic landscapes and finally, a seascape that engulfs all the figures that compose a virtual crowd at the end of the poem, when even the voice of the narrator disappears.

The poem's abrupt and highly dramatic beginning launches the fully developed form of Baudelaire's allegory. Its two forms—personification and abstraction—shape his revision of classical, medieval, and baroque allegory for modern poetics. At the instant of the narrator's thought, the apostrophe of Andromache, the Trojan heroine, resurrects the past and calls forth a series of associations. The poem situates these associations and events in vivid images that are mirrored within its nearly symmetrical two-part structure. Through the evocation of the heroic exiles of Troy and Rome in the banal, noisy street-work of present-day Paris, the poem suggests the intersection of antiquity and modernity in the streets of Paris. In the course of the poem, the banal present will expand to melancholy, spleen, and commodification, while the heroic past will expand in several layers of poetry and the ideal. The fates of Andromache and the strange talking Swan enter the consciousness of the narrator: they resonate through the modern forms of exile that he associates with the transformation of Second-Empire Paris and the experience of the black woman far from her native Africa. The evocative magic of allegory allows the swan to speak and other conjured figures to appear to the narrator; allegory allows thoughts and images of the past to appear more real to the narrator than the phenomenal evidence of the present. These conjured figures resonate as abstractions in the montage of images that Benjamin explores as Woman, the City, and Death. At the same time, the exiled characters of the poem personify idealized heroism, tragic loss, and painful longing. Allegory allows the "douleurs" and "souvenirs" of the early stanzas to flow downstream into the oceans of "Douleur" and "Souvenir" at the crescendo of the last stanzas of the poem. Abstraction and personification bring the two worlds together, in a rush of water, a terrible premonition of death for the crowd of exiles, and a final whispered invocation at the end of the poem—"bien d'autres encor!"—as the narrator's voice fades out.

Note

The author gratefully acknowledges research support from the University of California, Irvine.

Works Cited

Baudelaire, Charles. *Œuvres complètes*. Ed. Claude Pichois. 2 vols. Paris: Gallimard, 1975–6.

Benjamin, Walter. *The Writer of Modern Life: Essays on Charles Baudelaire*. Ed. Michael W. Jennings. Trans. Howard Eiland, Edmund Jephcott, Rodney Livingston, & Harry Zohn. Cambridge, MA & London: The Belknap Press of Harvard UP, 2006.

Chambers, Ross. "'Je' dans les Tableaux Parisiens de Baudelaire." *Nineteenth Century French Studies* 9 (1980–81): 59–68.

_____ . "Baudelaire's Street Poetry." *Nineteenth-Century French Studies* 13 (1985): 244-59.

_____ . *Mélancolie et opposition: les débuts du modernisme en France*. Paris: José Corti, 1987.

Klibansky, Raymond, Erwin Panofsky, & Fritz Saxl. *Saturn and Melancholy*. London: Thomas Nelson & Sons Ltd., 1964.

Nelson, Lowry. "Baudelaire and Virgil: A Reading of *Le Cygne*." *Comparative Literature* 13 (1961): 332–45.

Segal, Charles. *Interpreting Greek Tragedy: Myth, Poetry, Text*. Ithaca, NY: Cornell UP, 1986.

Starobinski, Jean. *La Mélancholie au miroir*. Paris. Julliard, 1989.

Baudelaire's "Spleen et Idéal": A Brief Rhetorical Analysis

Maria Scott

The Linguist Roman Jakobson famously allied metaphor with poetry because both metaphor and poetry privilege what he calls the vertical axis. Metaphor does this by substituting one thing with another thing that resembles it (a beehive as a metaphor for a financial district) and poetry by, for example, arranging verses vertically and privileging end rhymes. Prose, on the other hand, and particularly realist fiction, was linked by Jakobson to metonymy, which is usually regarded as a particular type of metaphor, but which he opposed to metaphor on the basis that metonymy privileges adjacency or context rather than resemblance. A briefcase used to emblematize a financial district would be an example of a metonym; it does not resemble the thing it stands in for, but it is logically, contextually linked to it. Realist fiction is metonymic in structure, on account of its domination by what Jakobson frames as horizontal relations, or its prioritization of contextual detail over the logic of similarity. Barbara Johnson's very influential reading of the rhetorical differences between Charles Baudelaire's verse poetry and his prose poetry draws on and supports Jakobson's division of labor. She notes the privileging of metaphor in Baudelaire's verse poems and the contrasting prioritizing, in his prose poems, of metonymic features. According to Johnson, Baudelaire's prose poetry dismantles the metaphors and, therefore, the aesthetic appeal of his verse poetry, and partly replaces them with the metonymic structure that is, for Jakobson, characteristic of prose.

Johnson frames the distinction between Baudelaire's metaphorical verse poems and his more metonymic prose poems in terms of a divide between two attitudes or systems, the first of which is closely linked to aesthetic idealism, and the second of which deconstructs— without negating—that idealism from within, so that the distinction between the verse poems and the prose poems is less one of opposition than of difference. This second attitude might be aligned with Baudelairean "spleen"; one of the titles that Baudelaire gave to his planned collection of prose poems was, after all, "Le Spleen de Paris." The word "spleen" is a French borrowing from the English language and is defined by the *Petit Robert* as a "mélancolie sans cause apparente, caractérisée par le dégoût de toute chose." Eugene Holland echoes Johnson's alignment of metaphor with idealism and metonymy with a contestation of this idealism when he notes that Baudelaire's "characteristically modern poetry registers a trajectory away from the metaphoricity of romantic symbolism, via its decoding by a metonymic poetics" that is "most patent and severe in the prose poems," but that is "already at work in the verse collection" (*Baudelaire and Schizoanalysis* 76).

The "Spleen et Idéal" section of *Les Fleurs du mal* complicates, however, any Jakobson-inspired association of Baudelairean idealism with a metaphoric poetics, and the related connection that is often perceived in his work between disenchantment and the failure of metaphor. "Spleen et Idéal" is, by far, the most substantial grouping of poems in each of the three established configurations of the collection (1857, 1861, 1868). It also serves, in all three versions, as the gateway to the volume, being placed directly after the prefatory poem "Au Lecteur." The poems included in "Spleen et Idéal" describe what appear, at least at first, to be opposed emotional states. Many of the texts in this section describe feelings, such as bitterness, anger, irritation, and despondency; these can be aligned under the broad heading of "Spleen." Four of the poems in "Spleen et Idéal" are actually entitled "Spleen." By contrast, poems that describe the Baudelairean "Idéal" typically evoke a state of elation and harmonious plenitude. Poems, such as "La Beauté" and "Hymne à la beauté," which take aesthetic beauty as their focus, often gesture towards both states, in that they present aesthetic ideals as oppressive and tormenting.

As well as invoking seemingly antithetical states of mind or spirit, the "Spleen et Idéal" poems describe differing attitudes towards the self. The poems that most clearly belong to the "Idéal" subset typically describe a kind of dissolution or vaporization of the self; this is evident in texts like "Élévation," "Parfum exotique," and "Correspondances," where the movement is one of expansion. By contrast, the most straightforwardly splenetic poems characteristically involve an imprisonment in and materialization of the self, a movement of retraction and solidification. As a result, the "ideal" and "spleen" poems seem initially to align themselves easily with Sigmund Freud's two key operations of the unconscious, namely, displacement and condensation, which the French psychoanalyst Jacques Lacan associated respectively with metonymy and metaphor, as theorized by Jakobson. It makes intuitive sense that if displacement is associated by Lacan with metonymy and condensation with metaphor, then Baudelaire's light-footed, vaporizing poems must be fundamentally metonymic in character (even if the direction of their movement tends to be vertical, as in "Élévation"), and his concretizing, immobilizing poems essentially metaphorical (even if, despite Jakobson's schema, the failure of transcendence or verticality is regularly thematized in such texts, as for example in "L'Albatros"). The remainder of this essay will read three poems from "Spleen et Idéal" in an attempt to demonstrate that the splenetic poems are more intrinsically metaphorical than the idealizing poems, which arguably privilege metonymic relations.

The Rhetoric of Charm: "Le Parfum"

Lecteur, as-tu quelquefois respiré
Avec ivresse et lente gourmandise
Ce grain d'encens qui remplit une église
Ou d'un sachet le musc invétéré?

Charme profond, magique, dont nous grise
Dans le présent le passé restauré!
Ainsi l'amant sur un corps adoré
Du souvenir cueille la fleur exquise.

De ses cheveux élastiques et lourds,
Vivant sachet, encensoir de l'alcôve,
Une senteur montait, sauvage et fauve,

Et des habits, mousseline ou velours,
Tout imprégnés de sa jeunesse pure,
Se dégageait un parfum de fourrure.

The idealizing poem "Le Parfum" (*Œuvres complètes,* 1: 39) takes as its theme the intensely physical, sensual memory that can be stimulated by the sense of smell. The opening stanza refers to a grain of incense that cxpands to fill a church with its rich aroma, and to the heady scent released by a sachet of musk. The second stanza goes on to talk about the "Charme profond, magique" (line 5) that is released in the present, but that emanates from the "passé restauré" (line 6). This quatrain also conjures up the figure of a lover picking a flower of memory from his lover's body. The two tercets refer to a particular woman, whose full head of hair and whose clothes once released a powerful, feral, and youthful smell.

Does this idealizing poem evoke (metaphorical) fusion or (metonymic) juxtaposition? Assimilation or separation? The thematic juxtaposition of present and past in the second stanza is echoed in the syntax of its two first lines, where the adjectives "profond" and "magique" are separated by a comma, and where the words "le présent" and "le passé" sit slightly awkwardly alongside one another, their connection established only by the preceding and subsequent words. In the next two lines of the second stanza, contiguity is again foregrounded:

Ainsi l'amant sur un corps adoré
Du souvenir cueille la fleur exquise (lines 7–8).

The remembered woman doesn't stand in for the present woman ("un corps adoré"), doesn't replace her as if in a metaphorical substitution; instead, the lover picks what he calls the flower of memory from her body. The representation of memory as a flower is a loosely metaphorical device, but the construction "la fleur [du souvenir]" (line 8) does not allow the image of the flower to substitute itself for memory; the two components of the metaphor (tenor and vehicle, or memory-concept and flower-image) remain juxtaposed rather than assimilated into one another. Furthermore, the connection being established between a flower and a memory originates not in any intrinsic similarity between the two elements, but in the wider context of the poem; in other words, the link between flower and memory is provided by the idea of smell, which is not a feature shared by both, but rather an effect of one and a trigger for the other. Flowers do not resemble memories, but through the smell, they release flowers can trigger memories. No element in this poem replaces any other element, as it would in the case of a text governed by metaphorical logic: the body that is adored by the lyric subject in the present is represented in the poem as contiguous to the flower, which (the context suggests) produces a heady perfume, just as the hair and clothes of the woman evoked in the tercets produced, because of their adjacency to her body, a dizzying smell. The overwhelming impression is one of metonymic juxtaposition rather than metaphorical fusion.

In the first tercet, the mistress' elastic and heavy hair, described as a "Vivant sachet, encensoir de l'alcôve" (line 10), is presented as releasing a feral kind of fragrance. The image of the hair as living sachet is metaphorical, harking back to the fragrant sachet of musk evoked in the first stanza. The resemblance between the mistress' hair and a sachet of musk is visual, olfactory, and also tactile: both are "élastiques" (line 9). However, the metaphor of the censer, "encensoir de l'alcôve" (line 10), which also refers back to the first stanza, is not based on any visual or tactile resemblance to the woman's hair, and it is difficult to imagine much similarity between the scent released by a censer and the kind that emanates from hair. The disappearance of the visual linkage to the hair, a similarity that the sachet maintained, means that the censer is less metaphor than metonym: its link to the hair is more context-based than resemblance-based.

The second tercet refers to the muslin and velvet clothes worn by the mistress in the past: impregnated by the scent of her youthful body, they released a smell of fur. This animal smell only comes from the clothes because the muslin and velvet have been in touch with the woman's body, impregnated with its smell. Again, the logic is one of contiguity. The use of the imperfect tense in the two tercets, and the reference to the youth of the woman, indicate that, in the tercets, the lyric subject is remembering his mistress' former body, prompted by her smell in the present... he is remembering her past body *from* her present body: "Dans le présent le passé restauré" (line 6). The past woman does not replace the woman in the present; the first two stanzas suggest, by implication, that it is the scent of the present woman that conjures up—via the flower of memory found on her beloved body—the remembered woman, so that both are somehow present, adjacent to one another, the same and yet different. "Le Parfum" does not conflate past and present, but makes them contiguous to one another, metonymically linked through the sense of smell.

I have tried to show that, in the idealizing poem "Le Parfum," the logic is metonymic rather than metaphorical, in the sense that metonymy relies on relations of contiguity and context while metaphor involves absorption, conflation, and substitution. A similar logic of contiguity can also be shown to govern other idealizing poems like "Correspondances," where the word "comme" appears seven times, maintaining differences and distances even while establishing links. It is more customary, admittedly, to argue that "Correspondances" expresses a fusional, Symbolist aesthetic, but it is interesting to note that the word "comme" is associated by Barbara Johnson with the metonymic logic of Baudelaire's prose poetry rather than with the allegedly metaphorical logic of his verse. Paul de Man, furthermore, highlights the partly enumerative, rather than purely substitutive functioning of the final "comme" in "Correspondances" (248–50). In the idealizing poem "Le Cadre," the adornments of a woman are *compared* to, though not conflated with, the frame of a painting; in "Le Beau Navire," the woman is likened to, but not identified with, a beautiful boat, her legs likened to two witches, and her arms likened to gleaming boas. Similarly, in the idealizing poem "Le Serpent qui danse," the woman is compared to a dancing snake, a boat, a young elephant, and so on, but never actually identified with any of these things. In "Le Chat," similarly, she is only *compared* to a cat. In "La Géante," woman and landscape are never entirely collapsed into one another... the giantess lies across the countryside, her breasts are *like* mountains.

It is true that in "La Chevelure," one of the verse poems analysed by Barbara Johnson, metaphor seems to play the dominant role, but if the lock of hair becomes, through the operation of metaphor, an aromatic forest, an ebony sea, and a noisy port, it is also metonymized, continually made into something adjacent, ancillary. It is not just an ocean, but "ce noir ocean où l'autre est enfermé" (line 22), always pointing towards something else. The hair is figured not as a destination in itself, but as a place found along the way towards a destination. I would suggest that if the woman implied by this poem is excluded by its logic, as Barbara Johnson argues, it is not so much because she is metaphorically suppressed or replaced as because she is only metonymically represented. As Johnson herself points out, the woman is never present in person. Her connection to the lock of hair is only metonymic, as is the connection between the lock of hair and the exotic land, to which the poet is imaginatively transported. In more spleen-centred poems, by contrast, the mistress is metaphorically rendered, for example as a "vase de tristesse" (line 2), as a "bête implacable et cruelle" (line 9) ("Je t'adore à l'égal de la voûte nocturne"), or as a "Machine aveugle et sourde" (line 9) ("Tu mettrais l'univers entier dans ta ruelle").

Eugene Holland observes that even idealizing verse poems, such as "La Chevelure" and "Correspondances" deploy a metonymic poetics that seems to undermine their metaphorical logic (43–79). A reading of Baudelaire's idealizing poems as primarily metonymic rather than primarily metaphorical in character goes against a tradition of reading them as fusional, as proto-Symbolist, and as repressive of difference and insistent on sameness and identity. But a metonymic reading of Baudelaire's "ideal" poems seems logical in view of the fact that metonymy was associated by Sigmund Freud with the avoidance of censorship and, therefore, with an escape from constraints. In addition, Jacques Lacan may have associated metonymy with the never-ending and quasi-oppressive chain of desire, but the dynamism of desire is preferable to the immobilization of desire that occurs in the case of the clinical symptom in psychoanalysis, a symptom that is defined by him as a metaphor: "le symptôme *est* une métaphore, que l'on veuille ou non se le dire, comme le désir *est* une métonymie, même si l'homme s'en gausse" (528). Metaphors, for Lacan, are points of stasis, fixation, or inertia in the unending, metonymic chain of desire; symptoms are metaphors because they materialize our pain, attesting to the irremediable absence of the object of desire.

Turning now to two spleen-centred poem that take as their focus the same theme as "Le Parfum," namely memory, I'd like to suggest very briefly that the governing logic is metaphorical, in that what is at stake is not the maintenance of separation between different things but rather their conflation and absorption.

The Rhetoric of Desolation: "Spleen"

J'ai plus de souvenirs que si j'avais mille ans.

Un gros meuble à tiroirs encombré de bilans,
De vers, de billets doux, de procès, de romances,
Avec de lourds cheveux roulés dans des quittances,
Cache moins de secrets que mon triste cerveau.
C'est une pyramide, un immense caveau,
Qui contient plus de morts que la fosse commune.
—Je suis un cimetière abhorré de la lune,
Où comme des remords se traînent de longs vers
Qui s'acharnent toujours sur mes morts les plus chers.
Je suis un vieux boudoir plein de roses fanées,
Où gît tout un fouillis de modes surannées,
Où les pastels plaintifs et les pâles Boucher
Seuls, respirent l'odeur d'un flacon débouché.

Rien n'égale en longueur les boiteuses journées,
Quand sous les lourds flocons des neigeuses années
L'ennui, fruit de la morne incuriosité,
Prend les proportions de l'immortalité.
—Désormais tu n'es plus, ô matière vivante!
Qu'un granit entouré d'une vague épouvante,
Assoupi dans le fond d'un Sahara brumeux;
Un vieux sphinx ignoré du monde insoucieux,
Oublié sur la carte, et dont l'humeur farouche
Ne chante qu'aux rayons du soleil qui se couche.

In the second of the four poems bearing the title "Spleen" (*Œuvres complètes,* 1: 73), there is only a very limited use of comparison, or simile; instead, metaphors predominate. The first line states that the lyric subject contains an absurdly large volume of memories, and the various metaphors of the poem develop this point. An opening simile compares the lyric subject's "triste cerveau" to a large chest of drawers full of romantic keepsakes. Then the lyric subject's head is described, metaphorically, as a pyramid and a huge tomb full of dead people. The subject then announces that he *is* a cemetery where long worms or lines of verse weave around his favorite corpses. He goes on to state that he *is* an old boudoir full of withered roses. These images all share a crucial point in common: in each case, the lyric subject is presented as a container of the past. The poet's head is the chest of drawers, the pyramid, the tomb, the cemetery, and the boudoir; pyramid, tomb, and cemetery share obvious features in common, while the chest of drawers evoked at the beginning of the poem could easily be found in the boudoir that comes later. In the next stanza, the lyric subject presents himself as a block of granite and an old forgotten sphinx, both images harking back to metaphors deployed previously in the text. The overwhelming sense is one of a collapse into non-differentiation: the long-neglected boudoir is essentially equivalent to the long-neglected sphinx; bodies in the graveyard are gnawed by worms, the colors of the Boucher prints fade, and the outlines of a sphinx are obscured by the desert mist. There is little thematic evidence of verticality here (objects lie around the place, bodies lie in the graveyard, the sphinx is "assoupi," the sun is setting), and yet relations of similarity (associated by Jakobson with metaphor and the vertical axis) predominate.

The subject as forgotten sphinx recalls the metaphor of the soul as gravestone that appears in "Le Mauvais Moine." Similarly striking metaphors characterize other spleen-centred poems too, such as the metaphor of the lyric subject as an old bottle in "Le Flacon," as a broken bell in "La Cloche fêlée," or as a knife in "L'Héautontimorouménos." Such substitutions of inanimate objects for the lyric subject often border on personification, and indeed are regularly accompanied by personifications in the spleen poems. In the "Spleen" poem "J'ai plus de souvenirs," for example, the soul is materialized as a series of inanimate objects, but there is also a recurring use of personification: the moon hates the poet-cemetery; plaintive pastel sketches and pale Boucher prints breathe in the emanations of an opened bottle; days limp along; the world is carefree; even the sun may well go to bed rather than set in the ordinary way. The reference to "ennui," described in the poem as taking on the proportions of immortality, recalls, furthermore, the personification of "Au lecteur," the opening (and splenetic) poem of *Les Fleurs du mal*, in which boredom is personified as a houka-smoking monster, in which sins are stubborn and repentance cowardly, and where our vices appear as a menagerie of horrible beasts.

Personification is a rhetorical device that is far more prevalent in the "spleen" poems of "Spleen et Idéal" than in the more idealizing texts. We might think, for example, of the complaining bell and sickly clock of "Pluviôse, irrité," and the various personifications of "Le Goût du néant." It is true that beauty is personified in both "La Beauté" and "Hymne à la beauté," but these poems are only ambiguously idealizing… beauty has a sinister, splenetic aspect in both.

The Rhetoric of Desolation: "L'Horloge"

Horloge! dieu sinistre, effrayant, impassible,
Dont le doigt nous menace et nous dit : « *Souviens-toi!*
Les vibrantes Douleurs dans ton cœur plein d'effroi
Se planteront bientôt comme dans une cible;

Le Plaisir vaporeux fuira vers l'horizon
Ainsi qu'une sylphide au fond de la coulisse;
Chaque instant te dévore un morceau du délice
À chaque homme accordé pour toute sa saison.

Trois mille six cents fois par heure, la Seconde
Chuchote: *Souviens-toi!*— Rapide, avec sa voix
D'insecte, Maintenant dit. Je suis Autrefois,
Et j'ai pompé ta vie avec ma trompe immonde!

Remember! Souviens-toi! prodigue! *Esto memor!*
(Mon gosier de métal parle toutes les langues.)
Les minutes, mortel folâtre, sont des gangues
Qu'il ne faut pas lâcher sans en extraire l'or!

Souviens-toi que le Temps est un joueur avide
Qui gagne sans tricher, à tout coup! c'est la loi.
Le jour décroît; la nuit augmente; *Souviens-toi!*
Le gouffre a toujours soif; la clepsydre se vide.

Tantôt sonnera l'heure où le divin Hasard,
Où l'auguste Vertu, ton épouse encor vierge,
Où le Repentir même (oh! la dernière auberge!),
Où tout te dira Meurs, vieux lâche! il est trop tard!»

"L'Horloge" (*Œuvres complètes*, 1: 81) is the last poem in the *Spleen et idéal* section of both the 1861 and 1868 editions of *Les Fleurs du Mal*. As in "Le Parfum" and the "Spleen" poem just examined, the broad theme is memory. The clock is personified in the first quatrain as a sinister god, warning us to remember the passing of time and the imminence of suffering. The clock then speaks directly in the poem, personifying Pleasure for us, going on to personify the Second hand, then "Maintenant" (line 11), then Time itself is personified as "un joueur avide" (line 17), and finally, in the last quatrain, Chance, Virtue, and Repentance are all personified.

"L'Horloge" offers, then, a particularly striking (so to speak) example of a rhetorical device that is especially characteristic of the spleen-centred poems. But does the prevalence of personification in the spleen poems support the argument proposed thus far, namely that these texts are governed by a metaphorical rather than metonymic logic? A quick detour via psychoanalysis suggests that it does. The metaphorical function is, for Lacan, fundamental to the institution of the human being as a social subject. He or she needs to substitute something for the mother—a bobbin, for example, as in the fort-da game described by Freud in *Beyond the Pleasure Principle*—to enable proper functioning in society. If the subject never manages to master the metaphorical function, then what Lacan calls the paternal metaphor, or the *Nom-du-Père*, is never internalized, and the subject goes through his or her life as a psychotic, though the psychosis may never be activated. In other words, psychosis is founded on "l'échec de la métaphore paternelle" (Lacan 575). Psychosis is not only the result of a failure of metaphor, it also causes a malfunctioning of metaphor that can manifest itself as delusions. Interestingly, as well as being a literary device, personification is a term in psychiatry designating a compound hallucination experienced by shizophrenics. There is certainly something hallucinatory about the personifications that feature in splenetic poems like "L'Horloge." If the paternal prohibition that is so necessary to the human subject's formation from a psychoanalytic perspective (Lacan calls this prohibition the *Non-du-Père*), were to be made into an image, it might look very like the figure of the "dieu sinistre, effrayant, impassible" (line 1), threatening us with his finger and telling us to remember the fact of our own imminent death.

Baudelaire's spleen-centred poems, in which this essay has argued the logic of metaphor predominates and personification prevails, might thus be read as expressions of a quasi-psychotic state of mind. This is not at all to propose a clinical diagnosis of the poet's own state of mind; he did have fears of encroaching madness towards the end of his life, but the condition that afflicted him was aphasia rather than psychosis. It is worth noting that Roman Jakobson links this linguistic disorder, which reduced Baudelaire to silence throughout his final months, to the malfunctioning of either the metaphorical or the metonymic cognitive function.

This essay has used the work of Jakobson and Lacan to argue that Baudelaire's idealizing poems obey a metonymic logic and that his splenetic poems place more of an emphasis on the metaphorical function. This claim contests—or at least complicates—a more usual tendency in Baudelaire criticism to align poetic metaphor with idealism and metonymy with the failure thereof.

Works Cited

Baudelaire, Charles. *Œuvres complètes*. Ed. Claude Pichois. 2 vols. Paris: Gallimard (Bibliothèque de la Pléiade), 1975–6.

De Man, Paul. "Anthropomorphism and Trope in the Lyric." *The Rhetoric of Romanticism*. New York: Columbia UP, 1984. 239–62.

Holland, Eugene W. *Baudelaire and Schizoanalysis: The Socio-Poetics of Modernism*. Cambridge, UK: Cambridge UP, 1993.

Jakobson, Roman. "Two Aspects of Language and Two Types of Aphasic Disturbances." *Language in Literature*. Eds. Krystyna Pomorska and Stephen Rudy. Cambridge, MA: Belknap Press, 1987. 95–114.

Johnson, Barbara. *Défigurations du langage poétique: la Second Révolution baudelairienne*. Paris: Flammarion, 1979.

Lacan, Jacques. *Écrits*. Paris: Éditions du Seuil, 1966.

Forests of Symbols and Patterns of Meaning: Reading Poetry through Baudelaire's "Correspondances"

David Evans

When the first edition of *Les Fleurs du mal* appeared on June 25, 1857, the memorable sonnet "Correspondances," one of fifty-two previously unpublished poems, was quickly taken by readers and critics as a sort of *art poétique* and has since been read as the central pillar of the poet's whole *œuvre*, as if it encapsulated, in a mere fourteen lines, Baudelaire's entire poetics. The poem has been the subject of countless exegeses—thematic, symbolic, structural, intertextual—illuminating the ways in which it explores the relationships between humankind, the natural world, and the poet, between belief, meaning, and art. Moreover, scholars have amply demonstrated that the poem provides a conceptual bridge between the Romantics' yearning for transcendence in the early years of the nineteenth century and the hermetic theories of the Symbolist generation in its closing decades. Such a wealth of previous scholarship can be daunting for any reader, not least the undergraduate student overwhelmed by an extensive reading list, pressing essay deadlines, and an impending examination. A comprehensive analysis of this poem's significance to Baudelaire's complete works, whole poetic movements, and successive generations of writers would require many hundreds of pages and may be pieced together from the excellent work of scholars, such as Austin, Broome, Culler, Leakey, and Pommier. Let us instead take as our starting point a close reading of the text itself, since its suggestion that complex patterns of meaning may be perceived in nature provides the perfect analogy for how to read any poetry, no matter how familiar—or unfamiliar—it may seem.

La Nature est un temple où de vivants piliers
Laissent parfois sortir de confuses paroles;
L'homme y passe à travers des forêts de symboles

4   Qui l'observent avec des regards familiers.

  Comme de longs échos qui de loin se confondent
  Dans une ténébreuse et profonde unité,
  Vaste comme la nuit et comme la clarté,
8   Les parfums, les couleurs et les sons se répondent.

  Il est des parfums frais comme des chairs d'enfants,
  Doux comme les hautbois, verts comme les prairies,
  – Et d'autres, corrompus, riches et triomphants,

12   Ayant l'expansion des choses infinies,
  Comme l'ambre, le musc, le benjoin et l'encens,
  Qui chantent les transports de l'esprit et des sens.

On first reading, the text does little to dispel the prejudices of the skeptic, for whom poetry talks of little else but nature. Indeed, given the comparison of Nature, with its idealizing capital N, to a temple in line 1, it might be tempting to dismiss the sonnet as yet another ode to vegetation, were it not for Baudelaire's barbed response to Fernand Desnoyers, who in 1854 invited submissions to a volume of nature poetry. Explaining his rather perverse contribution of two resolutely urban poems, "Le Crépuscule du matin" and "Le Crépuscule du soir," Baudelaire wrote:

> Vous savez bien que je suis incapable de m'attendrir sur les végétaux et que mon âme est rebelle à cette singulière religion nouvelle [...]. Je ne croirai jamais que *l'âme des Dieux habite dans les plantes*, et, quand même elle y habiterait, je m'en soucierais médiocrement, et considérerais la mienne comme d'un bien plus haut prix que celle des légumes sanctifiés. J'ai même toujours pensé qu'il y avait dans la *Nature*, florissante et rajeunie, quelque chose d'impudent et d'affligeant (*Correspondances* I 248, Baudelaire's emphasis).

This is a far cry from the poetry of Baudelaire's Romantic predecessors, Alphonse de Lamartine and Victor Hugo, which reads as a hymn to the divine glory of the natural world, interpreting the fields and forests, mountains and valleys, rivers and lakes, as God's wondrous creation. As Culler (120) has shown, the opening line of Baudelaire's sonnet seems to belong to this intertextual network:

> Dieu caché, disais-tu, la nature est ton temple!
> > (Lamartine, *Méditations poétiques* [1820], "Dieu," line 113)
> C'est Dieu qui remplit tout. Le monde, c'est son temple.
> > (Hugo, *Les Feuilles d'automne* [1831], "Pan," line 37)

In his letter to Desnoyers, three years before the publication of "Correspondances," Baudelaire seems to refute this interpretation of the natural world as infused with a divine soul. Yet *Les Fleurs du mal* does not articulate a simple rejection of belief in transcendent meaning out there in the world—rather, the poet constantly oscillates between belief and skepticism, hope and despair. For every poem of mournful existential emptiness, such as "La Cloche fêlée," the four "Spleen" poems or " Le Goût du néant," we can find another that sings of a higher realm of understanding, where an invigorating sense of life's beauty and purpose emerges as acute sensual or aesthetic experience, as in "Harmonie du soir" or "Élévation," the poem placed directly before "Correspondances" in *Les Fleurs du mal* and which concludes:

> Heureux celui [...]
> — Qui plane sur la vie, et comprend sans effort
> Le langage des fleurs et des choses muettes!
> > (*Œuvres complètes*, 1: 10, lines 15–20)

While the natural world, then, can no longer be taken as incontrovertible proof of divine meaning, it is not simply dismissed as indifferent or meaningless. Rather, it speaks a mysterious, subtle language—non-verbal patterns of meaning to be deciphered by those few souls sensitive, or artistic, enough to be attuned to it, as feature frequently in *Le Spleen de Paris*, Baudelaire's posthumous volume of prose poems: "Un œil expérimenté ne s'y trompe jamais" ("Les Veuves," *Œuvres complètes*, 1: 292). "Correspondances," then, marks a turning point between the stable beliefs of Romanticism and the instability of post-Romantic modernity, as Baudelaire shifts our understanding of poetry away from a celebration of meaning already placed in the world by a divine presence. Reading poetry now becomes an active search for meaning, or a continuous process of constructing fragile, tentative readings based on fleeting insights, a process that happens first and foremost in poetic language itself, "le langage des fleurs (*du Mal*)."

The first quatrain establishes our place in the world as interpreters of forests of symbols, suggesting immense living structures, complex ecosystems where light occasionally breaks through the shadows. For Hugo and Lamartine, the rhythms and harmonies of this ecosystem were evidence of a divine hand at work behind all nature's colors and textures, ensuring a delicate balance between the cyclical changing of the seasons, the waters, the wind in the trees, birdsong, the clouds, and the stars. In "Correspondances," however, these patterns of meaning are much less clear, darker, and more elusive. Rather than a verb of direct expression such as *dire* or *parler*, the expression "Laissent [...] sortir" (line 2) suggests a hazy kind of emanation, while "de confuses paroles" indicates a message, which is difficult to decipher, of which neither the receiver nor, indeed, the speaker is sure. Furthermore, the adverb "parfois" suggests that nature does not always offer itself up to be interpreted, but rather, opens up only at certain privileged moments of acute sensory insight.

The rest of the poem describes, in greater detail, these moments of heightened sensitivity, which appeal to more than one sense at once, through sound, sight, and scent. In the second quatrain, the poet insists on disparate elements coming together in unforeseen and mysterious ways: "de longs échos" (line 5), whose original source is lost, and which reverberate in the distance so that when they come together, their unity remains "ténébreuse et profonde" (line 6), leaving their meaning half concealed. Line eight provides an example of a phenomenon—or perhaps, rather, a picturesque figure of speech that appeals to the poetic imagination—for which Baudelaire has become famous, namely synaesthesia, or the perception of one sense in terms of another, such as perceiving colors when hearing sounds. The tercets illustrate this phenomenon with two sorts of scent: those as soft as the sound of oboes, or as green as prairies, and others so important that they occupy twice as many lines as the first group, which call to mind "des choses infinies" (line 12). These are sensual perfumes and the incense used in religious ceremonies, scents which transport the mind and the senses in a transcendental experience where disparate elements fuse together, and the harmonies hidden beneath the surface of the world resonate as one. In this poem, such moments of heightened intensity do not serve to reveal the divine, but rather, to give mind and body some sense of the ungraspable mysteries beyond our earthly sphere, beyond time, space, language and human experience, mysteries for which the poet yearns, in order to provide relief from the physical and mental suffering which, throughout *Les Fleurs du mal*, appears to be the condition of modern man in an urban, industrial, materialist society.

That such sensory "correspondances" occur only at privileged moments of heightened sensitivity is confirmed by Baudelaire's writings on the effects of beauty, sensual or sexual experience, art, music and artificial intoxicants, such as wine and hashish. In the poem "Tout entière," the poet refuses to answer when the devil asks which part of his lover's body he prefers, replying instead:

"Et l'harmonie est trop exquise,
Qui gouverne tout son beau corps,
Pour que l'impuissante analyse
En note les nombreux accords.

Ô métamorphose mystique
De tous mes sens fondus en un!
Son haleine fait la musique,
Comme sa voix fait le parfum!" (lines 17–24)

Just as the scents, colors, and sounds form an indivisible unity in "Correspondances," genuinely sensual, or erotic, experience does not divide the lover's body into separate parts for analysis and evaluation, but rather, merges the senses in a moment of transcendent ecstasy. In his essay, *Du vin et du hachisch* (1851), Baudelaire claims that hashish also inspires this sensory fusion: "Les équivoques les plus singulières, les transpositions d'idées les plus inexplicables ont lieu. Les sons ont une couleur, les couleurs ont une musique" (*Œuvres complètes,* 2: 392). And in his famous essay on Wagner (1861), Baudelaire makes a similar claim for music:

> Ce qui serait vraiment surprenant, c'est que le son *ne pût pas* suggérer la couleur, que les couleurs *ne pussent pas* donner l'idée d'une mélodie, et que le son et la couleur fussent impropres à traduire des idées; les choses s'étant toujours exprimées par une analogie réciproque, depuis le jour où Dieu a proféré le monde comme une complexe et indivisible totalité (*Œuvres complètes,* 2: 784, Baudelaire's emphasis).

While Baudelaire certainly recommends all sorts of artificial stimuli for achieving the sort of "transports" (line 14) described in "Correspondances," when he returns to hashish in *Les Paradis artificiels* (1860), he makes an important qualification:

> Puis, arrivent les équivoques, les méprises et les transformations d'idées. Les sons se revêtent de couleurs, et les couleurs contiennent une musique. Cela, dira-t-on, n'a rien que de fort naturel, et tout cerveau poétique, dans son état sain et normal, conçoit facilement ces analogies (*Œuvres complètes,* 2: 419).

A poetic mind, Baudelaire claims, can easily conceive of such "correspondances" and sensory amalgamations without using artificial intoxicants. Indeed, in the prose poem "Enivrez-vous," poetry itself acts as a possible stimulant for this kind of *ivresse*: "enivrez-vous sans cesse! De vin, de poésie ou de vertu, à votre guise" (*Œuvres complètes,* 1: 337). But what is a poetic mind, and how does it differ from a non-poetic mind? Does that necessarily hierarchical idea not sit uneasily alongside improvements in education and literacy which meant that successive generations of nineteenth-century French schoolchildren were able to churn out passable verse in composition class, based on the models they studied? If verse production is within the grasp of anyone with a basic level of education, genuine poets need a way to mark themselves out from inferior writers and imitators. Baudelaire's notion of a "cerveau poétique," therefore, re-defines poetry not as a piece of writing in metrical, rhyming verse, but rather, as a way of seeing, feeling, and imagining humankind's relationship with the world. Indeed, in a letter to Alphonse Toussenel, he argues that "*l'imagination* est la plus *scientifique* des facultés, parce que seule elle comprend *l'analogie universelle*, ou ce que la religion mystique appelle la *correspondances*" (*Correspondances* I 336, Baudelaire's italics). Poetic language, therefore, functions for Baudelaire both as the site of these mysterious "correspondances" and as a source of sensual pleasure. Thus we might conceive of poetry, like nature, as being made of "de vivants piliers" which occasionally emit "de confuses paroles" and "de longs échos" and inspire in the reader "l'expansion des choses infinies."

Except, perhaps, for the obfuscatory discourses of politics and advertising, language, in its everyday uses, often serves to transmit messages in as clear a form as possible. Such language is entirely inappropriate, then, for imagining the hidden truths of this universal analogy beyond the limits of our regular experience. Poetic language, in its attempt to express these elusive "correspondances" must necessarily resist reduction to one simple meaning, ensuring it remains as complex, elusive and unanalyzable as the barely decipherable realities towards which it points. Referential meaning is only one aspect of language—in literature and poetry, as well as rhetoric, rhythm and sound can play an equally important role in suggesting other layers of meaning, and on this level, the "vivants piliers" of "Correspondances" have a lot to say.

If we begin with rhythm and peer carefully enough into the dark forest of the text, a number of patterns, which were not immediately apparent, start to appear. The sonnet is written in alexandrines, lines of twelve syllables, which enjoy a similar cultural prestige in French literature to iambic pentameter in English. Alexandrines are used frequently in poetry from the Renaissance to the twenty-first century, as well as in theatre from the seventeenth-century classics—Molière,

Racine and Corneille—to the eighteenth and nineteenth centuries. The defining structural feature of the alexandrine is a subtle, but palpable, mid-line break—the caesura—which divides the line into two hemistichs of six syllables, with an accent on the final syllable of each: xxxxxX / xxxxxX. Within each hemistich, it is customary to identify a secondary accent, which usually falls on the final syllable of a word, so that within the predictable 6/6 structure, other, more flexible patterns are created:

La Na-ture / est un **temple** // où de vi-vants / pi-**liers**   (3/3//4/2)
1 2 <u>3</u> / 4 5 <u>6</u> // 7 8 9 <u>10</u> / 11 <u>12</u>

In contrast to standard spoken French, where the "e" at the end of words is rarely pronounced, in verse, it contributes to the syllable count if followed by a consonant, but not if followed by a vowel, or at the end of a line:

Lai-ssent par-fois sor-tir // de con-fu-ses pa-rol(es);
2 3 4 5 6 7 8 9 10 11 12 x

L'homm(e) y pass(e) à tra-vers // des fo-rêts de sym-bol(es)
1 x 2 3 x 4 5 6   7 8 9 10 11 12 x

Qui l'ob-ser-vent a-vec // des re-gards fa-mi-liers.
1 2 3 4 5 6 7 8 9 10 11 12

While syllable counting can appear confusing at first, it becomes much simpler once one is accustomed to the fact that the caesura normally follows a word which carries enough semantic meaning for it to bear an accent. It rarely appears in the middle of an indivisible sense unit; this 6/6 structure is such a fundamental rhythm in French verse that, once the reader becomes used to it, the caesura can usually be identified without painstakingly counting out the syllables. Vowel pairs can cause a little uncertainty, but if the 6/6 structure is identified first, it should be clear which are to be read as one syllable, with synaeresis ("pil*iers*," line 1, "famil*iers*," l. 4, "n*ui*t," l. 7), and which as two syllables, with diaeresis ("triomphants," line 11, "expansi-**on**," line 12). Finally, although a word may end in an "e," with unpronounced consonants "s" or "nt," this so-called mute "e," or *e caduc*, cannot be accentuated, and so when scanning rhythmic segments, it belongs to the following unit: "de confus/*es* paroles" (3/3) not "de confus*es* / paroles" (4/2), "Qui l'observ/*ent* avec" (3/3) not "Qui l'observ*ent* / avec" (4/2).

A rhythmic reading of "Correspondances" allows several patterns to emerge from the "vivants piliers" of the verse:

La Nature / est un temple // où de vivants / piliers	3 3 4 2
Laissent parfois / sortir // de confus/es paroles;	4 2 3 3
L'homme y passe / à travers // des forêts / de symboles	3 3 3 3
Qui l'observ/ent avec // des regards / familiers.	3 3 3 3
Comme de longs / échos // qui de loin / se confondent	4 2 3 3
Dans une ténébreuse // et profonde / unité,	6 3 3
Vast/e comme la nuit // et comm/e la clarté,	1 5 2 4
Les parfums, / les couleurs // et les sons / se répondent.	3 3 3 3
Il est des parfums / frais // comme des chairs / d'enfants,	5 1 4 2
Doux / comme les hautbois, // verts / comme les prairies,	1 5 1 5
– Et d'autr/es, corrompus, // rich/es et triomphants,	2 4 1 5
Ayant / l'expansi-on // des chos/es infinies,	2 4 2 4
Comme l'ambr/e, le musc, // le benjoin / et l'encens,	3 3 3 3
Qui chant/ent les transports // de l'esprit / et des sens.	2 4 3 3

The first noteworthy feature is the preponderance of highly regular 3/3//3/3 rhythms in the first quatrain. The chiasmus (*abba* structure) in the first four hemistichs (3/3-4/2-4/2-3/3) establishes the 3/3 rhythm as a framing device for the first complete utterance (main clause / relative clause / semi-colon). Given the rhythmic diversity, which Hugo claimed he had brought into French verse from the 1820s onwards—"Et sur les bataillons d'alexandrins carrés, / Je fis souffler un vent révolutionnaire" ("Réponse à un acte d'accustion," *Les Contemplations* [1856], lines 64–65)—the insistent regularity of lines 3–4 is striking. Given the subject of these lines—the reciprocal process by which we are observed by the natural world, of which we are also the observers—we might imagine that this succession of identical metrical units performs rhythmically the sense of perfect oneness with the universe which occurs at such fleeting moments of symbiosis.

The rhythmic fabric of the second quatrain demonstrates just how fragile and elusive these moments of communion are, as the pattern which seems so insistent in lines three and four threatens to disintegrate at precisely the moment the poem describes disparate elements coalescing (lines 5–6), although it recurs in the second hemistich of lines five and six. Are we to understand that the unity, of which the poem offers us a glimpse, slips out of focus no sooner than we have sensed it, or even that it is simply a fiction which the poetic imagination projects onto the world? The difficulty of locating a secondary accent in the first hemistich of line six, however, might suggest a different reading. Neither "Dans" nor "une" are semantically important or syntactically independent enough to carry an accent, and although we might be tempted to accentuate "tén-," the accent in French usually falls on the final syllable of polysyllabic words. As such, line six lends itself most naturally to a 6//3/3 reading, which pulls the reader irresistibly towards the second hemistich, thereby embodying in its very resistance to accentual subdivision the "unité," which it expresses. In the same way, the rhythmic destabilization of line seven is recuperated in the rhythmic regularity of line eight. Whereas the former begins with a monosyllabic jolt, throwing the adjective "Vaste" into relief before the rest of the line amplifies the idea with a double simile, line eight returns to the regularity of lines three and four at the precise moment the mysterious concord between scents, colors, and sound is evoked.

We should be wary, however, of overvaluing the 3/3//3/3 structure—is it necessarily, inherently meaningful simply because its pleasing regularity has caught our attention? Baudelaire writes in his account of the 1855 Exposition universelle in Paris of "La variété, condition *sine qua non* de la vie," thanks to which "il y a dans les productions multiples de l'art quelque chose de toujours nouveau qui échappera éternellement à la règle et aux analyses de l'école"

(*Œuvres complètes,* 2: 578). From this point of view, what might appear to be several awkward, unbalanced rhythms in the tercets— "Il est des parfums / frais" (5/1), "Doux / comme les hautbois" (1/5), "verts / comme les prairies" (1/5), "rich/es et triomphants" (1/5)— might simply provide the sort of rhythmic variety which guarantees genuine art. Indeed, Baudelaire writes in his sketches for a preface to *Les Fleurs du mal* that "le rythme et la rime répondent dans l'homme aux immortels besoins de monotonie, de symétrie et de surprise" (*Œuvres complètes,* 1: 182). As such, when that striking 3/3//3/3 rhythm occurs again in line thirteen, underlining the sense of amplification as the rich, triumphant perfumes accumulate, we might see it not necessarily as the perfect regularity towards which poetry should strive, but rather, as part of a constant play between rhythmic features, sometimes monotonous, sometimes surprising, which allows the "confuses paroles" of both the world and the text to remain elusive.

Similarly mobile, fragile "correspondances" can be observed at the rhyme, which appears to follow an irregular form for the sonnet: *abba cddc efe fgg.* Nineteenth-century French theorists of poetry recognized only one rhyme pattern for the regular sonnet— *abba abba ccd ede*—but as Robb demonstrates, Baudelaire was a pioneer of the irregular sonnet as early as the 1840s, experimenting with many different rhyme combinations throughout *Les Fleurs du mal,* with the quatrains of more than forty of his seventy-six sonnets featuring four, rather than two, different rhyme sounds (229–241). That Baudelaire should choose an irregular form to write about the mysterious harmonies beneath the surface of the natural world is surely significant. As Théophile Gautier asked in his preface to the posthumous third edition of *Les Fleurs du mal* (1868), "L'irrégulier dans le régulier, le manque de *correspondance* dans la symétrie, quoi de plus illogique et de plus contrariant?" (Robb 241, my emphasis). Rather than propose a normative model of the universal analogy by suggesting that the rhythms and harmonies of the world necessarily correspond to regular sonnet form, Baudelaire appears to suggest that while these elusive patterns certainly obey a structural logic, they are perhaps not fixed in a simplistic, easily reproducible way.

This is certainly the reading to which the rhyme sounds point: while the *a* and *d* rhymes should definitely be labelled as two different pairs, since they are spelled differently—"piliers / familiers," "unité / clarté"—their final vowel sound, the acute /e/, is identical. This adds an extra layer of complexity, whereby the structural elements of one part of the pattern call out to others, creating "de longs échos qui de loin se confondent" (line 5).

A similar echo is created between the *e* and *g* rhymes, graphically distinct but phonetically identical: "enfants / triomphants," "encens / sens." While this appears to offer another extra layer of harmony, which resists classification within simple rhyme categories, that harmony falters slightly on the poem's final word, whose function, one might imagine, would be to confirm the sense of "correspondances" with a strong rhyme. Yet what the text actually offers us is a slightly malfunctioning rhyme, since the final "s" of "encens" is not usually pronounced, whereas that of "sens" is. This sort of poetic license was common in French poetry, as many poets rhymed "Vénus" /venys/ with the adjective "nus" /ny/, and is thus relatively uncontroversial. In the context of this poem, however, this phonetic hesitation allows the "correspondances" between textual elements to flutter uncertainly, as the final "s" is both heard and unheard. This faltering echo effect between the closing rhyme words is a far cry from the emphatic *rime léonine* (a rhyme over two whole syllables) which opens the poem: "**pil**iers / fam**iliers**" (/ilje/). Indeed, throughout the poem the rhymes are not as strong as one might expect for a poem dealing with the harmonies of the natural world: three *rimes suffisantes* (two identical adjacent phonemes)—"par**oles** / symb**oles**" (/ol/), "conf**ondent** / rép**ondent**" (/od/), "en**fants** / triom**phants**" (/fa/)—and one *rime pauvre* (one identical phoneme): "prair**ies** / infin**ies**" (/i/).

Yet just as the "confuses paroles" emitted by the "vivants piliers" of the natural world set us an irresolvable interpretative challenge, so too the malfunctioning harmony of the poem's final rhyme participates in another network of meaning, which has the opposite effect of actually increasing the harmony: the remarkable frequency of nasal vowels, especially /a/, which, after a striking crescendo through the first three stanzas, overwhelms the final stanza:

temple, vivants (l. 1)	/ ɑ̃ /, / ɑ̃ /
confuses (l. 2)	/ ɑ̃ /
symboles (l. 3)	/ ɔ̃ / 4
*	
longs, loin, confondent (l. 5)	/ ɔ̃ /, / ɔ̃ /, / ɔ̃ /, / ɑ̃ /
Dans, profonde (l. 6)	/ ɑ̃ /, / ɔ̃ /
parfums, sons, répondent (l. 8)	/ œ̃ /, / ɔ̃ /, / ɔ̃ / 9
*	
parfums, enfants (l. 9)	/ œ̃ /, / ɑ̃ /, / ɑ̃ /
corrompus, triomphants (l. 11)	/ ɔ̃ /, / ɔ̃ /, / ɑ̃ /
6	
*	
expansion, infinies (l. 12)	/ ɑ̃ /, / ɑ̃ /, / ɑ̃ /
l'ambre, benjoin, encens (l. 13)	/ ɑ̃ /, / ɑ̃ /, / ɑ̃ /, / ɑ̃ /, / ɑ̃ /
chantent, transports, sens (l. 14)	/ ɑ̃ /, / ɑ̃ /, / ɑ̃ / 11

The effect, thanks to which the vowel of "**sens**" appears twice in its rhyme partner "**encen**s," also features in two other rhyme pairs: "**confond**ent / rép**ond**ent" and "**enfan**ts / triomph**an**ts." Of course, the doubt that most often perturbs students of poetry, when textual analysis leads to this level of detail is: did the poet mean it? Are all these patterns meaningful? Might it be that we are projecting meaning onto structures in a way that distorts what the poet intended?

The poem itself provides the most encouraging answer to these concerns: while Romantic poets saw such subtle patterns in nature as part of a divine authorial intention, this post-Romantic poetry is not to be read as a search for the meaning which a quasi-divine author has hidden in the text for us to uncover. Rather, the text offers us the opportunity to interrogate the ways in which humankind looks for meaning in a universe that, at times, seems impenetrable, and at other, privileged moments, appears to offer up spontaneous flashes of "correspondances." Just as the universe only talks in symbols, with "confuses paroles," we should not expect the author of the poetic text to confirm or deny our intuitions. Thus our reading of poetry mirrors our existential encounter with the universe, and what might, at first, appear overwhelmingly frightening is, in fact, liberating: if I identify a structural pattern, which I can meaningfully interpret through the conceptual framework that the poem offers me, then who is to tell me that my insight is false, especially if, as Baudelaire suggests, "l'imagination est la plus scientifique des facultés"? If, having explored the phonetic properties of the rhymes, and the rich network of nasal vowels, I see a "correspondance" between "des **ch**airs d'**enfa**nts" (line 9) and "**chan**tent" (line 14), which confirms the relationship between scent and touch in the first instance and sound in the second, then the poem's own celebration of the fragility of the human search for meaning is enough to give me the courage of my convictions.

Similarly, it matters little if it is a coincidence that the only two examples of diaeresis in the whole poem occur on the same vowel sounds in two words placed closely together, separated by three occurences of the same key nasal vowel on which the poem concludes, themselves separated by other vowels, giving a AB-c-x-c-x-c-AB pattern: "t**ri-om**ph**a**nts / Ay**a**nt l'exp**a**ns**i-on**" (lines 11–12). Since pronunciation with diaeresis is highly unnatural, these lines, if read with scrupulous attention to the artifice of the metrical imperative, illustrate phonetically the sense of "expansion" that the poem's final lines celebrate. Certainly, the lengths to which Jakobson and Lévi-Strauss push their remarkable structural analysis of another sonnet, "Les Chats," confirm that the more carefully one looks, the more potentially valid patterns emerge. Baudelaire himself tells us, in his sonnet "Obsession," that the projection of meaning onto forms is a fundamentally human endeavor. In a moment of skepticism about meaning in the universe, he tries to imagine a perfectly black night sky without any stars:

Comme tu me plairais, ô nuit! sans ces étoiles
Dont la lumière parle un langage connu!
Car je cherche le vide, et le noir, et le nu!

Mais les ténèbres sont elles-mêmes des toiles
Où vivent, jaillissant de mon œil par milliers,

Des êtres disparus aux regards familiers
(*Œuvres complètes,* 1: 75, lines 9–14).

Yet despite his best efforts, he sees not an enormous black void, nor even a random jumble of stars, but rather, constellations: patterns that humankind has, for centuries, identified among the stars and that have played a central role in so many of the mythical narratives which we have used to explore the most fundamental questions about our humanity.

The construction of literary meaning, therefore, is not a search for a single answer that the author has hidden in the text and would guarantee if only we could ask him, but an actively imaginative activity, as our restless and inquisitive analytical minds seek to infer meaning from, or attribute meaning to, the patterns we identify. If these patterns are read within the interpretative framework, which the text offers us—the present sonnet encourages us to read formal echoes as an illustration of other sorts of correspondances—then the question of coincidence becomes redundant: I, as reader, am the source of the poem's meaning, which I have deduced to the best of my ability, but which must necessarily remain as fragile, and ultimately unstable, as any other potential reading. Poetic language offers the perfect framework for exploring the connections we make between external phenomena, not only thanks to the way it foregrounds formal structures as non-semantic patterns of meaning, but also thanks to two key poetic devices—metaphor and simile—which themselves create "correspondances" between phenomena that, until their appearance together in the text, might not have appeared to have any obvious connection.

Baudelaire is well known as the poet of the simile, with comparisons introduced by "comme," which is featured over one hundred times in *Les Fleurs du mal* and six times in "Correspondances" alone (the seventh "comme," in line thirteen, simply introduces a list of scents). Whereas many of these similes are quite straightforward and do not add much that is new to our understanding of the world, others force us to reflect on new "correspondances," which might not have occurred to us before:

Elle éblouit comme l'Aurore
Et console comme la Nuit;
      ("Tout entière," *Œuvres complètes,* 1: 42, lines 15–16)

Mais la tristesse en moi monte comme la mer
      ("Causerie," *Œuvres complètes,* 1: 56, line 2)

Grands bois, vous m'effrayez commes des cathédrales
      ("Obsession," *Œuvres complètes,* 1: 75, line 1)

Son parfum doux comme un secret
      ("Le Guignon," *Œuvres complètes,* 1: 17, line 13)

Et le ver rongera ta peau comme un remords
      ("Remords posthume," *Œuvres complètes,* 1: 35, line 14)

While the first and third of these similes offer a clear, almost clichéd relationship between tenor (what is being compared) and vehicle (what it is being compared to)—the poet's lover dazzles him like the dawn, his sadness engulfs him like an unstoppable tide—none of the other similes here provide such obvious comparisons. How, exactly, does the night console? Why would a cathedral inspire terror? What is particularly pleasurable about a secret? Indeed, the final example seems to invert the customary tenor and vehicle completely—whereas it is a commonplace to talk of feelings gnawing away at us, like a worm, it is far less obvious to compare a real worm, which the poet imagines eating his deceased lover's flesh, to remorse.

Thus the "forêts de symboles" (line 3), with which poetry presents the reader, invite us to construct both the text and the world afresh with each reading. We accept this challenge, knowing that the meaning of the structures we observe may only be provisional within the limits of our own capacity to observe, to analyze, and to interpret imaginatively and with confidence. As such, "Correspondances" provides the ideal starting point for these poetic encounters, since as Rimbaud tells Paul Demeny in a letter of May 1871, "Baudelaire est le premier voyant, roi des poètes, *un vrai Dieu*" (93, Rimbaud's italics). The poem, and the poetics it articulates, had such a profound influence on Baudelaire's contemporaries and subsequent generations of writers that, by the 1880s, it had become one of the central pillars of an entire poetic movement, Symbolism, whose very title picks up a key word from line three of the sonnet. At their worst and most simplistic, the minor Symbolist poets quite misunderstood the principle behind Baudelaire's *correspondances*, creating fixed systems of analogy between moods, objects, and symbols, as if the text were a puzzle to be solved, or a mystery to be unravelled. As we have seen, Baudelaire's poetry invites us to an infinitely subtler experience, active and open-ended: the constant *remise en question* of the world, and our relationship with it.

Works Cited

Austin, Lloyd James. *L'Univers poétique de Baudelaire*. Paris: Mercure de France, 1956.

Baudelaire, Charles. *Correspondances. Choix et présentation de Claude Pichois et Jérôme Thélot*. Paris: Gallimard, 2000.

_____. *Œuvres complètes*. Ed. Claude Pichois. 2 vols. Paris: Gallimard (Bibliothèque de la Pléiade), 1975–6.

Broome, Peter. *Baudelaire's Poetic Patterns*. Amsterdam: Rodopi, 1999.

Chesters, Graham. *Some Functions of Sound Repetition in "Les Fleurs du mal."* Hull: U of Hull, 1975.

Culler, Jonathan. "Intertextuality and Interpretation: Baudelaire's 'Correspondances'." *Nineteenth-Century French Poetry: Introductions to Close Reading*. Ed. Christopher Prendergast. Cambridge: Cambridge UP, 1990. 118–37.

Evans, David. *Rhythm, Illusion and the Poetic Idea: Baudelaire, Rimbaud, Mallarmé*. Amsterdam: Rodopi, 2004.

Forest, Philippe. *Le Symbolisme, ou, Naissance de la poésie moderne*. Paris: Bordas, 1989.

Guyaux, André. *Baudelaire: un demi-siècle de lectures des Fleurs du mal, 1855–1905*. Paris: Presses de l'Université Paris-Sorbonne, 2007.

Jakobson, Roman and Claude Lévi-Strauss. "'Les Chats' de Charles Baudelaire." *L'Homme* 2:1 (Jan. –Apr. 1962): 5–21.

Leakey, F. W. *Baudelaire and Nature*. Manchester, UK: Manchester UP, 1969.

Martino, Pierre. *Parnasse et symbolisme (1850–1900)*. Paris: Colin, 1935.

Michaud, Guy. *Message poétique du symbolisme*. Paris: Nizet, 1947.

Murphy, Steve, ed. *Lectures de Baudelaire: Les fleurs du mal*. Rennes: Presses universitaires de Rennes, 2002.

Pommier, Jean. *La Mystique de Baudelaire*. Geneva: Slatkine, 1967.

Rimbaud, Arthur. *Poésies*. Paris: Gallimard, 1999.

Robb, Graham. *La poésie de Baudelaire et la poésie française: 1838–1852*. Paris: Aubier, 1993.

Scott, Clive. *French Verse-Art: A Study*. Cambridge: Cambridge UP, 1980.

Baudelaire's *Les Phares* Revisited: Creating an Artistic Canon for the Romantic Era_____

Frances Fowle

"Glorifier le culte des images (ma grande, mon unique, ma primitive passion)."

—Charles Baudelaire, *Mon coeur mis à nu*, LXIX

Baudelaire was celebrated as an art critic, and his poetry provided inspiration for a whole generation of artists at the fin de siècle. He wrote with confidence and authority about art, and yet had no art historical training. He never visited the great museums of Italy, Spain, Germany, and the Netherlands (his only journeys outside France were to Mauritius and Belgium), and his knowledge of art was limited to pictures that he could see at the Salon, the Louvre, the Palais du Luxembourg, or those that were disseminated through black-and-white prints. As the art theorist André Malraux wryly commented, "Baudelaire never set eyes on the masterpieces of El Greco, Michelangelo, Masaccio, Piero della Francesca or Grünewald; or of Titian, or of Hals or Goya." (Werner 654–5) He favored "colorito" over "disegno, " but was never able to appreciate the work of the greatest Venetian painter. He wrote instinctively about paintings that enthralled or repelled him. Those that failed to move him were omitted from his "Salons," published in 1845, 1846 and 1859, and his review of the *Exposition Universelle* of 1855. He believed that "the best criticism is that which is both amusing and poetic: not a cold, mathematical criticism which, on the pretext of explaining everything, has neither love nor hate, and voluntarily strips itself of every shred of temperament … the best account of a picture may well be a sonnet or an elegy" (Werner 656).

In *Les Phares*, Baudelaire describes or evokes several works of art, some of which can be identified; others are composites, or even the poet's own creations. As Carrier points out, Baudelaire summarizes each artist by "condensing" features from the best known works; a contrast to Walter Pater's approach in *The Renaissance* (1893), whereby the *Mona Lisa* is used metonymically to stand for the entire history of European art and culture (Carrier 56–7).

Baudelaire's aim in this poem is to celebrate for posterity the greatest artists of all time. His selection, however, is not only unorthodox, but clouded by his subjective judgement. His appreciation of art was not that of the scrupulous connoisseur who would pour over a single canvas for hours on end. Often, he would form an opinion based on a cursory glance. What he valued in a painting was evidence of the artist's temperament; what the painters and sculptors in his canon have in common is their sensuality, their passionate, brooding temperaments, their dramatic use of light and shade and their expressive application of color. Rational classicism has no place in Baudelaire's pantheon; Leonardo da Vinci and Michelangelo take precedence over Raphael; Claude and Poussin are side-lined in favor of Rubens and Rembrandt; Chardin makes way for Watteau; Delacroix's passion and Goya's dark Romanticism supersede Ingres' clarity and idealization. Baudelaire's notion of artistic genius is linked closely to his perception of Romanticism as (in Brookner's words) "infinitely heroic, melancholy and profound enough to carry men on to some further goal" (Brookner 59). Artists who fail to engage on this emotional level are excluded. Thus, Ingres, whom Baudelaire later described as "quite devoid of that energy of temperament which constitutes the fatality of genius" (Mayne, *Charles Baudelaire* 133), is rejected from the canon.

Structurally the poem disregards any art historical chronology. It is as if the poet is leading us round a private art gallery, hung with examples of his chosen artists. Our emotions ebb and flow as the shifting colors, contrasting shades of light and dark, and the different "tones" of the poem wash over us. The Flemish master of the Baroque, Peter Paul Rubens leads us in, and the listener is intoxicated from the outset by Baudelaire's description of a "fleuve d'oubli, jardin de paresse" (line 1) (a river of oblivion, a garden of indolence). His inspiration was the great Marie de Médici cycle which he was able to see at the Palais du Luxembourg. He describes the "Oreiller de chair fraîche ... /ou la vie afflue et s'agite sans cesse" (lines 2–3) (Pillow of cool flesh ... /where life moves and whirls incessantly), evoking the voluptuous Naiads born aloft by the billowing waves in *The Disembarkation at Marseilles*. Rubens was the master of "colorito," and in the "Salon of 1846," Baudelaire praised him, not only for his rich palette, but for his sense of drama and fantasy.

With the next stanza the mood of *Les Phares* shifts, as the poet transports us from the heady, sensuous world of Rubens, back in time, to the mysterious realm of Leonardo da Vinci. Baudelaire associates Leonardo with a "miroir profond et sombre" (line 5), "a dark, unfathomable mirror," perhaps an oblique reference to the Renaissance concern with mimesis, "holding a mirror up to nature"; or even to Leonardo's esoteric practice of recording his notes in mirror writing. In his paintings, we discover that:

> ... des anges charmants, avec un doux souris / Tout chargé de mystère, apparaissent à l'ombre / Des glaciers et des pins qui ferment leur pays (lines 6–8)
> (... charming angels, with sweet smiles / Full of mystery, appear in the shadow / Of the glaciers and pines that enclose their country.)

The "doux souris" reminds us of Leonardo's most enigmatic work *The Mona Lisa* (1503–17, Musée du Louvre), but the description is closer to the *Madonna of the Rocks* of 1483–6 (Musée du Louvre, Paris), which Baudelaire would have known well from his trips to the Louvre. Only one angel inhabits this painting and Baudelaire is less interested in the mystery of incarnation than in the imaginary landscape in which the Virgin, Christ Child, and St. John the Baptist are seated. Indeed, his atmospheric description prefigures the brooding pines of later Symbolist works, such as Arnold Böcklin's *Isle of the Dead* of 1880 (Kunstmuseum, Basel).

The solemn tone is maintained in the poet's next image, attributed to Rembrandt van Rijn·

"…triste hôpital tout rempli de murmures,/ Et d'un grand crucifix décoré seulement / Où la prière en pleurs s'exhale des ordures, / Et d'un rayon d'hiver traversé brusquement" (lines 9-12).

(… gloomy hospital filled with murmuring, /Furnished only with a large crucifix,/ Lit for a moment by a winter's ray /Where tearful prayers rise up from the filth.).

It is impossible to identify this work, but it recalls Rembrandt's famous etching of *Christ Healing the Sick* (c.1647–9), also known as the *Hundred Guilder Print*. Rembrandt was a gifted painter, celebrated for his dramatic use of chiaroscuro, to which Baudelaire alludes, and one might have expected the poet to choose (rather than a hybrid of Rembrandt's etchings) an oil painting, such as the Louvre's *The Philosopher in Meditation* of 1632, highly imaginative and charged with atmosphere. This painting was greatly admired by writers throughout the nineteenth century, above all by Symbolists Paul Valéry and Paul Claudel and would have been a fitting addition to the poet's canon. On the other hand, the etching was well known and perhaps more representative of Rembrandt's sympathy for the less fortunate in society.

From the greatest Dutch artist of the Baroque period, Baudelaire transports us back again to the sixteenth century:

Michel-Ange, lieu vague ou l'on voit des Hercules / Se mêler à des Christs, et se lever tout droits / Des fantômes puissants qui dans les crépuscules / Déchirent leur suaire en étirant leurs doigts (lines 13–16).

(Michelangelo, shadowy place where one can see Herculeses / Mingling with Christs, and rising up, / Powerful phantoms, who in the twilight / Rend their winding-sheets with outstretched fingers)

Baudelaire may have heard of Michelangelo's colossal marble statue of Hercules, which disappeared from France in the eighteenth century, but the reference in his poem is to Michelangelo's *Last*

Judgement in the Sistine Chapel, which he could have known from Giulio Bonasone's engraving. In Michelangelo's masterpiece, figures such as Saint Bartholomew, seated astride a cloud, derive from the famous Apollo Belvedere, itself a classical representation of Hercules. Baudelaire admired the theatrical drama of Michelangelo's greatest achievement. His contorted, muscular torsos challenged the serene complacency of the High Renaissance and ushered in the Mannerist period.

One might have expected Baudelaire to allude to Michelangelo's enigmatic sculptures of *The Slaves*, which entered the Louvre's collection towards the end of the eighteenth century. Instead, he evokes the "winding sheets" of his famous *Pietà* in Rome before descending to another level altogether; for the fifth stanza introduces the "boxers" and "fauns" of the relatively minor seventeenth-century sculptor Pierre Puget, that "mélancolique empereur des forçats" (line 20). The line refers to Puget's formation as a ship's carver, sculpting ornaments for the galleys built in the shipyards of Marseilles, his native city. Baudelaire would have known his masterpiece, the *Milo of Croton* (Musée du Louvre, Paris), hewn from a large block of marble abandoned in the dockyards of Toulon (Herding 93).

He perhaps chose Puget over a greater sculptor such as Bernini (or indeed Michelangelo) because he instinctively recognized, in his work, the expression of a complex and tortured soul, but the choice is somewhat anomalous. By contrast, Antoine Watteau was celebrated as the leading French artist of the early eighteenth century. His "fêtes galantes" evoke the carefree life of the French aristocracy and the court of Louis XIV:

> … ce carnaval où bien des cœurs illustres/Comme des papillons, errant et flamboyant" (lines 21–22).

> (… this carnival where the loves of many famous hearts /Flutter capriciously, like gaudy butterflies).

Baudelaire knew and admired Watteau's Rococo masterpiece, the *Embarkation for the Island of Cythera* of 1717 (Musée du Louvre, Paris), to which he briefly alludes in his "Salon of 1846." Like the majority of Watteau's paintings it is a *fantaisie* set in the open air, and it was this imaginative, even theatrical aspect that Baudelaire so admired, together with Watteau's essentially colorist technique. However, neither Puget nor Watteau were artists to whom Baudelaire refers extensively in his art criticism; they appear to have been added as an afterthought, as two (albeit French) artists who bridge the gap between the world of the Old Masters and the modern era. As Porter has pointed out, if Baudelaire had included in *Les Phares* the artists most discussed in his "Salons," then Raphael and Veronese would surely have replaced these two artists in the pantheon (Porter 51).

From Watteau's "Décors frais et légers" (line 23), the mood darkens once again as Baudelaire reaches the climax of his poem: the art of the Romantic era. The next stanza reflect his admiration for Goya's satirical suite of prints *Los Caprichos* (the Caprices), a set of eighty acquatints, first published as an album in 1799 and intended to satirize the follies of contemporary Spanish society. The "cauchemar plein de choses inconnues…" (line 25) (nightmare full of unknown things…) refers to Plate 43, *The Sleep of Reason Produces Monsters* (1797–8), which shows a sleeping man tormented by nightmares, an image that has come to symbolize the darker, irrational strain in Romantic art. Baudelaire described the *Caprichos* as "a marvellous work, not only on account of the originality of their conceptions, but also on account of their execution" (Mayne, *Charles Baudelaire* 181). In particular, he admired Goya's feeling for "the blank horrors of nature and for human countenances weirdly animalised by circumstances" (Mayne, *Charles Baudelaire* 181). In *Les Phares* the "foetus qu'on fait cuire au milieu des sabbats" (line 26) alludes to the *Caprichos*, but perhaps also to the painting *The Witches Sabbath* in the Prado. The "vieilles au miroir" (old women with a mirror), is a theme reproduced in the *Caprichos*, but the poet may also have known the deeply satirical *Old Women Looking in a Mirror* or *Que Tal?* (Musée des Beaux Arts, Lille), which features a syphilitic old maidservant holding a mirror up to her hag-like mistress.

To Baudelaire, Goya was "a great and often … terrifying artist," but it was Eugène Delacroix who had reached the apex of artistic achievement. In the "Salon of 1845," he describes Delacroix as "décidément le peintre le plus original des temps anciens et modernes" (Brookner, "Art Historians" 274). For the poet-turned-critic, Delacroix represented modernity, not only through his expressive use of color, but because of his romantic temperament and powerful imagination. His paintings were a summation of all that had preceded him, combining the color and drama of Rubens, the brooding chiaroscuro of Rembrandt, the mysterious skill of Leonardo, and the temperamental theatricality of Michelangelo.

At the Louvre, Baudelaire was able to admire at leisure Delacroix's masterpieces: *The Barque of Dante* (1822), the *Massacre at Chios* (1824), the *Death of Sardanapalus* (1827), *Liberty at the Barricades* (1830), and the *Women of Algiers* (1834). He was close to the artist and familiar with his color theory, admiring his sense of the suggestive, emotional power of paint and its synaesthetic qualities. Indeed, in both the "Salon of 1846" and "Les Phares" (line 32) Baudelaire evokes—in relation to Delacroix—the music of the German composer Carl Maria von Weber, whose emphasis on myth and nature would influence Wagner.

When praising Delacroix, Baudelaire adopted a particular phraseology in both the poem and in his art criticism. In the "Salon of 1846," the artist's color is "toujours sanglante et terrible" (always bloody and terrible), while in *Les Phares* he describes a "lac de sang hanté des mauvais anges" (line 29) (a lake of blood haunted by bad angels). The actual painting described by Baudelaire in the poem is a fantasy, impossible to identify, but the description of a "lac de sang ... ombragé par un bois de sapins toujours vert" (lines 29–30) (a lake of blood ... shaded by evergreen pine trees) surely inspired the Belgian artist William Degouve de Nuncques to paint his darkly Symbolist landscape *The Pool of Blood* (Musées royaux des Beaux-Arts de Belgique, Brussels) in 1894. This mysterious painting is shrouded in death: a pool of blood (symbolizing a loss of vitality) surrounded by waving cypresses, with a small shrine set at a crossroads.

In conclusion, therefore, it becomes clear that Baudelaire's canon of artists is determined by his own Romantic imagination and by his overweening admiration for Delacroix. His descriptions are deliberately devoid of narrative; they are also a-historical and markedly a-political. Although "Les Phares" may have been written as early as 1846, *Les Fleurs du Mal* was published in 1857 at the height of the Second Empire. By then, the revolution of 1848 had ushered in a new, Realist era, embodied in the art of Courbet. Baudelaire was viewed as a participant in the modern movement and is featured in Courbet's *Atelier d'un Peintre* (Musée d'Orsay, Paris), exhibited in the artist's controversial 'Pavillon du réalisme' at the 1855 Exposition Universelle. His shadowy profile is also evident in Manet's *Jardin des Tuileries* of 1862 (National Gallery, London) and he is appropriately included (in the company of Manet and Whistler) in Fantin-Latour's *Hommage à Delacroix* of 1864 (Musée d'Orsay, Paris).

Indeed, Baudelaire's artistic canon was of its time and several of the artists in *Les Phares*—Rubens, Rembrandt, Watteau, Goya, and Delacroix—were later admired by the Impressionists for their expressive handling and bold application of color. Celebrated for his essay on Constantin Guys, *The Painter of Modern Life* (1863), Baudelaire nevertheless clung to a definition of modernity that incorporated his personal, Romantic vision. Romanticism, for Baudelaire, resided "neither in choice of subjects nor in exact truth, but in a mode of feeling" (Mayne, *Charles Baudelaire* 46), and in many ways his art theory, and certainly his poetry, had more impact on the Symbolists than on the Impressionists. Indeed, as early as 1881 Baudelaire was recognized by Paul Bourget as "a theoretician of decadence" (Dorra 129). The final lines of *Les Phares* foretell the poem's posthumous fame, as much as that of the artists it celebrates, but above all, it sends its "ardent sanglot" through the ages, to be echoed and repeated by the Symbolist generation.

Works Cited

Bourget, Paul. "Essai de psychologie contemporaine: Charles Baudelaire." *La Nouvelle Revue* 13 (1881): 398–417.

Brookner, Anita. "Art Historians and Art Critics VII: Charles Baudelaire." *The Burlington Magazine*, 106.735 (June 1964): 274.

_____. *The Genius of the Future*. London: Phaidon, 1971.

Carrier, David. *High Art: Charles Baudelaire and the Origins of Modernist Painting*. University Park: Pennsylvania State UP, 1996.

Dorra, Henri. *Symbolist Art Theories: A Critical Anthology*. Berkeley, CA: U of California P, 1995.

Herding, Klaus. "Puget sculpteur" *Pierre Puget, Peintre, Sculpteur, Architecte 1620–1694*. Marseille : Musées de Marseille/Réunion des Musées Nationaux, 1994: 88–99.

Mayne, Jonathan, ed. *Charles Baudelaire, The Mirror of Art: Critical Studies by Charles Baudelaire*. Oxford, UK: Phaidon, 1955.

_____ , ed. *Art in Paris 1845–1862: Salons and other Exhibitions Reviewed by Charles Baudelaire*. Oxford, UK: Phaidon, 1981.

Porter, Laurence M. "The Anagogic Structure of Baudelaire's *Les Phares*." *The French Review* 46.5 (Spring 1973): 49–54.

Werner, Alfred. "Baudelaire: Art Critic." *The Kenyon Review* 28.5 (November 1966): 650–61.

Re-Reading Baudelaire's "Peintre de la vie moderne": Guys, Modernity, and Baudelaire's "Spiritual Art"

Juliet Simpson

Baudelaire's critical 1863 portrait of the illustrator Constantin Guys, "Le Peintre de la vie moderne" (*Œuvres complètes,* 2: 683–722), is arguably the best-known, most widely read of Baudelaire's writings on visual art. As the emblematic "peintre de la vie moderne," modern-life hero, the *flâneur* par excellence, bearer of artistic and cultural modernity, Baudelaire's "Guys" has become, for so many students of French literature and art, a trailblazer of nineteenth-century "modernism," freighted with ideas of historical and artistic rupture, detachment, modernism, and its legacies.[1] From Walter Benjamin's symbol of the Baudelairean *flâneur*'s "alienated" modernity to T. J. Clark's modern-life artist-dandy, we think we know Guys' creation through Baudelaire's eyes as the consummate anti-bohemian Dandy, the substitute for Edouard Manet's even greater modernity. But what do we really understand about the modernity of the artist and his presentation in the essay, which, for many scholars, has become a founding text in studies of modern French literature and art? This essay explores this question through reconsidering afresh some central, yet neglected artistic contexts for and thematic interests in Baudelaire's "Peintre de la vie moderne," including their links with his earlier and contemporary writings on art. The aim is to suggest alternative approaches to reading "Le Peintre de la vie modern," which shed new light on the essay's apparent binaries of "modernity" to "reaction"; Romantic synthesis to "alienation"; of transcendence to banality; of form to ephemera, creating instead, fresh insights into its more complex and nuanced engagement with its central theme of a modern poetic and artistic creation as *spiritual*.

Baudelaire's "Peintre de la vie moderne," published in 1863, in common with Edmond and Jules de Goncourts' 1873 monograph, *Gavarni: l'homme et l'oeuvre*, was unquestionably modern in both subject-matter and its artistic and critical mission. Its concern to promote the art of illustration, press, and ephemera through Guys' example, to centre-stage importance in the art world of Second-Empire Paris, ostensibly fulfils Baudelaire's new, non-Bohemian artistic vision of the "epic" beauty of modern-life, first developed in his 1846 Salon and call to an expanding bourgeois public to apprehend this "spectacle de la vie élégante et des milliers d'existences flottantes qui circulent dans les souterrains d'une grande ville" and recognize its "héroisme" (*Œuvres complètes,* 2: 495). To this new politics and art of the modern, Baudelaire links a parallel poetic-critical one, using the emblem of the artist-illustrator—as vignettist, improviser, caricaturist, a capturer of fashions and big city "existences flottantes"—as a figure operating between expanding bourgeois and élite tastes, between "marginal" and high art forms, to emblematize a new aesthetics and philosophy of both literature and art, glimpsed in the potency of passing fashion. Indeed, it is this vision of art, as subsumed by commodity and fashion, that Benjamin sees as Baudelaire's central inspiration as the archetypal poet of "urban capitalist modernity" (Jennings 1). Yet a closer exploration of "Le Peintre de la vie moderne's" engagement with these ideas in both text and its contexts, points to overlooked tensions and complexities in Baudelaire's response to Guys' illustrations as "art" and the suggestive, poetic appeal of their modernity. These are tensions, in fact, which highlight the persistence of Baudelaire's earlier efforts in 1846 to revitalize Romantic art,[2] to find a point of connection between this Romantic quest, incarnated above all for Baudelaire in Eugène Delacroix's ability to synthesize an eternal and transitory beauty, and the "spirituality" he sees as central both to Guys' dandyism and modern vision.

Romantic "modernities": Reframing Baudelaire's "Guys"

The contexts for Baudelaire's essay are apparently well known. Its focus is directly related to Baudelaire's developing interest in an expanding visual-cultural world of the July Monarchy and the Second Empire, especially to a burgeoning in popular illustration within the period's expanded press and publishing culture.

Serialized in *Le Figaro* in three installments between November and December 1863,[3] it also has a particular significance in Baudelaire's development as a poet and art critic. It represents his most sustained exploration of themes first broached in early critical writings in his 1845 and 1846 Salons, calling for an art to express a new "heroism" of modern life, counterpointing Baudelaire's mature poetic engagement with modern-life socio-political experience in his 1869 *Petits poèmes en prose* (Stephens 72–107). This chronology is well-charted and extensively explored. But of particular interest to this essay are thematic patterns and relationships in "Le Peintre de la vie moderne" that still merit closer attention. These concern the problem of Baudelaire's Romantic treatment of his presentation of Guys' modernity and its connections with Baudelaire's mature poetic and critical preoccupations with the value and cultural meanings of a contemporary "spiritual" art and its experience.

By the early 1860s, Guys could hardly be characterized as a "Romantic" figure. Rather, he was one of the period's growing ranks of newspaper illustrators, distancing themselves from a vogue for physiognomies, typologies, and portraits of *moeurs*, which an earlier generation, notably Henri Gavarni, had popularized as "modern" during the 1830s and 1840s. He had become known for his scenes of fashionable types and gatherings, as well as his visual reportage of the Crimean War, executed in what emerged as his trademark drawing style—sketch-like, abbreviated, cursive, bold, with little of the graphic detail and expressive characterization developed by the vignette-forms of earlier illustrators: by, for example, Monnier, Grandville, and Gavarni. Moreover, Guys was also well-connected to an élite London establishment milieu through his illustrations for *The Illustrated London News*, placing him in the vanguard of a graphic reportage revolution, destined "au cœur de la population" (Ingram, Dufilho 75), as well as by his membership in the period's fashionable gentleman's clubs and sets. In short, in social and artistic status, Guys was the antithesis of Baudelaire, whom, in 1857, his near contemporary, erstwhile friend, Théodore de Banville described to the Goncourts as "farouche," a savage living on the margins of the period's literary groups. Banville's label, meant to humiliate, had some justification. But it also highlights something else: an emerging, rivalrous battle for modernity, one in which Baudelaire's "modern" could be appropriated as it would by the Goncourts in promoting their modern, Gavarni, and thereby divested of the subversive and prescient force of its complex spiritual subtexts.

According to Claude Pichois, Baudelaire's first knowledge of Guys' work dates from April 1859 (*Œuvres complètes*, 2: 1,414). By December 1859, he was writing to his publisher Poulet-Malassis of his order and purchase, through Champfleury, of "de superbes dessins à Guys" for himself and Malassis (*Œuvres complètes*, 2: 1,414). In March 1861, this had grown to some 2,000 illustrations in several albums and included many of Guys' Crimean War scenes, prompting Baudelaire's further efforts, on Guys' behalf, to publicize his services as "un observateur" in a context, including at the Imperial level, he saw as potentially receptive to Guys' *œuvre* (*Œuvres complètes*, 2: 1,415).[4] But Baudelaire was also fascinated by what he referred to in a letter to Edmond Texier of 1861 as Guys' singular, "fantastique"[5] quality as an artist. He had become obsessed with him as an illustrator for his *Spleen de Paris*; the same letter to Texier outlines Baudelaire's plans for a large-scale exhibition of Guys' work to accompany the study in preparation, first titled "Guys, peintre de moeurs," offered to *Le Siècle*, *La Presse*, eventually published in *Le Figaro* as "Le Peintre de la vie moderne" (*Œuvres complètes*, 2: 1,416–1,417).

Despite Baudelaire's evident interest in Guys' art of "observation" as an illustrator of types and *mœurs*, his perception of their fantastic and strange elements indicate, by 1861, his response to Guys' illustrations and already hints at a duality of vision: a duality, which—in David Carrier's post-formalist reading of it—sees Baudelaire's view of Guys' "modernity" as double-edged and ambiguous, capturing fleeting existences and pleasures past and present, moving between what is experienced as transient and contingent, yet capturing this through processes (of memory and artistic synthesis), which are eternal and durable.[6] And there is another, barely mentioned context for Baudelaire's preoccupation with Guys' modernity. This is his interest in ideas and sources

apart from the immediately contemporary, notably the Goncourts'
La Femme au dix-huitième siècle (1856). Their study also on the
"marginal" art of vignettes demonstrates, through their collation
of documents, fashion and social life scraps, a new type of history
of eighteenth-century life and customs, constructed from transient
phenomena, from apparent trivia. The relationship between the two
interests—eighteenth-century and mid-nineteenth-century ephemera
as "art" forms—is persuasive. Baudelaire read the Goncourts'
history in 1862—the period coterminous with projects on Guys
and his sketch—never developed—on eighteenth-century fashions,
toilettes, and spectacles.[7] Such interests, alongside Baudelaire's
other evolving poetic preoccupations at this period, notably in the
work of Thomas de Quincey and especially Edgar Allan Poe's short
stories and writings (Baudelaire translation of Poe's "Philosophy of
Furniture" appeared in 1852, followed by "The Raven" in 1853), also
shape his dualistic attitude to Guys' art in ways that, by 1863, have
moved beyond Guys' initial appeal for Baudelaire as an "illustrator
of moeurs."

So far from Guys' illustrations as emblematic of an art of modern
fragmentation or disconnection, as a substitute for Manet's or as
merely dualistic and ephemeral, Baudelaire's central innovation in
"Le Peintre de la vie moderne" is arguably his perception of Guys'
illustrations as *art*. He sees them as constantly suggestive sources for
new ideas of both artistic and poetic unity, synthesis and recreation.
In short, Guys emerges through these interests as a pendant creator
to the permeating themes of synthesis and transcendence in
Baudelaire's almost contemporary "1859 Salon" review and 1863
essay on Delacroix. This places Guys as an innovator at the limits of a
Romantic view of art, who takes trivial materials and ephemera only
to transfigure them into experiences that are not merely transient,
but synthetic and visionary.

"Le Peintre de la vie moderne": Observation, Vision, and Spiritual Modernity

What is striking about "Le Peintre de la vie moderne" is its sense
of a formal unity of poetic language and ideas, its tightly-structured

composition around central patterns of ideas and words: "transitoire, éternel, profondeur, beau, laide, observation, philosophie, homme-enfant, beauté, harmonie, spiritualité," imposing on Guys a substance, vision, and depth of insight, which translates the rapid and bold facility of his style, yet suggestively synthesizes the strange, unsettling visionary qualities of Guys' work, captured notably in his urban "demi-monde" subjects of 1855–1865 (see Figs. 1 & 2). The theme is insistent and recurrent throughout the thirteen sections comprising "Le Peintre de la vie moderne" (imposed just prior to publication) and is developed in three main areas of interest (philosophy—beauty—"spiritualité"/synthesis). First, while Guys' illustrations are identifiably "modern" in depicting the subjects of a transforming modern urban world—as the observer with war, of fashions, crowds, modern women, modern beauty, artifices of fashion, toilettes, dandyism, and dilettantism—as "l'observateur passionné" (*Œuvres complètes*, 2: 691), he is, in Baudelaire's terms, not a reporter, but a philosopher of his world: "Je le nommerais volontiers un dandy [...] car le mot dandy implique une quintessence de caractère et un intelligence subtile" (*Œuvres complètes*, 2: 691). The distinction here, a critical one, also makes a larger art-political point, anticipated in an 1860 letter to Malassis where Baudelaire

Figure 1 – *Box Seats (pen and ink wash on paper), Constantin Guys (1802–92) /Musee de la Ville de Paris, Musce Carnavalet, Paris, France/Giraudon/The Bridgeman Art Library*

Figure 2 – *Half length portrait of a woman (w/c and ink on paper), Constantin Guys (1802–92) /Musee de la Ville de Paris, Musee Carnavalet, Paris, France/Giraudon/The Bridgeman Art Library*

uses an encounter between Guys, Champfleury and Duranty to distinguish the "observateur" and "realist," which becomes one of "vision" and philosophy to banality; as he insists, "décidement, les réalistes ne sont pas des observateurs […] ils n'ont pas la patience philosophique nécessaire."[8]

Baudelaire's second main area of interest, the particular, moderne beauty of Guys' art, is also closely related to his first, his "philosophy" and dandyism. Guys, for Baudelaire, is first and foremost, the illustrator of transience, immersed in ephemeral beauty, "la beauté fugace," its "vie multiple et la grâce mouvante de tous les éléments de la vie" (*Œuvres complètes*, 2: 692)—capturing its endlessly changing fashions, types of female beauty, its artifices, its "élégance provocante et barbare" (*Œuvres complètes*, 2: 720); "les attitudes du riche" and "les pompes du dandysme" (*Œuvres complètes*, 2: 722). Yet, more than this: Guys also becomes the artist and poet of this "beauté passagère, fugace de la vie présente" (*Œuvres complètes*, 2: 724). While, therefore, it is possible to see Guys as an incarnation of Benjamin's Baudelairean *flâneur*-dandy, "who strolls through the urban crowd as a prosthetic vehicle of a new vision" (Jennings 9), taking "un bain au multitude" ("Les Foules," *Œuvres complètes*, 1: 291), Guys' innovation is his capacity to express and transpose this multiplicity into an act of vision. Thus, for Baudelaire, Guys' very "modernity," his expression of "beauté fugace" as developed in Section V's central focus on "La Modernité," involves synthetic acts of transposition (by the Baudelairean "observateur") that serve to recreate commonplace materiality, its superficial banality into visionary experiences of it in ways that evoke the brief transcendence , "un éclair," the poetic flash that irradiates the transient moment of desire in Baudelaire's *A Une passante* (1860): "Un éclair ... puis la nuit !— Fugitive beauté/ Dont le regard m'a fait soudainement renaître." (*Œuvres complètes*, 1: 93). Here, the poet as both witness and one drawn into an intense "folie" of glimpsed passion is also, in a sense, recuperated by a beauty, which although fleeting, still rejuvenates him, "m'a fait soudainement renaître." Similarly, from Section III onwards in "Le Peintre de la vie modern," there is an insistent emphasis on Guys' developed "faculté de voir" (*Œuvres complètes*, 2: 693–93), which enables him to be both active perceiver and transformed subject of his vision.

This movement of ideas—from the commonplace to its transcendence—is thus metaphorized from Section III in the insistent emphasis on Guys' developed "faculté de voir." We are told that, when Guys awakes, he experiences everyday things as "éclairées" (Baudelaire's emphasis), artistically and poetically. He sees illuminated, for example, "la vie dans des capitales" now as "l'étonnante harmonie" and as transfigured into "l'éternelle beauté" (*Œuvres complètes*, 2: 692). He captures its fleeting appearances,

---

expressions and forms (emblematized by beauties of fashion, artifice of toilettes, of social and military life) only to transform them synthetically, to "extract" ("extraire" in Baudelaire's expression) their "beauté mystérieuse," "le fantastique réel de la vie" (*Œuvres complètes*, 2: 697). Indeed, here Guys' art is implicitly linked with Baudelaire's romanticized and visionary Balzac's (1859), as well his earlier interest in German Romantic writers (Hoffmann) in Guys' seeming capacity to express dualities, yet transform them. These ideas, for example, are strikingly expressed in Guys treatment of female beauty (Fig. 2), in his evocation of fragments— gestures, fashions, tissues of materiality ("une lumière, un regard, une invitation au Bonheur"), which are in themselves nothing, yet suggestive of "une harmonie générale" (*Œuvres complètes*, 2: 714).

In turn, both themes—Guy's 'philosophy' and expression of modern beauty— are developed in the text's third, arguably most significant concern. This is Baudelaire's recurrent emphasis on Guys' "spiritualité" as man and as "artist." What this idea means is suggestively and perhaps deliberately elusive. While it echoes the Romantic "spiritualité," linked earlier in Baudelaire's 1846 Salon review with poetic and visual art that intimate transcendent states of being and creation—"c'est-à-dire, intimité, spiritualité, couleur, aspiration vers l'infini" (*Œuvres complètes*, 2: 421)—in "Le Peintre de la vie moderne," "spiritualité" acquires an amplified sense, now intimating a movement towards an interior unity expressed by attributes of concentration, distillation, and the dandy's austerity. For Baudelaire, Guys, therefore, becomes emblematic of a double synthesis. He is both "[un] citoyen spirituel de l'univers" (*Œuvres complètes*, 2: 689)—he aspires to transcendent creativity, to a condition of greater vision, but as "un homme-enfant" (a man-child/ a child-man) he also recuperates a primary unity of being and perception linked here with infancy, harnessing it to the synthesizing "quintessence de caractère" (*Œuvres complètes*, 2: 691) identified with Guys' dandyism. If the child as "génie retrouvée" is a well-worn Romantic cliché, Baudelaire also develops it, positioning Guys' dandyism as a cipher for an expanded "spiritualité" of being and creation. Indeed, this is intimated as a model of subjectivity, which engages with dualism (inherent in subject-object relations), but overcomes it by acts of vision that possess and synthesize it: a process Baudelaire sees as emblematized by Guys' art—his urban and military scenes—which are absorbed into and become coterminous with his subjectivity: "Le tableau de la vie extérieure le pénétrait [...] et s'emparait de son cerveau" (*Œuvres complètes*, 2: 691). ("The picture of exterior life penetrated him and took hold of his being.") Thus, while ephemera may captivate by its sensory and artistic allure, it poses an ontological problem of synthesis, which leads to its recuperation and recreation in a movement away from a fragmentary vision of art or being.

Not only this: Guys' art is seen as a model of "spiritualité" in this subjectively, internalized synthetic sense. Guys' improvisatory *métier,* his liking for strong outline, silhouette, "l'arabesque du contour," for unfinished states: sketches ("croquis") and vaporous watercolor washes ("ébauches") is attributed with larger powers of vision and distillation. As a "harmoniste," his art becomes a metamorphosis of its subjects as "cette traduction légendaire de la vie extérieure" ("a legendary translation of exterior life") (*Œuvres complètes*, 2: 698). It transposes "la mode," for example, into "le goût de l'idéal" (*Œuvres complètes*, 2: 716), make-up, "laquelle unité," into the agency of "un être divin et supérieure" (*Œuvres complètes*, 2: 717) and makes the artifices and props of female beauty resemble the mysterious beauty of the "priestess." In short, for Baudelaire, Guys' art, in this way, stands at the head of a whole tradition of "petites arts de la vie" of illustration, one which—synthesized with a genealogy of Romantic art extending via selected High Renaissance and eighteenth-century masters to contemporaries—assumes epic Wagnerian and proto-Symbolist implications in its potential for legendary visions and translations of contemporary life.

In the context of this essay's themes, what this treatment of Guys suggests is of two-fold significance. It indicates an expansion of the territory of Baudelaire's Romanticism. Further, in creating a model of "spiritualité" that is clusive, suggestive, and complexly interwoven with the fragmentary banality of "la vie quotidienne," It poses an alternative to the pervasive spiritualism promoted by Victor

Cousin as part of a Second Empire ideology of legislated morality and culture. This is why Guys is "written-up" by Baudelaire—imposing on him a poetic philosophy, patterning of ideas, and a textual architecture that transforms the ostensible superficiality of Guys' subjects and his facility of style. In sum, Guys did not need to be Manet fully to inhabit Baudelairean modernity. Rather, his insubstantial, improvisatory pageant of types, with their rapid transitions of mood, atmosphere, and strangely uncanny metamorphoses of image and identity, are, for Baudelaire, expressive of his virtues because they leave room for something else: for a suggestive "spiritualité" of vision, for a new philosophy and art of modernity co-opted— although not exclusively Baudelaire's—that extends and offers the last viable home for Romanticism.

Notes

1. See, notably, Walter Benjamin's seminal treatment of this theme, *Charles Baudelaire: A Lyric Poet in the Era of High Capitalism*. London: Verso Classics. 1997. For responses to Benjamin's influential perspective in relation to art, see T. J. Clark. *The Painting of Modern Life*: *Paris in the Art of Manet and his Followers* (1984). Princeton, NJ: Princeton UP. 1999; and in Baudelaire's art criticism and *Petits poèmes en prose*, cf. Ross Chambers. "The *flâneur* as hero." *Australian Journal of French Studies* 28 (1991): 142–153.

2. Notably, in section II of his *Salon de 1846*, "Qu'est-ce que le Romanticisme" in defining Romantic literature and art as to be found in "la manière de sentir" (*Œuvres complètes*, 2: 420).

3. *Le Figaro*, 26, 29 November; 3 December 1863: first published in *L'Art romantique*. Michel Lèvy Frères, 1868 (*Œuvres complètes*, 2: 1,413).

4. Baudelaire and Guys had also met in Paris in late 1859; it appears they also exchanged ideas about Baudelaire's promotion of Guys' work: see letter to Malassis, 23 December 1859: "je dîne ce soir avec M. Guys [...] il serait heureux de porter des babioles chez les amis." Baudelaire, *Correspondances*. I. Paris: Editions Gallimard, 1973: 643.

5. See Baudelaire, *Correspondances*. Vol. 2. Paris: Editions Gallimard, 1973: 212–3.

---

6. David Carrier. *High Art: Charles Baudelaire and the Origins of Modernist Painting.* University Park: Pennsylvania State UP, 1996: 76–78.

7. In his "Notes sur le XVIIIe siècle," which includes mention of examples of works of art by artists (collections and sources) of particular interest to Goncourts; by Cochin, Lancret (*Œuvres complètes*, 2: 725–28).

8. Baudelaire, letter to Poulet-Malassis. 16 February 1860. *Correspondances*, 1: 670.

Works Cited

Baudelaire, Charles. "A Une passante": XCIII. *Les Fleurs du mal* (1861).

_____. "Les Foules": XII. *Le Spleen de Paris*. 1862. *Petits poèmes en prose*. Ed. H. Lemaître. Paris: Garnier, 1862.

_____. "L'Oeuvre et la vie d'Eugène Delacroix." 1863. *L'Art romantique*. Paris: Michel Lévy frères, 1868.

_____. "Le Peintre de la vie moderne." 1863. *L'Art romantique*. Paris: Michel Lévy frères, 1868.

_____. "Salon de 1846." 1846. *L'Art romantique*. Paris: Michel Lévy frères, 1868.

_____. *Œuvres complètes*. Ed. Claude Pichois. 2 vols. Paris: Gallimard (Bibliothèque de la Pléiade), 1975–6.

_____. *Correspondances*. Eds. Claude Pichois & Jean Ziegler. 2 vols. Paris: Gallimard (Bibliothèque de la Pléiade), 1973.

Benjamin, Walter. *Charles Baudelaire: A Lyric Poet in the Era of High Capitalism*. London: Verso Classics, 1997.

Carrier, David. *High Art: Charles Baudelaire and the Origins of Modernist Painting*. University Park: Pennsylvania State UP, 1996.

Chambers, Ross. "The *flâneur* as hero." *Australian Journal of French Studies* 28 (1991): 142–153.

Clark, Timothy J. *The Painting of Modern Life: Paris in the Art of Manet and his Followers* (1984). Princeton, NJ: Princeton UP, 1999.

Dufilho, Jérôme. "Constantin Guys: Artist-Reporter." *Constantin Guys: Fleurs du mal*. Eds. Jérôme Dufilho & Christine Lancha. Paris: Editions des musées de la Ville de Paris, 2002: 75–92.

Goncourt, Edmond. *Gavarni*: *l'homme et l'oeuvre*. Paris: Charpentier, 1873.

Jennings, Michael W., ed. *Essays on Baudelaire*: *The Writer of Modern Life*. Harvard, MA: Harvard UP, 2006.

Stephens, Sonya. *Baudelaire's Prose Poems*. Oxford, UK: Oxford UP, 1999.

Baudelaire and Music

Randolph Paul Runyon

Baudelaire makes many allusions to music in the *Fleurs du mal*. In *Correspondances*, he proclaims: "Il est des parfums frais comme des chairs d'enfants, / Doux comme les hautbois" (lines 9–10), a combination he repeats in "J'aime le souvenir de ces époques nues . . ." in speaking of youth exuding "Ses parfums, ses chansons et douces chaleurs" (line 40). According to "Les Phares," in a Delacroix painting, "des fanfares étranges / Passent, comme un soupir étouffé de Weber" (lines 31–32). The poet's muses in both "La Muse malade" and "La Muse vénale" have a musical connection. He wants his ailing muse's blood to flow rhythmically "Comme les sons nombreux des syllabes antiques, / Où règnent tour à tour le père des chansons, / Phoebus" and Pan, the lord of harvests (lines 12–14). The other muse's venality in part consists in being obliged, like a choirboy, to "Chanter des Te Deum" (line 11), in which she does not believe to earn her daily bread.

In that passage from "La Muse malade," Baudelaire alludes to the mathematics of poetry when he writes of "les sons *nombreux* des syllabes antiques." Louis-Nicolas Bescherelle, in his *Dictionnaire universel* (dating from 1856 and thus contemporary with Baudelaire), defines "nombreux" in a literary context as:

> Harmonieux, qui flatte l'oreille par un heureux choix et une habile disposition de mots . . . . Les maîtres dans l'art de parler appellent *nombreux* tout ce que les oreilles aperçoivent de proportionné dans la prononciation du discours, soit pour la proportion des mesures du temps, soit pour la juste distribution des intervalles de la respiration.

Boileau, in his *Épître IX* (1675) describes his own poems as composed of sounds "agréables" and "nombreux" (203).

In "Le Chat" *("Dans ma cervelle se promène . . .")* "nombreux" reappears in both a poetic and musical context. The cat's purring is

music to the poet's ears: "il n'est pas d'archet qui morde / Sur mon cœur, parfait instrument, / Et fasse plus royalement / Chanter sa plus vibrante corde" (lines 17–20). It is poetry, too: "Cette voix . . . / Me remplit comme un vers *nombreux*" (lines 9, 11). But the most striking (and the only remaining) iteration of the word in the *Fleurs du mal* occurs in *Tout entière*. Hoping to trip him up, the Devil asks the poet to name the sweetest part of his mistress' charming body. He refuses, claiming to be ravished by all of it. Besides,

> . . . l'harmonie est trop exquise,
> Qui gouverne tout son beau corps,
> Pour que l'impuissante analyse
> En note les *nombreux* accords (lines 17–20).

It is not that the chords are too numerous to count, but that the harmony is too exquisite to submit to detailed analysis. The musicality of the beloved is reasserted a few lines later: "Son haleine fait la musique" (line 23).

Music of a different sort, "une étrange musique," emerges from the rotting carcass in "Une charogne," crawling with larva and flies that rise and fall like a wave and move like a breathing body. Though as in "Tout entière," the source of that music is related to his beloved, for as he reminds her: "telle vous serez . . . / Quand vous irez . . . / oisir parmi les ossements."

In the previous existence, recalled in *La Vie antérieure*, the swells of the sea, "en roulant les images des cieux, / Mêlaient d'une façon solennelle et mystique / Les tout-puissants accords de leur riche musique / Aux couleurs du couchant reflété par mes yeux" (lines 5–8). Here we see a synesthesia akin to that in *Correspondances* of the odors sweet as oboes (which were also "verts comme les prairies" [line 10]) and to the experience in "Les Phares" of looking at a painting of Delacroix and hearing Weber.

In notes for a preface to the *Fleurs du mal* that he never completed, Baudelaire envisions showing "comment la poésie touche à la musique par une prosodie dont les racines plongent plus avant dans l'âme humaine que ne l'indique aucune théorie classique." A few lines later, he asserts that "la phrase poétique .

. . touche à l'art musical et à la science mathématique" (*Œuvres complètes,* 1: 183). He connects music with mathematics as well in the "Salon de 1859": "L'art du coloriste tient évidemment par de certains côtés aux mathématiques et à la musique" (*Œuvres complètes,* 2: 625). But there is something poetic, too, about the colorist's art, for in the "Salon de 1846" Baudelaire declares that "Les coloristes sont des poètes épiques" (*Œuvres complètes,* 2: 426). In the same discussion (the chapter "De la couleur"), he writes of the musicality of nature itself as colors change in relation to each other in the course of a day. As the sun rises and then makes its way across the sky, the colors change their intensity. While respecting their natural sympathies and antipathies, they continue to live "en harmonie par des concessions réciproques." Colors "multiplient à l'infini leurs mariages mélodieux." At sunset, "de rouges fanfares s'élancent de tous côtés; une sanglante harmonie éclate à l'horizon." Summing up,

> Cette grande symphonie du jour, qui est l'éternelle variation de la symphonie d'hier, cette succession de mélodies, où la variété sort toujours de l'infini, cet hymne compliqué s'appelle la couleur.

> On trouve dans la couleur l'harmonie, la mélodie et le contrepoint (*Œuvres complètes,* 2: 423).

Baudelaire's interest in reciprocity, seen here in the "concessions réciproques," through which colors continue to live in harmony with each other, resurfaces in his one venture into music criticism, "Richard Wagner et *Tannhäuser* à Paris." He had just quoted at length from a text of Franz Liszt's about *Lohengrin*, and in particular about Wagner's compositional technique of repeating leitmotifs (a term, however, that Wagner never used to describe his own works and was not in general use until after Baudelaire's death). The quotation concludes with Liszt saying, "même si la musique de cet opéra devait être privé de son beau texte, elle serait encore une production de premier ordre." Baudelaire then comments:

En effet, sans poésie, la musique de Wagner serait encore une œuvre poétique, étant douée de toutes les qualités qui constituent une poésie bien faite; explicative par elle-même, tant toutes choses y sont bien unies, conjointes, réciproquement adaptées, et, s'il est permis de faire un barbarisme pour exprimer le superlatif d'une qualité, prudemment *concaténées* (*Œuvres complètes*, 2: 802–803; italics Baudelaire's).

This is a remarkable statement, a veritable *ars poetica*. Philippe Lacoue-Labarthe writes that Baudelaire here "very accurately speaks of music, of the musical 'system' of Wagner, in terms of concatenation." Despite the poet's lack of musical knowledge,

he will have *recognized* in Wagner's music, explicitly, a quality that made it to his eyes the *equal* of poetry: that of being able to *present ideas*, something like the way in which Liszt said that certain melodic sections, in Wagner, are the "personifications of ideas." . . . But that was only the case inasmuch as the melody-ideas of this sort of music-writing were "prudently concatenated." In other words, the sign was quite clear all the same; it was less the ideas in themselves than their being put together that permitted music to accede to meaning and, thus, to become an oeuvre of poetry. Ultimately, each *opera* of Wagner tends to resemble the *livre* as Baudelaire conceived it. That is to say, in fact, the work of art (38–40; italics his).

By "une œuvre poétique" Baudelaire appears, in Lacoue-Labarthe's estimation, to mean not (or not just) a single poem, but a *livre*, such as *Les Fleurs du mal*. But what did Baudelaire mean by concatenation, exactly? Bescherelle defined it thus:

CONCATÉNATION. s. f. (ét. lat., *cum*, avec; *catena*, chaîne). *Philos*. Enchaînement, liaison. La concaténation des causes secondes est un effet de la Providence. Ce mot est aujourd'hui hors d'usage. *Rhét*. Figure qui consiste à reprendre dans une période quelques mots du premier membre pour commencer le second, et à lier ainsi successivement tous les membres entre eux, jusqu'au dernier.

How might that be comparable to Wagner's compositional style? In his essay on the composer, Baudelaire says that what first drew

him to his music was "certaines phrases mélodiques dont le retour assidu, dans différents morceaux tirés de la même oeuvre, avait vaguement intrigué mon oreille" (*Œuvres complètes,* 2: 801). It was the repetition itself that intrigued him, and concatenation is characterized by an insistent repetition.

Yet there is also repetition in the sonata-allegro form exploited in the classical era by such composers as Mozart and Haydn, but it is a kind of repetition from which Wagner departs. The two themes are repeated after their initial exposition, so the listener can be sure to remember them. In the development section, fragments of the two themes are juxtaposed and taken to distant tonalities; in the recapitulation, both themes are restated, the second now transposed from its original tonality into that of the first. It is a hierarchy, in which the first theme always wins out over the second, forcing or persuading it to adopt its tonality. Nearly every note has an identifiable place in this structure, and as long as he or she knows the rules of the game, the attentive listener can follow along. Thomas Grey, basing his analysis on the work of Carl Dahlhaus, describes the listener's experience as "tectonic hearing," in which "the ear traces and seeks to retain an accumulating hierarchy of levels" (208). It is as if the listener were in a maze, to which he has the blueprint and, therefore, will have no trouble finding his way out. It is as if he were looking down at the labyrinth from above.

But when listening to a Wagner opera (or a Liszt symphonic poem), the ear no longer has a blueprint and is no longer above the maze, but in it. To find the way out, the listener must engage in what Grey calls "*anknüpfendes Hören*": hearing by knotting or tying a thread (*knüpfen* is to tie, knot, braid, weave, fasten, knit), the Ariadne's thread that leads one out of the labyrinth. Grey calls this:

> additive or hypotactic hearing: successive events or phrases are heard "each as the consequence of what came before and the premise of what follows," so that they appear as links in a chain. . . . The hypotactic or "chain" model dispenses with a long-term memory of musical events, and focuses only on the immediate experience of threading one's way through these events as they occur (209).

Thus, according to Grey, Wagner's music is indeed what Baudelaire appears to say it is: concatenated.

According to Alain Vaillant, so too are the *Fleurs du mal*. Vallant traces echoes from one poem to the next in both the 1857 and 1861 editions:

> En termes de rhétorique, on parle d'anadiplose pour désigner la reprise en début de phrase d'un élément final de la phrase précédente, et de concaténation lorsque l'anadiplose est poursuivie tout au long d'un texte. La composition des *Fleurs du mal* repose sur un art, à la fois original, parfaitement maîtrisé et à visée ironique, de la concaténation (273).

I make the same argument in *Intratextual Baudelaire: The Sequential Fabric of the* Fleurs du mal *and* Spleen de Paris.

There is more to be said about the concatenation of the *Fleurs du mal*, but let us first note the curious fact that Baudelaire applies the same term to Edgar Allan Poe: "Dans les livres d'Edgar Poe, le style est serré, *concaténé* ; la mauvaise volonté du lecteur ou sa paresse ne pourront pas passer à traver les mailles de ce réseau tressé par la logique" (*Edgar Allan Poe, sa vie et ses ouvrages*, 2: 283; italics Baudelaire's). Here, the concatenation is not an assiduous return of the same, but the interlacing meshes of a net. In another essay, he praises Poe's style yet again for being both "serré" and composed of "mailles," in this instance, links of chain mail: "son admirable style, pur et bizarre,—serré comme les mailles d'une armure,—complaisant et minutieux,—et dont la plus légère intention est de pousser doucement le lecteur vers un but voulu" (*Œuvres complètes*, 2: 316).

In Baudelaire's quotation from Liszt, the latter likewise praised Wagner's style for being "serré:"

> Le spectateur, préparé et résigné à ne chercher *aucun de ces morceaux détachés qui, engrenés l'un après l'autre sur le fil de quelque intrigue, composent la substance de nos opéras habituels*, pourra trouver un singulier intérêt à suivre durant trois actes la combinaison profondément réfléchie, étonnamment habile et poétiquement

intelligente, avec laquelle Wagner, *au moyen de plusieurs phrases principales*, a serré *un nœud mélodique* qui constitue tout son drame. Les replis que font ces phrases, en se liant et s'entrelaçant autour des paroles du poème, sont d'un effet émouvant au dernier point (*Œuvres complètes*, 2: 801; italics Baudelaire's).

Margaret Miner argues that this "noeud," in Baudelaire's estimation if not Liszt's, was not exactly a good thing:

> Baudelaire oddly underlines the already strange statement that the motifs form "a melodic *knot*" [*un noeud mélodique*] that Wagner has pulled tight [serré], with "twists" [replis] that are bound and woven around the libretto. . . . [A] tightened "*knot*" "binding itself" around the libretto sharply calls to mind a noose, or at least a rope that constricts and lacerates limbs rather than embracing them. Taken together, then as strands of an ominously resonant "*knot*" that tightens around and between the words sung on stage, the motifs apparently have as much power to stifle as to support or caress. Instead of joining in the stage drama, the motifs might succeed only in immobilizing and eventually choking it; the melodic knot might create a drama of its own that paradoxically tears the opera apart (82–83).

Indeed the knot does create a drama of its own, and that is precisely the point Liszt was making: "Wagner . . . a serré un nœud mélodique *qui constitue tout son drame.*" This is not traditional opera, where the music is parceled out into "ces morceaux détachés . . . engrenés l'un après l'autre sur le fil de quelque intrigue." That intrigue is merely the libretto, and Wagner's music as a higher calling than to serve it. As Lacoue-Labarthe wrote:

> it was less the ideas in themselves than their being put together that permitted music to accede to meaning and, thus, to become an oeuvre of poetry." Their being put together, their combination and recombination is the concatenation that for Baudelaire creates the poetry: "sans poésie, la musique de Wagner serait encore une œuvre poétique (*Musica Ficta*).

That's what excited Baudelaire about Wagner, and it is strangely similar to what excited Baudelaire about Poe. That the latter's style is "serré" is what he likes about it: "serré" like the meshes of a net (made by tying knots), "serré comme les mailles d'une armure" (made of links in a chain and thus concatenated). That he uses the same language in speaking of Poe and Wagner (in the latter instance, using Liszt's language) is perhaps more pertinent than that a knot might put someone in mind of a noose. As Grey suggests, it is precisely by paying attention to the melodic knot, by a practice of "*anknüpfendes Hören*" (knotted listening), that the listener can make sense of the music.

Wagner's new style of operatic composition, knots and all, is quite literally compelling. It is forceful, as Liszt asserts: "Wagner, *forçant* notre méditation et notre mémoire à un si constant exercice, arrache, par cela seul, l'action de la musique au domaine des vagues attendrissements et ajoute à ses charmes quelques-uns des plaisirs de l'esprit" (Baudelaire, *Œuvres complètes*, 2: 802; my italics). Similarly, Poe's "style serré" manages to "pousser doucement le lecteur vers un but voulu." There is no escaping its net or its logic. "Le lecteur, *lié* par le vertige, est contraint de suivre l'auteur dans ses entraînantes déductions" (*Œuvres complètes*, 2: 317; my italics). In Wagner's *Lettre sur la musique*, to which Baudelaire amply refers in his Wagner essay, the composer says that what he admires in a Beethoven symphony is its power to draw the listener into its chain, its *enchaînement*:

> Les instruments parlent dans cette symphonie une langue dont aucune époque n'avait encore eu connaissance ; car l'expression, purement musicale jusque dans les nuances de la plus étonnante diversité, *enchaîne* l'auditeur pendant une durée inouïe jusque-là. [. . .] La symphonie [. . .] nous dévoile un *enchaînement* des phénomènes du monde qui diffère absolument de *l'enchaînement* logique habituel ; et *l'enchaînement* qu'elle nous révèle présente avant tout un caractère incontestable : c'est de s'imposer à nous avec la persuasion la plus irrésistible et de gouverner nos sentiments avec un empire si absolu qu'il confond et désarme pleinement la raison logique (Wagner xxxiii–xxxiv).

Wagner writing about Beethoven sounds like Baudelaire writing about Poe, and like Liszt and Baudelaire writing about Wagner.

But when Baudelaire praises Wagner's operas for being, even without their words, a poetic work and goes on to list the qualities of "une poésie bien faite," he is writing of Baudelaire as well. And that self-description extends to other parts of "Richard Wagner et *Tannhäuser* à Paris" than that one passage. As André Ferran has remarked, "Il s'agit pour Baudelaire beaucoup moins de juger Wagner que de se réfléchir lui-même en Wagner" (341). What he was drawn to in Wagner was his own reflected image. He said as much in his letter to the composer of February 17, 1860:

> La première fois que je suis allé aux Italiens pour entendre vos ouvrages . . . j'ai été vaincu tout de suite. Ce que j'ai éprouvé est indescriptible, et si vous daignez ne pas rire, j'essaierai de vous le traduire. D'abord il m'a semblé que je connaissais cette musique, et plus tard en y réfléchissant, j'ai compris d'où venait ce mirage; il me semblait que cette musique était *la mienne*, et je la reconnaissais comme tout homme reconnaît les choses qu'il est destiné à aimer. Pour tout autre que pour un homme d'esprit, cette phrase serait immensément ridicule, surtout écrite par quelqu'un qui, comme moi, *ne sait pas la musique*, et dont toute l'éducation se borne à avoir entendu (avec grand plaisir, il est vrai) quelques beaux morceaux de Weber et de Beethoven (*Correspondance*, 2: 1452n; italics Baudelaire's).

His own reflection is what drew him to Poe as well. In presenting his translation of the American's stories to the public, he wrote:

> Pour conclure, je dirai aux Français amis inconnus d'Edgar Poe que je suis fier et heureux d'avoir introduit dans leur mémoire un genre de beauté nouveau; et aussi bien, pourquoi n'avouerais-je pas que ce qui a soutenu ma volonté, c'était le plaisir de leur présenter un homme qui me ressemblait un peu, par quelques points, c'est-à-dire dans une partie de moi-même ? (*Avis au lecteur*, 2: 348).

He expressed it in stronger terms in his correspondence:

Ce qu'il y a d'assez singulier, et ce qu'il m'est impossible de ne pas remarquer, c'est la ressemblance intime, quoique non positivement accentuée, entre mes poésies propres et celles de cet homme, déduction faite du tempérament et du climat (letter to his mother, 8 March 1854; *Correspondances* 1: 269).

Savez-vous pourquoi j'ai si patiemment traduit Poe? Parce qu'il me ressemblait. La première fois que j'ai ouvert un livre de lui, j'ai vu, avec épouvante et ravissement, non seulement des sujets rêvés par moi, mais des PHRASES pensées par moi, et écrites par lui vingt ans auparavent (letter to Théophile Thoré, 20 June 1864; *Correspondances*, 2: 386).

Baudelaire, as he admits to Wagner, was not very knowledgeable about music. He had not heard more than one of his operas, *Tannhäuser,* presented in Paris in March 1861 under less than ideal conditions. He had attended three concerts, conducted by the composer, in January and February of 1860, which featured: the overture to *The Flying Dutchman*; the Arrival of the Guests, the Pilgrims' Chorus, and the Venusberg music from *Tannhäuser*; the prelude to *Tristan*; and the prelude and the Bridal Chorus from *Lohengrin* (*Correspondances* 2: 1,456). In the days following those concerts, he did what he could to hear more Wagner.

Ceux de mes amis qui possédaient un piano furent plus d'une fois mes martyrs. Bientôt, comme il en est de toute nouveauté, des morceaux symphoniques de Wagner retentirent dans les casinos ouverts tous les soirs à une foule amoureuse de voluptés triviales. La majesté fulgurante de cette musique tombait là comme le tonnerre dans un mauvais lieu. Le bruit s'en répandit vite, et nous eûmes souvent le spectacle comique d'hommes graves et délicats subissant le contact des cohues malsaines, pour jouir, en attendant mieux, de la marche solennelle des *Invités au Wartburg* ou des majestueuses noces de *Lohengrin* (*Correspondances,* 2: 786).

In his letter to Wagner, Baudelaire says that his musical education was limited to hearing some fine pieces by Beethoven and Weber. He refers to those two again in his essay on Wagner when he writes of the profound effect that first hearing Wagner's music had on him:

> A partir de ce moment, c'est-à-dire du premier concert, je fus possédé du désir d'entrer plus avant dans l'intelligence de ces œuvres singulières. J'avais subi (du moins cela m'apparaissait ainsi) une opération spirituelle, une révélation. Ma volupté avait été si forte et si terrible, que je ne pouvais m'empêcher d'y vouloir retourner sans cesse. Dans ce que j'avais éprouvé, il entrait sans doute beaucoup de ce que Weber et Beethoven m'avaient déjà fait connaître, mais aussi quelque chose de nouveau que j'étais impuissant à définir, et cette impuissance me causait une colère et une curiosité mêlées d'un bizarre délice (*Correspondances,* 2: 785).

The case of Carl Maria von Weber is especially significant, for as Grey writes, "Weber's operas . . . were . . . the most significant models for the development of Wagner's own technique of motivic reminiscence" (192). Wagner himself writes, in his *Lettre sur la musique*, that if *Tannhäuser* was welcomed by the Parisian public (alas, it would not be), he would owe that success "grande partie, aux analogies très-visibles qui relient cet opéra à ceux de mes devanciers, et parmi ceux-ci je vous signale avant tout Weber."

The poem in *Les Fleurs du mal*, in which Baudelaire most obviously seems to concentrate his thoughts on music is "La Musique," a poem I would like to discuss in some detail. Here is the poem as it appeared in the 1861 edition, in the version most readers know it (and most commentators have analyzed):

> La musique souvent me prend comme une mer!
> Vers ma pâle étoile,
> Sous un plafond de brume ou dans un vaste éther,
> Je mets à la voile;
>
> La poitrine en avant et les poumons gonflés
> Comme de la toile,
> J'escalade le dos des flots amoncelés
> Que la nuit me voile;

Je sens vibrer en moi toutes les passions
    D'un vaisseau qui souffre;
Le bon vent, la tempête et ses convulsions

Sur l'immense gouffre
    Me bercent. D'autres fois, calme plat, grand miroir
De mon désespoir!

Previous commentators have noted that it is in the form of a sonnet except that it is cast in the unusual combination of alexandrines alternating with lines of five syllables and that the enjambments become increasingly marked until the reader experiences something analogous to falling into an "immense gouffre" at the very moment (at the end of line 12) that he pronounces those words (for such a poem demands to be read aloud). The cradling that awaits in the *rejet* at the beginning of line 13 comes as a surprise, though perhaps not a greater one than the disappointment of learning in the poem's last words, after all the exultation at the beginning, that the sea reflects despair. No analysis of the poem fails to draw attention to the night that surrounds the poet like a veil in lines 7–8 and the insistent rhymes in *-oile* in lines 2, 4, 6, and 8.

But few have noted that, in the 1857 edition, both night and its veil are absent because Baudelaire almost entirely rewrote the second quatrain for the 1861 edition. In 1857, it had been:

La poitrine en avant et gonflant mes poumons
De toile pesante,
Je monte et je descends sur le dos des grands monts
D'eau retentissante;

Why did he make such an elaborate change? The answer is that the poems of the *Fleurs du mal* are, as Baudelaire said, what well-made poetry must be: "conjoined, reciprocally adapted" and "prudently concatenated." The reciprocal adaptation is of particular importance in this instance, for the order of the poems is different in the two editions, a change necessitated by the court-enforced removal of six offending sonnets and the addition of poems written since the first

---

edition. Here are the two segments of the part of the chain where "La Musique" appears:

1857: *Tristesses de la lune, La Musique, La Pipe*
1861: *La Pipe, La Musique, Sépulture*

Connections between "La Musique" and "La Pipe" will not concern us here, since Baudelaire kept them together. What is relevant is that in 1857, "La Musique" was connected to "Tristesses de la lune," a propinquity that was replaced in 1861 by one with "Sépulture." "Tristesses de la lune" remained essentially unchanged in the two editions:

Ce soir, la lune rêve avec plus de paresse;
Ainsi qu'une beauté, sur de nombreux coussins,
Qui d'une main distraite et légère caresse,
Avant de s'endormir, le contour de ses seins,

Sur le dos satiné des molles avalanches,
Mourante, elle se livre aux longues pâmoisons,
Et promène ses yeux sur les visions blanches
Qui montent dans l'azur comme des floraisons.

Quand parfois sur ce globe, en sa langueur oisive,
Elle laisse filer une larme furtive,
Un poète pieux, ennemi du sommeil,

Dans le creux de sa main prend cette larme pâle,
Aux reflets irisés comme un fragment d'opale,
Et la met dans son coeur loin des yeux du soleil.

The poet's "pâle étoile" in "La Musique" is a reincarnation of the "larme pâle" that falls from the moon and that he hides in his heart, as if it were a precious relic. The poet floating on the waves in "La Musique" parallels the moon's floating on the clouds, a parallel Baudelaire underlined in 1857 by creating an extended verbal echo that, in that edition, existed only between these two poems, the words "Sur le dos": "Sur le dos satiné des molles avalanches" (line 5) and "sur le dos des grands monts" (line 7 of "La Musique").

In the 1861 "La Musique," the poet "escalade le dos des flots amoncelés," words that replace the 1857 poem's "Je monte et je descends sur le dos des grands monts." In addition, as the clouds (figured as "visions blanches") "montent" in the sky in "Tristesses de la lune," the poet in "La Musique" "monte" on the waves. But both echoes disappear in 1861, as "La Musique" loses its connection to what had been its immediate predecessor. The precision of the 1857 echo between "Sur le dos" and "sur le dos" is no longer needed, for the poems are no longer next to each other.

Instead, "La Musique" gains a new neighbor, with which its newly-acquired "nuit" will serve to create a link, "La Sépulture":

> Si par une nuit lourde et sombre
> Un bon chrétien, par charité,
> Derrière quelque vieux décombre
> Enterre votre corps vanté,
>
> A l'heure où les chastes étoiles
> Ferment leurs yeux appesantis,
> L'araignée y fera ses toiles,
> Et la vipère ses petits ;
>
> Vous entendrez toute l'année
> Sur votre tête condamnée
> Les cris lamentables des loups
>
> Et des sorcières faméliques,
> Les ébats des vieillards lubriques
> Et les complots des noirs filous.

And the newly-rhyming "toile" and "voile" (lines 6, 8) of "La Musique" are echoed by the rhyming "étoiles" and "toiles" (lines 5, 7). "La Sépulture" was also in the 1857 edition, and, in fact, was a neighbor to "Tristesses de la lune," whose "poète pieux," who saves and conceals the moon's pale tear, finds a counterpart in the "bon chrétien," who charitably protects the woman's body by hiding it underground. But now the new proximity of "La Musique" and "La Sépulture" suggests a similarity between the poet, who perceives without actually seeing the events transpiring around him—the passions of the suffering ship, both favorable winds and threatening tempests—and the woman addressed in "La Sépulture," who cannot see, yet can perceive what is taking place above her grave.

In the changes Baudelaire made to prepare "La Musique" for its new place in the sequence, we can see his continuing concern for the reciprocal adaptation and concatenation characteristic of the *Fleurs du mal* as a whole. Perhaps only in his essay on Wagner (and to a lesser extent in his writings on Poe), when he describes the poetic qualities of that music whose discovery was so momentous for him and yet so strangely familiar, does he reveal his deepest poetic intention.

Works Cited

Baudelaire, Charles. *Correspondances*. Eds. Claude Pichois & Jean Ziegler. 2 vols. Paris: Gallimard/Pléiade, 1973.

_____. *Œuvres complètes*. Ed. Claude Pichois. 2 vols. Paris: Gallimard/Pléiade, 1975–76.

Bescherelle, Louis Nicolas. *Dictionnaire universel de la langue française*. Paris: 1856.

Boileau, Nicolas. *Satires, Épîtres, Art poétique*. Ed. Jean-Pierre Collinet. Paris: Gallimard/Folio, 1985.

Ferran, André. *L'Esthétique de Baudelaire*. 1933. Paris: Nizet, 1968.

Grey, Thomas. "*. . . wie ein rother Faden*: On the Origins of 'leitmotif' as Critical Construct and Musical Practice." *Music Theory in the Age of Romanticism*. Ed. Ian Bent. Cambridge, UK: Cambridge UP, 1996: 187–210.

Lacoue-Labarthe, Philippe. *Musica Ficta (Figures of Wagner)*. Trans. Felicia McCarren. Stanford, CA: Stanford UP, 1994.

Miner, Margaret. *Resonant Gaps: Between Baudelaire and Wagner*. Athens: U of Georgia P, 1995.

Runyon, Randolph Paul. *Intratextual Baudelaire: The Sequential Fabric of the Fleurs du mal and Spleen de Paris*. Columbus, OH: Ohio State UP: 2010.

Vaillant, Alain. *Baudelaire, poète comique*. Rennes: Presses Universitaires de Rennes, 2007.

Wagner, Richard. "Lettre sur la musique." *Quatre poèmes d'opéras, traduit en prose française, précédés d'une Lettre sur la musique.* Paris: Librairie Nouvelle, 1861.

Song-settings of Baudelaire's Poetry

Helen Abbott

Baudelaire's poetry has often been set to music, but how and why his work is set to music, and by which kind of composers, is not always clear. We know that of the one-hundred-twenty or so poems in *Les Fleurs du mal*, not all have been set to music. Even fewer of the prose poems from *Le Spleen de Paris* have attracted song-settings. It is difficult to pin down an exact figure; databases, which seek to capture Baudelaire song-settings, largely focus exclusively on classical music settings. For example, the RecMusic database lists one-hundred-thirty-eight different settings from seventy-two separate Baudelaire texts (both verse or prose poems). Meanwhile, the Mélodie française database lists a significantly higher number of two hundred-sixty-one different Baudelaire settings. These differing statistics are testament to the fact that the full extent of how Baudelaire has been set to music has not yet been uncovered, including a wealth of popular music settings and of settings in translation across many different languages. What we do know is that a core set of his poems have attracted an unusually high number of song-settings, across all musical genres and languages. These poems are: "L'Invitation au voyage," "Harmonie du soir," and "La Mort des amants." During the nineteenth-century in France alone, on the basis of surviving evidence, "L'Invitation au voyage" attracted ten nineteenth-century settings, "La Mort des amants" five, and "Harmonie du soir" at least three (there is anecdotal evidence of a further setting, but no score remains) by composers as renowned as Henri Duparc and Claude Debussy. The actual numbers of settings to date of each of these poems is, however, much higher. We know that these three poems have also captured the imagination of numerous popular songwriters across the generations, from the French *chansonnier* Léo Ferré ("L'Invitation au voyage," "Harmonie du soir," "La Mort des amants," 1957), to the American experimental electronic composer Ruth White ("Evening Harmony," 1969), and the contemporary

French singer-songwriter-arranger BabX ("La Mort des amants," 2010).

Strangely, Baudelaire's poetry has often been considered *difficult* to set to music. We find this opinion in an important interview with a number of French composers that was conducted by journalist and author Fernand Divoire in *Musica*, published in 1911. Divoire asked the challenging question: "Sous la musique que faut-il mettre? De beaux vers, de mauvais, des vers libres, de la prose?" The response given by the opera composer Camille Erlanger about Baudelaire is revealing. He states that "Baudelaire [...] se suffit totalement à soi-même" (Divoire 60). This implies that Baudelaire's poetry does not benefit from having music attached to it because his poetic language is self-sufficient. It also suggests that composers will find it difficult to know what to do with Baudelaire's poetry if it is indeed so self-sufficient. This view is echoed by the important German philosopher and musicologist Theodor Adorno, who addressed the issue of setting Baudelaire to music in a 1937 study of the Austrian composer Alban Berg, who had twice set Baudelaire's poetry (in German translation) to music in the 1920s. Adorno's critique of what composers do to Baudelaire's poetry is not entirely positive, suggesting instead that they are unable to deal effectively with his complex poetry: "To this day music has hardly been a match for the secular quality of Baudelaire's poetry. With atrocious success, the best-known settings, those by Henri Duparc, relegate the *Fleurs du mal* to the sphere of salon music. The five Baudelaire songs by Debussy are certainly not among his chefs d'œuvre" (119). Here, Adorno mentions two of the most famous settings of Baudelaire's poetry from the 1870s and 1880s in France: he talks of Henri Duparc's extremely famous 1870 setting of "L'Invitation au voyage" and his 1874 Baudelaire setting of "La vie antérieure," and Claude Debussy's set of five complex songs, known as the *Cinq poèmes de Baudelaire,* which date from 1887–1889 (these are settings of "Le Balcon," "Harmonie du soir," "Le Jet d'eau," "Recueillement," and "La Mort des amants"). Adorno goes even further in his critique of settings of Baudelaire, landing the blame on the poet himself, slating him for his difficulty:

The question arises whether the reasons may not lie with Baudelaire. [...] It remains uncertain whether [...] music is tolerated or paralyzed. In any event Baudelaire's dialectical attitude toward Romanticism makes setting him very much more difficult; the attempt to do so will almost invariably contradict one or the other of his opposing impulses (119).

By raising the issue of whether or not Baudelaire's poetry is driven by Romantic ideals, Adorno highlights an aesthetic question that lies right at the heart of the challenge we face in understanding how and why Baudelaire's poetry is set to music.

Chanson or *Mélodie*: "L'Invitation au voyage"

The story starts right back during Baudelaire's own lifetime and what happened with his poetry in relation to music in the mid nineteenth century. The now relatively unknown military composer Jules Cressonnois was the first to publish a setting of Baudelaire's poetry during the poet's lifetime. The poem that he chose was, in fact, "L'Invitation au voyage," and his setting dates from 1863, four years before the poet's death in 1867. We do not know for certain whether or not Baudelaire heard this song-setting, but we do know from his correspondence with Madame Charles Hugo, a pianist and singer and daughter-in-law of Victor Hugo, that Baudelaire was aware of Cressonnois' work. In about 1865 or 1866, Baudelaire writes to her asking her to perform some Cressonnois songs for him: "Madame, voici des mélodies de mon ami Cressonnois, que je n'ai jamais entendu exécuter. Je compte un peu sur vous pour me faire cette grâce" (*Correspondances* 2:559). What would Baudelaire have heard if she had performed Cressonnois' "L'Invitation au voyage" for him? It is a simple, strophic song, on the level of what is known in French as a *chanson*. It sets all three verses of the poem, interspersed with the refrain repeated twice in each instance. Musically, it offers simple harmonies and a lyrical tune, set over a very clear triple-time pulse in the verses. Sometimes, this triple time is, in fact, at odds with the Baudelairean verse line, creating some awkward emphases in the text, which nonetheless make sense musically. It is, therefore, a challenge for performers of the Cressonnois setting to smooth out these issues, in order to capture the overall charm of the song, rather than focusing on its imperfections. One of the key things we notice, when listening to the Cressonnois setting, is that he uses duple time for the refrain. This creates a contrast to the waltz-like feel that dominates in the verses; the refrain is more lyrical, with the melody and bass line moving upwards by step in a repetitive structure (the refrain words are repeated twice but with different music: "Là, tout n'est qu'ordre et beauté // Luxe, calme et volupté" lines 13–14). It culminates on a top F for the final syllable of the second instance of "beauté," which then creates a release back down the scale for the word "calme," which mirrors musically what the word itself suggests. This is a rare instance of word-painting. For the most part, the song does not illustrate in music what the words depict; in fact, when we analyze the words, it is difficult to know what it is that music could even attempt to illustrate because Baudelaire's choice of language is non-prescriptive: he writes of an exotic journey to an unknown land with an unspecified woman ("Mon enfant, ma sœur, // Songe à la douceur // D'aller là-bas vivre ensemble," lines 1–3). This is perhaps what Erlanger and Adorno are hinting at in their analyses of Baudelaire's poetry as "self-sufficient" or "difficult," namely that music is not capable of capturing the full range of interpretive possibilities instigated by Baudelaire's poetic language, but that it can only ever encapsulate certain aspects of it.

It would be unfair to use the Cressonnois setting as a sole example, however, especially when it is Henri Duparc's much richer setting of the same poem, just seven years after the Cressonnois one, which dominates on the recital stage still today. Duparc had greater training and skill as a composer than Cressonnois, whose work remained largely in the domain of popular *chanson*, military music, and music for the theatre. In contrast to Cressonnois, Duparc's work has stood the test of time, and his setting is often considered to be one of the finest French *mélodies*–a form of more erudite art song than the lighter *chanson*. Duparc's "L'Invitation au voyage" is also often considered to be the first successful setting of a Baudelaire poem (Bergeron 7). Interestingly, however, Duparc's setting throws up similar issues to those we have already identified in the Cressonnois. The choice of musical meter does not always match the accentuation of the verse line (there are some odd stresses on extended syllables such as the second syllable of "soleils" in the line "Les soleils mouillés" [line 7]), and the music cannot illustrate the full range of meanings latent within the poem. These kind of disruptions to Baudelaire's poem are to be expected, however, as they are an inevitable feature of what needs to happen when words are set to music. Yet alongside such minor disruptions, there is one major disruption to the overall coherence of the poetic text: Duparc cuts out the second stanza entirely, thus creating a new poetic structure that suits his musical one and that is to the detriment (perhaps) of the poem itself. The stanza that Duparc cuts out is the one that centers on the decor of the room, which Baudelaire imagines for himself and his lover—it describes the polished walls, the exotic flowers, the decorative ceilings, the mirrors, all in oriental style ("La splendeur orientale," l.23). Commentators have suggested that the reason Duparc omits this stanza is because the description of a fixed physical space does not suit the musical evocation of an ocean voyage (Youens 422). It is true that the outer stanzas have more "watery" imagery, which could support the fluid musical writing of Duparc's piano accompaniment, for example, but the reason for the omission is more likely to be structural than thematic. Other composers since Duparc have also omitted the second stanza, and there are many more examples of composers making similar cuts and omissions with other poems. This reveals something broader about composers' structural decisions when it comes to setting poetry: the text they select might resonate strongly with them, but simply be too long to capture in song form.

What Duparc does present us with in his setting is a harmonic richness and an evocative rippling texture that goes some way towards capturing the complexity of the Baudelairean imagery and ideas. The composer also negotiates the Baudelairean poetic form on other levels besides the overall structure. "L'Invitation au voyage" is an unusual poem in Baudelaire's œuvre: not only is it relatively rare to get a verse / refrain structure (which already hints at the idea of song form, especially popular songs which tend to have a collective refrain), but it is also an unusual choice of meter, alternating between lines of five syllables long and others of seven syllables long. Odd line lengths are not favored by Baudelaire (there are many more alexandrines, decasyllables, and octosyllables in his verse writing), but the choice of five- and seven-syllable lines suggests that Baudelaire was thinking of something more musical in the very fabric of his poetic text. As Jean-Michel Gouvard has pointed out in his article on verse meter and musicality, the pentasyllable (five-syllable line) is often used in song, especially in *chanson* (23). We cannot ignore the fact, also, that if you run on one of the pentasyllabic lines into a heptasyllabic (seven-syllable) one, it creates a twelve-syllable line, or alexandrine—the hallowed, traditional French verse meter, used most extensively in more highbrow poetry. What we see at work in Baudelaire's "L'Invitation au voyage," then, is a subtle, yet complex, interaction between highbrow poetry (the hints at alexandrine verse lines) and popular song (suggested by the verse-refrain form and the metrical choice of penta- and heptasyllables). It is this aspect, which composers struggle to capture in their song-settings because their musical setting inevitably conveys a decision about aesthetic status: Cressonnois opts for the simpler techniques of a more lyrical popular song or *chanson*, whereas Duparc opts for the more complex layers of art song or *mélodie*. Both engage with the Baudelaire text in different ways, and in so doing, they help fuel fresh interpretations of Baudelaire's poem.

To celebrate the centenary of the first publication of *Les Fleurs du mal* in 1957, the *chansonnier* (singer-songwriter) Léo Ferré released an album of his own settings of Baudelaire's poetry, which themselves offer a fresh take on Baudelaire. One of the most frequently played is his setting of "L'Invitation au voyage." Like both the Cressonnois and the Duparc settings, he opts for a triple-time feel, which creates a soothing, almost lulling, rhythm. He sets the full poem (all three stanzas plus refrains) and creates a lyrical melody, typical of the *chansonnier*-style of the 1950s. What is interesting about the Ferré setting is that the arrangement (by Jean-Michel Defaye) includes an accordion alongside piano, guitar, and double bass. For a poem that talks so much of the idea of going elsewhere, of travelling to more exotic locations, far away from France, this song maintains in its sound-world one of the strongest resonances of France: the accordion. We should not assume that this is completely at odds with the Baudelaire poem, however. At the end of the second stanza, we see Baudelaire commenting how "Tout y parlerait // À l'âme en secret // Sa douce langue natale" (lines 24–26). This idea that, for all the oriental exoticism, everything would still continue to secretly speak in its native tongue, is revealing: the French sound of the accordion runs through the background of the Ferré setting, subtly reminding us of the "native tongue" of the poetic text itself. For all that the poem dreams of foreign climes, it remains a poem rooted in its very Frenchness.

What this survey of three different settings reveals is how the same poem, which thematizes an imagined exotic voyage to a country other than France, has generated three different types of French song, whether *chanson* or *mélodie*, across three different eras, granting the poem a different aesthetic status on each occasion.

Musical translation: "Harmonie du soir"

But what might happen when Baudelaire's poetry is set to music in translation? There are many examples of how Baudelaire's poetry has been translated into other languages and then set to music. Important examples include Alexander Gretchaninov's 1909 settings in Russian, Alban Berg's 1920s settings in German, and Ruth White's 1969 settings in English. While we might be tempted to think that Baudelaire's poetry is the preserve of a certain idea of "Frenchness," in fact fittingly, given invitation to journey elsewhere through the powers of the imagination as seen in "L'Invitation au voyage," Baudelaire's poetry has itself travelled far afield. In the words of fellow French poet Paul Valéry, "Avec Baudelaire, la poésie française sort enfin des frontières de la nation. Elle se fait lire dans le monde" (39). Baudelaire himself privileged the idea of translation (he famously translated Edgar Allan Poe's work into French). Yet there is a particular type of translation, with which Baudelaire engages closely, and which is prompted by the work of an important composer: the monumental German opera composer

Richard Wagner. For Baudelaire, Wagner's work inspires a kind of "musical translation" of ideas, as the poet suggests in his famous 1861 article on Wagner's *Tannhäuser* opera, published shortly after the disastrous, disrupted performance of the work at the *Opéra de Paris* in that same year.[1] In championing Wagner, Baudelaire not only goes against the grain of much of the collective critical opinion of the mid nineteenth century in Paris, but he also takes a particular approach to accessing Wagner's work. Baudelaire examines an important phenomenon that emerges for him when he encounters Wagner's music. He perceives that the same piece of music enables different translations (into written language) of the same idea. He identifies how the same idea is conveyed even in the very different "translations" (or written texts about Wagner's music) by the French composer Hector Berlioz, the Hungarian composer Franz Liszt and Baudelaire himself. Baudelaire focuses one of his examples on the overture to the opera *Lohengrin*, about which he has already read in works by Berlioz and Liszt: "M'est-il permis à moi-même de raconter, de rendre avec des paroles la traduction inévitable que mon imagination fit du même morceau, lorsque je l'entendis pour la première fois, les yeux fermés, et que je me sentis pour ainsi dire enlevé de terre?" (*Œuvres complètes* 2:796). This "traduction inévitable" is founded on the notion of an emotional response to Wagner's music, which is somehow verbalized. Later on in the same article, Baudelaire writes of the translation process going in the opposite direction, and specifically of how both the "Pilgrims' Chorus" in *Tannhäuser* and the overture to that opera offer a "musical translation" of an idea: they depict the idea of a lost soul in musical language. In essence, Baudelaire sees the process of translation from music to text as moving from the abstract to the concrete, and that a "musical translation," a translation of a (textual) idea into music, is one that goes from the concrete (because it can be put into words, or verbalized) to the abstract (which is removed from the burden of words). This concept is an important one for Baudelaire. However, we must acknowledge that—typical of a number of nineteenth-century French poets—what we are actually dealing with in Baudelaire's article is a set of enticing, but frustratingly fluid concepts and imprecise terms. It is very difficult to pinpoint exactly what the relationship between text and music is (other than that they somehow relate to each other and can generate similar emotional responses). It is even more difficult to identify precisely what happens within that process of (musical) translation that Baudelaire identifies. Nonetheless, much as we might critique Baudelaire's apparent imprecision, he does touch right at the heart of what happens when poetry and music are pitted alongside each other: the process of interaction is never straightforward, and we can never assume an "untroubled" translation from one form into another, or from one language into another (Venuti 14).

By accepting that musical translation is never straightforward, we can understand instead how this lack of straightforwardness is, in fact, a necessary and integral feature of song-settings. The settings of "L'Invitation au voyage," which we examined above all, entail some form of disruption to Baudelaire's poem, whether small-scale issues with the amount of emphasis that is given to a particular word or syllable, or more structural issues with the omission of entire stanzas, for example. It is for this reason that we have to be very careful not to assume that there is ever a "perfect harmony" between a poem and its musical setting. Tempting though it may be to think, for example, that Debussy's 1887 setting of Baudelaire's "Harmonie du soir" offers an example of "perfect harmony" between poem and music—especially given the text which promotes the idea that all the senses can intermingle and somehow harmonize with each other—we can, in fact, find many instances, in which it does not. On a macrostructural level, the figure of repetition is key. Repetition is a technique that typically signals a common ground between structuring devices in music and structuring devices in poetry. In "Harmonie du soir," the poetic text is exceptionally repetitive because Baudelaire uses the unusual form known as the *pantoum*, a sequence of quatrains, in which lines two and four of the preceding stanza become lines one and three of the next stanza. This extensive use of line repetition is different from the technique of the refrain that we have seen in "L'Invitation au voyage" because the syntactical and semantic contexts for the repeated lines change as a result of the shift in position. This poses structural challenges for the composer because it is not clear whether or not the same sentiment or sense needs to be conveyed in the repeated instance of the same line. Debussy opts to largely maintain the same melody for the vocal line each time the same words repeat, but the piano underlay is modified a little at each repetition. Thematically, the poem also speaks of music with direct references to whirling sounds ("Les sons et les parfums tournent dans l'air du soir," line 3), a melancholy waltz ("Valse mélancolique et langoureux vertige!" lines 3 & 7), and a trembling violin, which tugs at the heart strings ("Le violon frémit comme un cœur qu'on afflige," lines 6 & 9). These brief instances of musical vocabulary are, of course, tempting in terms of word-painting, and Debussy does allow a little waltz-like flourish to embellish the triple-time figure under the "Valse mélancolique et langoureux vertige" line, for example, but there are points at which the supposed "perfect harmony" between poetic structures and musical structures cannot—and should not—comfortably match. "Harmonie du soir" is a poem in alexandrines, which is the longest possible line in standard French verse. Its length makes it harder to set to music, and to sing, as it causes problems with phrase length because a sung version usually has a longer duration than normal speech. For the most part, Debussy has expressly set the alexandrines to one musical phrase, but he does not always maintain this. The "violin" line ("Le violon frémit comme un cœur qu'on afflige," lines 6 & 9), for example, ends up being rather awkward with an extended note value granted to the definite article "Le," and the musical phrasing broken at a strange point in the vocal line, which does not match with the singer's breathing. This presents challenges for singers, who take on the Debussy setting, which is not a lyrical or melodic setting, but one that carefully, and provocatively, negotiates the notion that music and poetry can somehow "translate" each other's ideas and sentiments.

If we accept that even a famous French composer's song-setting will always be at odds with Baudelaire's poem on some level—even someone as skilled and sensitive to poetry as Debussy—then we can understand how other songs, which exist at much further remove from Baudelaire, are not necessarily *more* at odds with his poetry. Instead we need to remember that all combinations of poetry and music will always involve some kind of challenging process that has to take place in the space of a "musical translation," which is so difficult to pin down. It is simply that the process becomes even harder to unpack and analyze, when Baudelaire's poetry is taken out of its own language.

It is helpful, then, to consider Gretchaninov's 1909 setting of "Harmonie du soir." Here, we have a relatively rare case of a composer choosing to set the poem in two parallel versions—one in Russian and one in the original French. In order to accommodate the differences between the two languages, Gretchaninov has to add in optional notes for the singer in the vocal line, depending on whether s/he is performing the song in French or Russian. This has obvious implications, not only for the ensemble work between the piano accompaniment and the vocal line, but also for the musical stresses in relation to the textual accentuation. Unlike the Debussy setting, Gretchaninov does not maintain exactly the same melody for each of the repeated verse lines. This has two important ramifications: first, Gretchaninov erases, or at least reduces, the important status of repetition that is so central to the Baudelaire poem itself; second, Gretchaninov allows himself the chance to try out a different way of setting the same words (whether in French or Russian). On this second point, however, Gretchaninov's decisions are revealing— whilst he might change the pitch of the melodic line, he does not alter the metrical rhythm for the repeated version of the same phrase. This suggests that, for Gretchaninov, the metrical properties—in both language versions—take precedence over the overall structural properties of the poetic text.

Composers can, and do, go even further away from the Baudelairean original in "translating" the poem into music. The ground-breaking American electro-acoustic composer Ruth White creates an extraordinary setting of "Harmonie du soir" in English translation on her acclaimed 1969 album *The Flowers of Evil*. It begins with a two-minute long musical prelude, heavily laden with effects from the innovative use of the Moog synthesizer, before then launching into a swirling stereo-effect, spoken-voice English translation of the Baudelaire poem. White's setting raises questions as to whether we are still dealing with a song-setting or in fact something different, such as a performed musical reading. She shows us another way of bringing words and music into contact with each other, one that exploits the key notion of translation, but that retains the poem's inherent verbal quality over its musical possibilities, even in this poem, which directly refers to music. By choosing to retain the spoken voice, White's setting does something that the other settings we have examined by Debussy and Gretchaninov do not: White overtly acknowledges that the music that is referred to in the poem is not vocal music, but instrumental music, and so in her "musical translation" of the poem, she does not transpose the vocal line into music, but she develops a rich musical underlay to the poem. What we are presented with in White's rendition of the poem is something that seeks to retain the poem as poem rather than translate it musically into song because for all its combinatory powers, song always remains conflicted. The conflict that remains here is that Baudelaire's poem is nonetheless a little lost in translation—the poetic text has not been translated into music, but into the English language, which has its own sound properties far removed from the French sounds, rhythm, and meter Baudelaire constructed. In White's hands, "Harmonie du soir" is thus removed from its French context on a number of levels: it has an English text; it does not use a French song form (such as *chanson* or *mélodie*); and it relies on integral acoustic effects deployed by the composer-performer. In this way, White pushes right at the aesthetic boundaries both of Baudelaire's poetry and of music itself, experimenting with how far poetry and music can be pushed when they move beyond what might normally be expected of a song-setting.

Song-settings of Baudelaire, then, do not just conform to the type of popular or lyrical French song known as *chanson*, nor indeed do they exclusively sit in the category of more highbrow art song or *mélodie*. By examining six song-settings of Baudelaire, using three very different settings of two important poems, "L'Invitation au voyage" and "Harmonie du soir," we can better understand how setting Baudelaire's poetry to music can never be straightforward. This is, in part, because of the particular qualities of Baudelaire's poetry, which makes his texts somehow already "self-sufficient" (and, therefore, texts that do not need the support of music) or "difficult" to set to music. It is also in part because all song-settings always create a conflicted relationship between the poetic text and the music. Despite the aesthetic ideal of a "perfect harmony" between poetry and music, or of all ideas being somehow analogous or "translatable," no matter what format (what Baudelaire would elsewhere call the idea of "Correspondances" between different senses), there is always some level of disruption, whether to the verse meter and textual stresses, or to the overall structure of a poem. What is important to understand, however, is that these disruptions do not necessarily have a negative impact on Baudelaire's poetry; instead, they enable his poems to travel beyond the confines of the pages of *Les Fleurs du mal*, opening them up to new audiences across the globe, across generations, and across genres.

Note

1. Wagner's opera *Tannhäuser* opened in Paris on 13 March 1861. After only three performances, Wagner, who had been involved in the rehearsals and the production, withdrew it from the Paris stage because of the numerous disruptions caused by certain factions of the opera-going public (most notably the Jockey Club), whose objections to the opera centered primarily on the positioning of a ballet in Act I rather than in the more usual place of Act II.

Works Cited

Adorno, Theodor W., Juliane Brand, & Christopher Hailey. *Alban Berg, Master of the Smallest Link*. Cambridge, UK: Cambridge UP, 1991.

BabX. "La Mort Des Amants." *BabXofficiel*. BabX. Armel Hostiou. YouTube, 22 Feb. 2012. Web. 10 Dec. 2013.

Baudelaire, Charles. *Correspondances*. Eds. Claude Pichois & Jean Ziegler. Paris: Gallimard, 1973.

———, *Œuvres complètes*. Ed. Claude Pichois Paris: Gallimard, 1975–6.

_____. N.d. *RecMusic*. Web. 10 Dec. 2013. <http://www.recmusic. org/lieder/b/baudelaire/>.

_____. N.d. *Mélodie Française*. 10 Dec. 2013. Web<http://www. melodiefrancaise.com/encyclopedie/encyclopedie.php>.

Bergeron, Katherine. *Voice Lessons: French Meìlodie in the Belle Epoque.* Oxford, UK: Oxford UP, 2010.

Cressonnois, Jules. "L'Invitation au voyage." *Harmonies*. Paris: Retté, 1863. 27–33.

Debussy, Claude. "Harmonie du soir." *Cinq Poèmes de Baudelaire*. Paris: Librairie de l'Art Indépendant, 1890.

Divoire, Fernand. "Sous La Musique Que Faut-il Mettre? De Beaux Vers, De Mauvais, Des Vers Libres, De La Prose?" *Musica* 102.3 (1911): 58–60.

Ferré, Léo. "L'Invitation au voyage." Rec. 1957. Arr. Jean-Michel Defaye. *Les Fleurs du mal*. Léo Ferré. 1957. Vinyl recording.

Gouvard, Jean-Michel. "Mètre, rythme et musicalité." *Le Vers et sa musique*. Ed. Jean Foyard. Dijon: Centre de Recherches le Texte et l'Édition, Universiteì de Bourgogne, 2001.

Gretchaninov, Alexander. "Harmonie du soir." *Les Fleurs du mal*. Moscow: A. Gutheil, 1911.

Valeìry, Paul. "Situation De Baudelaire." *Varieìteì II*. Paris: Gallimard, 1948. 32–48.

Venuti, Lawrence. *The Translator's Invisibility: A History of Translation*. London: Routledge, 2008.

White, Ruth. "Evening Harmony." Rec. 1969. *Flowers of Evil*. Ruth White. 1969. Vinyl recording.

Youens, Susan. "From the Fifteenth Century to the Twentieth: Considerations of Musical Prosody in Debussy's *Trois Ballades De François Villon*." *The Journal of Musicology* 2.4 (1983): 418–33.

Baudelaire Translations by Three Maverick Poets: Roy Campbell, Robert Lowell, and James Robertson

Mario Relich

Baudelaire has always been a challenge for English-language translators; the main reason perhaps is that, particularly in *Les Fleurs du mal*, his poems explore a wide range of extreme emotional states and, at times, grotesque imagery, so accuracy of language is not enough to capture his uniquely special qualities. Laurence Lerner, himself a poet, has well described some of the difficulties. He makes the following observation regarding his translation of Baudelaire's "L'Invitation au Voyage" ("Invitation to the Voyage"): "This, one of the most famous of Baudelaire's poems, may well be one of the most difficult to translate, since its effect depends almost entirely on the word music." Something similar could be said of just about every other poem by Baudelaire, certainly in *Les Fleurs du Mal*. Fearing that the same could be true of his own efforts, at least with this particular poem, Lerner goes on to add, about his translation of the poem for his selection: "English versions tend to sound conventional and undistinguished (and I fear this one is no exception); but it seems wrong to omit it from any Baudelaire selection" (*Baudelaire* 96). The challenge for translators of Baudclaire, therefore, is to avoid English versions that sound "conventional and undistinguished," a problem that is bound to arise not just with "L'Invitation au voyage."

The South African Roy Campbell; Robert Lowell, who is generally regarded as one of the greatest twentieth-century American poets; and James Robertson, contemporary Scottish novelist and poet, are among the finest translators of Baudelaire not because of their accuracy, but because each has a strong affinity with Baudelaire's poctic persona. Before taking a closer look at their Baudelaire translations, what translating poetry entails needs to be discussed. One of the greatest authorities on this issue was

---

John Dryden, second only to John Milton as poet of the Restoration period, as well as a great critic, dramatist, and translator himself.

Dryden argued, in his "Preface to Ovid's *Epistles*," that there were three ways of translating poetry. The first, he called "metaphrase, or turning an author word by word, and line by line, from one language to another" (Dryden, *Of Dramatic Poesy*, 1: 268). His objection to this kind of what we would now call a "literal" translation is that it was too pedantic for translating any poem into English, and that translators attempting such supposed accuracy betray "a faith like that which proceeds from superstition, blind and zealous" (Dryden, *Of Dramatic Poesy*, 1: 268). The second method 'is that of paraphrase, or translation with latitude, where the author is kept in view by the translator, so as never to be lost, but his words are not so strictly followed as his sense, and that, too, is admitted to be amplified, but not altered'. This was, in fact, the method, which Dryden approved. A good example of what Dryden meant by amplified, occurs in Laurence Lerner's translation of the first "Spleen" poem. Here are two of Baudelaire's lines:

> Je suis un vieux boudoir plein de roses fanées,
> Où gît tout un fouilis des modes surannées,
> *(Baudelaire: Selected Verse* 175, lines 10–11)

Lerner renders these lines as follows:

> I am the room in which Miss Havisham
> Sits brooding and remembering ...
> *(Baudelaire* 37, lines 11–12)

Lerner brilliantly transforms the fusty image of an "old boudoir" ("un vieux boudoir") by substituting the voice of the frustrated spinster Miss Havisham in Dickens' *Great Expectations*, a novel moreover published in 1861, only a few years after the 1857 edition of *Les Fleurs du mal*. This certainly "amplifies," and makes vividly dramatic, Baudelaire's image for readers familiar with Dickens, but it is also very close to Dryden's third method of translation.

He defined it as "that of imitation, where the translator [...] assumes the liberty not only to vary the words and sense, but to forsake them both as he sees occasion; and taking only some general hints from the original, [...] as he pleases" (270). Just like Dryden calls the method of "paraphrase" "translation with latitude," one could call "imitation" a method of "translation with attitude." In the case of the three poet-translators discussed here, many of their Baudelaire translations display a combination of "paraphrase" and "imitation"; indeed, they are translations with "latitude" and "attitude."

To begin with Roy Campbell, he translated the entire *Les Fleurs du mal*, published as *Poems of Baudelaire*, in 1952. One of his biographers informs us that "he worked at tremendous speed on a translation of the poems of Baudelaire" (Alexander 224). Campbell himself declared: "I have been reading Baudelaire since I was fifteen, carried him in my haversack through two wars, and have loved him longer and more deeply than any other poet," adding that he translated Baudelaire "because he lived my life up to the same age, with similar sins, remorses, ostracisms, and poverty and pardon" (*Poems of Baudelaire* 134 [footnote 194]).

As a Catholic convert, Campbell was attracted to what he took to be the poet's Catholic pessimism about human nature; to put it another way, Baudelaire's focus on the "sinfulness" of humankind. This is a view of Baudelaire retailed by T. S. Eliot and the French novelist François Mauriac among others. This is how Mauriac puts it:

> Baudelaire's errors and transgressions would only exclude him from Catholicism if they were not sins. If he could have committed them without becoming a sinner, then he would not be one of ours. But in Baudelaire every fault becomes a sin; he confesses it as such. By that sign, acknowledge him as my brother (Peyre 57).

Mauriac here is, of course, alluding to the "mon frère" at the end of 'Au lecteur': But that Baudelaire was addressing the reader as a "fellow Catholic" is a rather dubious proposition. After all, it is generally recognized that to be human sometimes involves not being entirely sincere in our relationships, so religion doesn't necessarily come into it. For Eliot, Baudelaire's Catholicism is revealed in his rejection of any kind of secular optimism and willingness to risk damnation. He was not a pious Christian, and certainly not saintly, but he recognized the reality of choosing between good and evil. Jean-Paul Sartre perhaps had a better grasp of Baudelaire's moral/aesthetic complexity, as in this comment from his book on the poet:

Hell is all very well for the crude, smug sins, but the soul of a man who desires Evil for Evil's sake is an exquisite blossom. It would be just as much out of place among the mob of vulgar sinners as a duchess surrounded by 'tarts' at Saint Lazare (Sartre 71).

Baudelaire himself had this to say in an abandoned Preface to *Les Fleurs du mal*:

The Devil. Original sin. Man as good. If you would, you could be the Tyrant's favorite; it is more difficult to love God than to believe in Him. On the other hand, it is more difficult for people nowadays to believe in the Devil than to love him. Everyone smells him and no one believes in him. Sublime subtlety of the Devil (*The Flowers of Evil* xvii).

Whether he actually believed in God and/or the Devil is beside the point. His real concern seems to have been the ambivalence of being human and how we are torn between various conflicting impulses. Campbell, however, was attracted to what he took to be Baudelaire's orthodox Catholicism and was notorious for siding with the Francoists in the Spanish Civil War, while Baudelaire sided with the rebels in the failed Revolution of 1848.

Some of his Baudelaire translations were included by Matthiel and Jackson Matthews in their edition the entire *Les Fleurs du mal* in translation, which was published in 1955. They picked the "best" versions of each poem by various British and American translators and declared that "Roy Campbell is the first poet of reputation to attempt the whole of *The Flowers of Evil* in English" (*The Flowers of Evil* vii). They went on to say that, "he succeeds in a large number of poems, but that he is most successful in the hard-driving didactic ones" (*The Flowers of Evil* vii). Campbell is by far the largest contributor, with no less than 43 out of 161 poems, so they could not all have been the 'didactic' ones. The distinguished Baudelaire authority F. W. Leakey was rather less complimentary, when he wrote, "Roy Campbell has proved boisterously erratic as well as heroic: there is no single unflawed version in his whole volume, let alone among those figuring in the Matthews compilation" (Leakey 101). But this criticism is nothing compared to Campbell's own insouciance: "I beg the reader's indulgence if I have erred on the slangy side: but I feared to offend my great original who had a horror of the pompously poetic" (*Poems of Baudelaire*).

One of the most revealing of Campbell's translations is that of "Benediction," the first poem in Baudelaire's 'Spleen et ideal' section of *Fleurs du mal*. Leakey has acutely described the poem as '... that passionately self-inspired chronicle of the Poet's victimization on earth but *benediction* or apotheosis, in Heaven' (Leakey 26). Here are the first four stanzas:

> Lorsque, par un décret des puissances suprêmes,
> Le Poète apparaît en ce monde ennuyé,
> Sa mère épouvantée et pleine du blasphèmes
> Crispe ses poings vers Dieu, qui la prend en pitié:
>
> "Ah! que n'ai-je mis bas tout un nœud de vipères,
> Plutôt que de nourrir cette dérision!
> Maudite sous la nuit aux plaisirs éphémères
> Où mon ventre a conçu mon expiation!
>
> "Puisque tu m'as choisie entre toutes les femmes
> Pour être le dégoût de mon triste mari,
> Et que je ne puis pas rejeter dans les flammes,
> Comme un billet d'amour, ce monstre rabougri,
>
> "Je ferai rejaillir ta haine qui m'accable
> Sur l'instrument maudit de tes méchancetés,
> Et je tordrai si bien cet arbre misérable,
> Qu'il ne pourra pousser ses boutons empestés!"
>
> (Baudelaire, *The Flowers of Evil* 11)

Campbell's translation is as follows:

> When by an edict of the powers supreme
> A poet's born in this drab space,
> His mother starts, in horror to blaspheme
> Clenching her fists at God, who grants her grace.
>
> "Would that a nest of vipers I'd aborted
> Rather than this absurd abomination.
> Cursed be the night of pleasures vainly sported
> On which my womb conceived my expiation.
>
> Since ofall women I am picked by You
> To be my Mate's aversion and his shame;
> And since I cannot, like a billet-doux,
> Consign this stunted monster to the flame,
>
> I'll turn the hatred, which You load on me,
> On the curst tool through which You work your spite,
> And twist and stunt this miserable tree
> Until it cannot burgeon for the blight."

(Poems of Baudelaire 134)

This poem must have been an intriguing one for Campbell to translate. As Peter Alexander's biography tells us, like Baudelaire, he was close to his mother, and she encouraged his artistic tendencies when he grew up in South Africa, but his relationship to his mother does not appear to have been anywhere near as complicated and ambivalent as Baudelaire's. Campbell, however, did like to see himself as a man of action, and one devoted to the outdoors, so he succeeds in capturing Baudelaire's sense of vigorous implacability in this portrayal of a mother horrified to the point of blasphemy by the poet she has spawned. And she regrets giving suck to her derisory child ("nourrir cette derision!") rather than failing to abort him. What Campbell tends to distort, or fail to convey, is the subtlety and linguistic flexibility of the mother's vituperation. For instance, "this drab space" is perhaps more reminiscent of a possibly dreary South African veldt than "ce monde ennuyé," which suggests rather more the wider social world of relationships plagued by boredom. With "a nest of vipers I'd aborted," perhaps Campbell's translation strays more into an "imitation," one with more "attitude" than "latitude." Campbell seems to have the Catholic injunction against abortion in mind, but the mother is actually telling us that she'd *rather* spawn a nest of vipers ("nœud des vipères'), not abort them. The final line of the fourth stanza is somewhat abstract, like Christ's cursing of the fig tree in Mark, 12–25, but the mother's words in French are much more specific, and in tune with the natural world. Paradoxically, the cumulative effect, when Campbell's entire translated poem is read, is to render Baudelaire's deployment of blasphemy along more doctrinally orthodox lines.

Robert Lowell's translations of Baudelaire, which consist of fourteen poems from *Les Fleurs du mal*, were collected in *Imitations*. This was first published in 1961, and, at the time, attracted much criticism, making what could be called a "succès de scandale," which of course can also be said of Baudelaire's book. Apart from Baudelaire, according to the critics, Lowell translated Rimbaud, Rilke, and Heine, among others, with varying degrees of success. Lowell mentions Dryden very briefly in his Introduction, but it is evident that he used the word "imitation" in Dryden's sense. Unlike Dryden, who somewhat deplored the practice of "imitation," Lowell thought that poetry translators, in order to be effective, had to practice "imitation." He argues that the "tone" of the original is more important than literal accuracy. This is how he put it:

> I have been reckless with literal meaning, and labored hard to get the tone. Most often this has been *a* tone, for *the* tone, is something that will always more or less escape transference to another language and cultural moment. I have tried to write live English and to do what my authors might have done if they were writing their poems now and in America (Lowell, *Imitations* xi).

It is the last sentence, which is particularly important and one that some critics find controversial. But Lowell also emphasizes that technical proficiency must also be part of the process in the practice of imitation; as he puts it "I believe that poetic translation – I would

---

call it an imitation—must be expert and inspired, and needs at least as much technique, luck and rightness of hand as an original poem" (Lowell, *Imitations* xii).

However, George Steiner, who has a very distinguished reputation as a cultural critic, while not overly critical, made the following point in the *Kenyon Review*, interestingly identifying Roy Campbell as a better translator of Baudelaire:

> [...] modesty is the very essence of translation. The greater the poet, the more loyal should be his servitude to the original; Rilke is servant to Louise Labé, Roy Campbell to Baudelaire. Without modesty translation will traduce; where modesty is constant, it can transfigure (Hamilton 291).

Yet, as we have seen, "servitude to the original" was not entirely Campbell's forte.

Politically, as in his opposition to the Vietnam War and in just about every other way, Robert Lowell, was very much a rebel and, like Campbell, a maverick in his own way. For a brief time, he was even a Catholic convert.

But his affinities with the French poet went deeper than that. In a letter to the poet-critic Randall Jarrell, dated October 24, 1957, he declared: "I think the French poets from Baudelaire through Apollinaire have really renewed poetry, they are modern poetry (except for Hardy and Hopkins)" (Lowell, *Letters of Robert Lowell* 298). Lowell, in fact, didn't only translate the poets he admired, he also alluded to and borrowed from them in his own poetry. His ambition, in this respect, was anything but self-effacing, and his next step was to translate some of his admired European poets, in what could be called a maverick manner pretty remote from Steiner's recommended "servitude to the original." He did so in *Imitations*, which Ehrenpreis described as "Lowell's attempt to find his voice in the high places of literature, to fashion retrospectively a tradition for his accomplishments," adding that he thereby legitimized "his progeny, replacing the Lowells and Winslows by Baudelaire, Rimbaud and Rilke" (Ehrenpreis 90). In short, according to Ehrenpreis, Lowell adopted European poets as his artistic forebears in a bid to reject what he possibly considered to be his stuffy New England ancestors.

There is no doubt, in any case, that Lowell's *Imitations* are embedded in controversy. According to his biographer Ian Hamilton, some reviewers were particularly incensed by Lowell's translation of stanza five of "To the Reader" ('Au lecteur'), supposedly 'a crushing indictment of the Lowell method (Hamilton 291). Here is Baudelaire:

> Ainsi qu'un débauché pauvre qui baise et mange
> Le sein martyrisé d'une antique catin,
> Nous volons au passage un plaisir clandestin
> Que nous pressons bien fort comme une vieille orange.

And here is Lowell's version:

> Like the poor lush who cannot satisfy,
> we try to force our sex with counterfeits,
> die drooling on the deliquescent tits,
> mouthing the rotten orange we suck dry.

Hamilton implies that Lowell's lines are so obviously inferior that he didn't even need to comment on them. If Lowell's lines are taken in the spirit of "imitation" rather than "translation" in the literal sense, or what Dryden called "metaphrase," then Lowell's stanza has a logic of its own. He deflects focus on the "martyred" breast of an old prostitute ("Le sein martyrisé d'une antique catin"), which at least makes us visualize her as a woman with a ravaged body, with total focus on the "poor lush," in other words, someone very drunk and possibly destitute, who barely knows what he is doing. That he is a "lush," a much more colloquial or even slangy word than either "drunk" or "alcoholic," rather "un débauché pauvre," or "penniless lecher" in Scarfe's prose rendering (*Baudelaire: Selected Verse* 155), gives him even less dignity than in Baudelaire's poem. The phrase "plaisir clandestin" also suggests that the man is not quite as impotent as the one visualized by Lowell. Lowell also transposes the sardonic "lesson" in Baudelaire's third line to the second line in his version, and it is more aggressive. Baudelaire emphasizes the furtive nature of, basically, men taking their pleasures where they can find them, while Lowell is more concerned with how futile and frustrating casual sexual encounters can be. Whether Lowell's lines distort Baudelaire or not, he certainly comes across as much harsher than Baudelaire. Similarly, he ups the ante in the first line of the second stanza, where "nos repentirs sont lâches" becomes "our confessions lies." Baudelaire suggests that "repentance is cowardly," but this leaves some room for forgiveness, whereas in Lowell's version, the stage of "repentance" doesn't even occur. But what Lowell does get away from in Baudelaire's opening poem to *Les Fleurs du mal* is any kind of worldly elegance. Lowell's "imitation" does fail in this respect. Baudelaire often sounds harsh, even shocking, but he is never raw or embittered in Lowell's manner.

Ehrenpreis praises Lowell's achievement as a Baudelaire translator very highly, commending "the decorous violence" of Lowell's style (92), and declaring that his "confident metres, the bold catchy phrases, express not simply what Baudelaire felt, but what we still want: a power to transcend lust and decay by the imagination that digests them" (92). But while he argues that "in artistic sensibility Lowell seems peculiarly at home with Baudelaire" (92), he concedes that in technique, far from surpassing Baudelaire, he is not always the French poet's equal in his mastery of technique and sensuous imagery; for instance: "Lowell relies overwhelmingly on visual imagery, whereas Baudelaire appeals elaborately to sounds, and is remarkable for a synaesthetic use of smells" (95).

More secular-minded than either Campbell or Lowell, at least in his Catholic phase, is the novelist and poet James Robertson. But Robertson is very familiar with the Calvinism of the Presbyterians in Scotland. Among other things, Calvinism involves a belief in predestination, or the notion that some are saved and many are damned purely by the inscrutable workings of God's grace, and the reality of the Devil, a belief shared with traditional Catholicism. As will be seen shortly, the Devil gets his due in Robertson's rendering of "Le Jeu."

What also makes the Scottish novelist and poet James Robertson a different kind of maverick from the other two poets is that his translations are in Scots. He thereby renders a selection from *Les Fleurs du mal*, entitled *Fae The Flouers o Evil*, not merely into English, whether of a New England American, or that of a cosmopolitan white South African, but a distinctive variant of English, namely Scots. It was and is a language rather than a regional dialect, which was spoken by most Scottish people, apart from Highlanders who spoke Gaelic, before the union of the Scottish and English parliaments in 1707. But poetry written in Scots persisted, with Robert Burns as its greatest exemplar before the twentieth century. Burns, of course, is so international in stature that he cannot be regarded as merely a "regional" poet, and in Scotland, he is regarded as the "national" poet.

It was in the 1920s and 1930s that the poet C. M. Grieve, under his "'nom de guerre" Hugh MacDiarmid, revived Scots as a major literary language with his stylistically modernist lyrics in Scots, in collections like *Sangschaw* (1925) and *Penny Wheep* (1926), and his great polemical long poem in the first-person voice, *A Drunk Man Looks at the Thistle* (1926). Robertson, who lives in a village where the locals speak their own version of Scots does not replicate MacDiarmid's pyrotechnics in his translations of Baudelaire. Instead, he presents a more conversational, colloquial Scots, which is arguably closer to the vigor and street language of Baudelaire than either Campbell or Lowell.

To go on to "Le Jeu," here is the final stanza:

> Et mon cœur s'effraya d'envier maint pauvre homme
> Courant avec ferveur à l'abîme béant,
> Et qui, soûl de son sang, préférerait en somme
> La douleur à la mort et l'enfer au néant!

Robertson's title is 'Gamblin,' and he renders the final stanza as follows:

An ma hert is feart that it shud envy fowk
That breenge sae bauldly tae the gantin precipice,
Syne, fou wi bluid, select dule ower daith,
An Auld Nick's crucible ower naethin-ness

gantin: yawning
syne: therefore
fou wi bluid: full of blood
dule: suffering

If read aloud, most of the words can be understood, for instance "bauldly" means "boldly" and "bluid" means "blood." Robertson's main change is to bring the Devil into the last line, but if Baudelaire doesn't mention the Devil here, he certainly does so in other poems, and in this poem, he does mention the realm of the Devil, namely hell ("l'enfer"). "Le Jeu" suggests that we are trapped between choosing suffering or death, hell or nothingness. But Robertson's version is more dramatic, as it visualizes the Devil himself preparing a "crucible" of pain for the damned. Risking damnation in Robertson's version is very much a personal matter of confronting the Devil.

By doing so, Robertson also alludes to Scottish folk-lore, in which Devil sometimes features prominently, and poems by Robert Burns, particularly the phantasmagoric *Tam O'Shanter.* His versions of Baudelaire, moreover, are certainly visceral in their vigor. The Scots word for "vigor" happens to be "virr," and it occurs in the second stanza of "Parfum Exotique" (translated as "Exotic Perfume"): "men o virr." In Baudelaire's poem, the line is as follows: "Des hommes dont le corps est mince et vigoureux." Robertson's corresponding line is not as languidly elegant, but it gains in punchy male directness: "Wi men o virr an soupleness an ease."

As in Lowell's case, some of Robertson's translations are very free, and others are more literal, making for a sequence of twenty-three poems independent of Baudelaire's much longer collection. Apart from his commitment to Scots as a distinct language in contemporary Britain, Robertson is also intent on showing how life in today's Scotland can be envisioned through lenses provided by the French poet. He is particularly shrewd with Scots idioms, such as: "Big sea, I cannot thole ye!," in which "thole" means "endure;" "Dae us a favour, nicht, pit oot yer starns" in "Obsession," which has exactly the same title as Baudelaire's poem and where "Dae us a favour" has more or less the same exasperated connotations as "do me a favor," but tends to be menacing and threatening in, say, a Glasgow underworld milieu. The phrase is also a favored one of stand-up comic Billy Connolly. Such turns of phrase, and there are many in Robertson's selection, make Baudelaire seem much more contemporary.

Robertson's selection for the most part seeks culturally Scottish equivalents of Baudelaire's themes. Particularly powerful in this respect is "The Hun," Robertson's version of "L'Ennemi." It was the Germans in World War I who were disparagingly called "Huns" by the British, but Baudelaire died in 1867, so he did not even live to see the Franco-Prussian War between the French and the Germans in 1870–71. By the time of World War I, the French called the Germans "les Boches," their equivalent of "the Hun." There is, of course, no such phrase as "les Boches" in Baudelaire's poem. It is not about any external, or military, enemy, but time as "the enemy within." Here is the final stanza in "L'Ennemi:"

> Ô douleur! ô douleur! Le Temps mange la vie,
> Et l'obscur Ennemi qui nous ronge le cœur
> Du sang que nous perdons croît et se fortifie!

Robertson's version is as follows:

> Aw man! man! Time juist eats life haill,
> An aye oor herts are gnawed by thon Hun,
> Wha growes wi ivery drap o bluid we skail.

> haill: whole
> aye: constantly
> oor herts: our hearts
> skail: leak out

Both Baudelaire and Robertson personify time as the ravager of life, but the ravager in Robertson's version hints at how lives have been so wasted by war in the past and "thon Hun" or "that Hun" personifies time in terms of the enemy in a world war, in which the proportion of Scottish casualties was very high. By doing so, Robertson is even bolder than Lowell, whose own version, entitled "The Ruined Garden" personifies time as a virus, which "eats the heart out of our sides." Perhaps Lowell's rendering of Baudelaire's "l'obscur Ennemi" betrays a fear of sexually transmitted disease on his part. But all three poets focus powerfully on how we, as mortal humans, are all subject to the depredations of time.

The social and personal consequences of alcoholic excess are very prominent in Robertson's sequence, as he translates no less than three poems in this vein, "Le Vin des amants," "Le Vin de l'assassin," and "Le Vin du solitaire." His Scots versions emphasize the squalid even more than Baudelaire's. Devastatingly, the drunken killer in "The Killer's Bevy" gets rid of his wife "For auld lang syne (if naehin else)." "[F]or auld lang syne" is, of course, a line sung from Burns all over the globe every New Year's Eve, which is called Hogmanay in Scotland. By contrast, Baudelaire's killer seems more conscience-stricken in that he remorsefully hopes to forget his murdered wife: "Je l'oublierai si je le puis!" "The Loner's Bevvy" is starker than "Le Vin solitaire" in its exposure of "the rotten-hertit true-versed makar" rather than just telling us to "Garde au cœur altéré du poëte pieux." "The Luvers' Bevvy" renders the opening line of "Le Vin des amants,"

Aujourd'hui l'espace est splendide!

with wonderfully idiomatic irony:

Get up! The Warld's oor Loch Fyne oyster!

"The world is your oyster" is a common expression to congratulate anyone on their good fortune, and Loch Fyne oysters are regarded as great delicacies, but its very title, as well as the poem itself, in both Baudelaire's and Robertson's versions, suggest that the lovers are living in the fool's paradise of excessive drinking.

All three "Bevvy" poems to some extent are reminders of social deprivation in Scotland, partly because the word "bevvy" (drink), and its derivatives would remind readers of a famous industrial intervention by the trade unionist Jimmy Reid. He and his colleagues, in late 1971, decided to fight a Conservative government decision to close the Upper Clyde Shipbuilders consortium. Instead of recommending a strike, however, they proposed a "work-in" by the shipbuilding workforce, in order to show that the shipyards were economically viable. The result was that the shipyards were largely rescued from closure. For this virtually unprecedented move in a highly volatile situation, Reid wanted to ensure that discipline was maintained; hence, in February 1972, he made a famous speech, in which he admonished the workers as follows: "There will be no hooliganism, there will be no vandalism, and there will be no bevvying, because the whole world will be watching us!" It's the "no bevvying" that he emphasized.

It remains to conclude by taking a brief look at three of the best versions of Baudelaire poems by the respective poets and to assess them as distinctive poems in English and Scots rather than as translations, starting with Robertson's "Melt (Three)," which is his version of perhaps the best-known "Spleen" poem, with the first line being "'Je suis comme le roi d'un pays pluvieux […']" It was also translated by Lowell and Campbell, both reproducing the same title. Here is Robertson's version:

Melt (Three)

I'm like a lairdie in Lochaber, or somewhaur juist as wet:
A tweedy rich *im*potentate, young yet past his sell-by date,
Sneerin at the bou an scrape o factors,
Bored wi his dugs an paycocks, pigs an tractors.
Naethin can divert him, no huntin, fishin, falconry,
No even tenants drappin deid aneath his balcony.
His favourite gillie's cantrips, sangs an sports
Are nae distraction sin he's taen the dorts.
His rose-strewn bed's mair like a peat bog o despond,
An jet-set limmers, skeeled at makkin lairdies feel like Bond,

Rin oot o sexy ploys an skimpy claes
That uised tae raise a smile at least frae Greitin Face.
The alchemist that kens hou gowd's procured
Cudna howk the iron in him immured,
Even a bathe in bluid, that the Romans thocht
Cud refull ancient veins wi virr, wudna dae ocht
Wi sic a stuffed old stookie: I dout there's nae remeid
When, whaur bluid shud rin, fylt water flows insteid.

lairdie: titled small landowner
bou an scrape: bowing and scraping
factors: land agents
dugs an paycocks: dogs and peacocks
aneath: beneath
gillie's cantrips: servant's antics
taen the dorts: taken the huff
limmers: rogues
skeeled: skilled
claes: clothes
Greitin Face: moaning expression
kens how gowd's procured: knows how gold is produced
cudna: couldn't
howk: prise out
refull: refill
ocht: anything
stookie: stupid person, effigy
remeid: remedy
fylt: filthy

Robertson's version diverges quite a lot from the original, so much so that it is rather more of an "imitation" than Lowell's version. For a start, the Scots word "melt" connotes not only ennui or boredom, but also sperm and tongue, both words implicit in much of Baudelaire. Robertson's version is very grounded in rugged countryside living, Lochaber being an area in the Highlands. It is also about social envy and boredom with country life on the part of the "lairdie," more of a social portrait than the poet's own boredom, yet it remains true to the spirit of Baudelaire's poem. As Leakey has pointed out, the word "spleen," ironically an English one, is not only interchangeable with "ennui" as Baudelaire uses it, but also "inertia, deep melancholy, profound despair" (Leakey 23). Robertson's poem does suggest something of a social inertia in the lairdie's life and certainly reads like sardonic social comment. The "lairdie in Lochaber, or somewhaur juist as wet," like "le roi d'un pays pluvieux" in Baudelaire's poem is the poet's alter-ego when in a bad mood, but more grounded in humdrum social reality than Baudelaire's "le roi." Arguably, Robertson's poem is more humorous, indeed satirical. The rhymes "despond" and "Bond" in lines 9 and 10, for instance, are wittily bathetic. Lowell's translation of roughly these same lines is much closer to the original:

> his bed of fleur-de-lys becomes a tomb;
> even the ladies of the court for whom
> all kings are beautiful, ...

However, the blue-blooded landowner described by Robertson is very recognizable, and his translation more of a genuine, transformative "imitation" than Lowell's.

To a query I sent him about his interest in translating Baudelaire, Robertson responded by e-mail as follows:

> ... as soon as I started reading him I realized that I had found the kind of ground I was looking for. He offered the right combination of subject-matter and mood, and also he wasn't too abstract. I think Scots responds well to descriptions of, for example, the weather or human physical attributes, of both of which there are plenty in Baudelaire! Mood too: Scots excels at the dark, the threatening, the violent. No shortage of these either in Baudelaire (Oct. 25, 2013).

While Robertson's version emphasizes his deployment of the Scots tongue, it is also clear that culturally he finds many affinities with Baudelaire.

Roy Campbell's translation of "L'Albatros" reads like a faithful version of the original, one of "latitude" rather than "attitude," as in the case of Robertson's "Melt" poems. Here it is:

The Albatross

Sometimes for sport the men of loafing crews
Snare the great albatrosses of the deep,
The indolent companions of their cruise
As through the bitter vastitudes they sweep.

Scarce have they fished aboard these airy kings
When helpless on such unaccustomed floors,
They piteously droop their huge white wings
And trail them on their sides like drifting oars.

How comical, how ugly, and how meek
Appears this soarer of celestial snows!
One, with his pipe, teases the golden beak,
One, limping, mocks the cripple as he goes.

The Poet, like this monarch of the clouds,
Despising archers, rides the storm elate.
But, stranded on the earth to jeering crowds,
The great wings of the giant baulk his gait.

(Campbell, *Selected Poetry* 174)

Campbell's version is particularly good in recreating Baudelaire's
alternate rhyme-scheme in English. He would have identified himself
as "The Poet" in the final stanza, a prey to the crowds, or masses,
which he disliked. "Gait" rhymes with "elate," but it is also significant
that, in Baudelaire's poem, the albatross is described as "l'infirme qui
volait," which means that the albatross is prevented from flying rather
than walking. But while Baudelaire's albatross is metaphorically like
a disabled person, Campbell's is prevented from walking by his very
wings. For Campbell, it is not so much that the poet is like a disabled
person among the public, but that he is hampered from connecting
with the public by his very creativity. It is a subtle difference, more
in keeping with Campbell's desire for the poet to be heroic. As Tom
Hubbard puts it, regarding Baudelaire's original, "*The Albatross,* in
which the giant wings of the bird render it impressive in flight but
clumsy in shipdeck captivity, provides a metaphor for the poet/

artist whose very gifts cause him humiliation in a philistine society" (Hubbard 19). Campbell undoubtedly regarded the poem in this light.

Lowell's rendition of "Le Gouffre" as "The Abyss" is one of his best takes on Baudelaire. Baudelaire's poem plays with the seventeenth-century French philosopher and mathematician, who was a "Jansenist," or particularly strict Catholic, Blaise Pascal's speculations on what he considered to be the frightening immensity of the universe. Baudelaire's very first line alludes to Pascal's dread: "Pascal avait son gouffre [...]" Scarfe's foot-noted commentary to the poem quotes, from Baudelare's *Intimate Journal*, the poet's own sense of what could be called existential dread: "Both morally and physically I have always had the sensation of the pit (*gouffre*); not only the pit of sleep, but of action, dream, memory, desire, regret, remorse, beauty, number, etc.," but he adds almost flippantly that "I have cultivated my hysteria with enjoyment and terror" (Baudelaire, *Selected Verse* 245). "Le Gouffre" itself is more somber, and the same can be said of Lowell's version:

The Abyss

Pascal's abyss went with him at his side,
closer than blood—alas, activity,
dreams, words, desire: all holes! On every side,
spaces, the bat-wing of insanity!
Above, below me, only depths and shoal,
the silence! And the Lord's right arm
traces his nightmare, traceless, multiform.
I cuddle the insensible blank air,
and fear to sleep as one fears a great hole.
My spirit, haunted by its vertigo,
sees the spirit at every window,
vague, horrible and dropping God knows where ...
Ah never to escape from number and form!

Formally, Lowell's version is less harmoniously controlled. Where Baudelaire's has four stanzas, made up of two quatrains followed by two tercets, Lowell's version is continuous, and made up of thirteen lines, as if to emphasize a dizzying amorphousness. Lowell's version is also more explicit about the fear of madness, namely his own, as occasionally he did suffer from mental instability. It is, indeed, beyond "imitation," very much a personal poem.

The Scottish poet Don Paterson illuminated precisely what effective translation of poetry involves when he wrote about his own versions of the Spanish poet Antonio Machado:

> ... the only defensible fidelity to the entirely subjective quality of *spirit* or *vision,* rather than to literal meaning; though one can perhaps be truer, or at least not unfaithful, to the wider argument of a poem, and its images (Paterson 58).

Whatever their merits, or otherwise, of their translations, Roy Campbell, Robert Lowell, and James Robertson "transcreated" Baudelaire according to their own lights, as poets in their own right, and because they recognized in him "mon semblable – mon frère!"

Works Cited

Alexander, Peter. *Roy Campbell: A Critical Biography.* Oxford: Oxford UP, 1982

Baudelaire, Charles. *Poems of Baudelaire.* Trans. Roy Campbell. London: The Harvill Press, 1952.

_____. *The Flowers of Evil.* Eds. Mathiel & Jackson Matthews. London: Routledge & Kegan Paul, 1955.

_____. *Baudelaire: Selected Verse.* Trans. Francis Scarfe. Harmondsworth: Penguin Books, 1964.

_____. *The Flowers of Evil.* Trans. James McGowan. Oxford, UK: Oxford World's Classics, 1998.

_____. *Baudelaire.* Trans. Laurence Lerner. London: J.M. Dent, 1999.

_____. *Fae The Flouers o Evil: Baudelaire in Scots.* Trans. James Robertson. Glenrothes: Kettilonia, 2001.

_____. *Intimate Journals.* Trans. & Ed. Christopher Isherwood. New York: Dover Publications, Inc., 2006.

Campbell, Roy. *Collected Poems: Translation.* Vol. 3. London: The Bodley Head, 1960.

_____. *Selected Poetry.* Ed. J. M. Lalley. London: The Bodley Head, 1968.

_____. *The Selected Poems of Roy Campbell.* Ed. Peter Alexander. Oxford, UK: Oxford UP, 1982.

_____. *Selected Poems.* Ed. Joseph Pearce. London: The Saint Austin Press, 2001.

Clements, Patricia. *Baudelaire & The English Tradition.* Princeton, NJ: Princeton UP, 1985.

Dryden, John. *Of Dramatic Poesy and Other Critical Essays.* Ed. George Watson. London: J.M. Dent & Sons, Ltd., 1962. 2 vols.

Ehrenpreis, Irvin. "The Age of Lowell." *Stratford-Upon-Avon Studies* 7 (1965): 68–95.

Eliot, T. S. *Selected Essays.* 1934. London & Boston: Faber and Faber, 1980.

Hamilton, Ian. *Robert Lowell: A Biography.* London: Faber & Faber, 1983.

Hubbard, Tom. *The Integrative Vision: Poetry and the Visual Arts in Baudelaire, Rilke and MacDiarmid.* Kirkcaldy: Akros Publications, 1997.

Leakey, F. W. ed. *Baudelaire: Les Fleurs du mal.* Cambridge: Cambridge UP, 1992. Landmarks of World Literature Ser.

Lowell, Robert. *Imitations.* London: Faber & Faber, 1971.

_____. *Collected Poems.* Eds. Frank Bidart & David Gewanter. London: Faber & Faber, 2003.

_____. *The Letters of Robert Lowell.* Ed. Saskia Hamilton. London: Faber & Faber, 2005.

Mauriac, Francois. "Charles Baudelaire, the Catholic" *Baudelaire: A Collection of Critical Essays.* Ed. Henri Peyre. Englewood Cliffs, NJ: Prentice-Hall, Inc., 1962.

Paterson, Don. *The Eyes.* New York: Faber & Faber, 1999. Faber Poetry Ser.

Peyre, Henri, ed. *Baudelaire: A Collection of Critical Essays.* Englewood Cliffs, NJ: Prentice-Hall, Inc., 1962.

Sartre, Jean-Paul, *Baudelaire.* Trans. Martin Turnell. London: Horizon, 1949.

Smith, Rowland. *The Literary Personality of Roy Campbell.* Montreal & London: McGill-Queen's UP, 1972.

Baudelaire's Prose Poems: Scots as an Antidote to "French"

James W. Underhill

Translating the "poetry" in Poems

Poets and academics seem to feel an irrepressible tug towards the poems of Charles Baudelaire. The great contemporary specialist of comparative versification, Clive Scott, devoted an entire work to analyzing the act of translating Baudelaire. Surely, this bears witness to two things: to both the creative energy of Baudelaire himself as a poet, and to the capacity of translators to refashion poems in a foreign tongue. Poems can and do leap across the gulf between languages and cultures. Not only do Baudelaire's poems speak to English readers, they speak to a wide public of poetry-lovers without estranging the most sensitive specialists or most exacting critics. But what about the translations of Baudelaire's poems in prose?

Translating Baudelaire's prose poems proves to be a double challenge. Not only does it force translators to reevaluate what exactly Baudelaire and we are supposed to understand by the 'poetry' of prose poems, it forces us to face up to the whole question of free verse as a practice in both writing and translating poems. Translation has always been considered as translating the meaning, extracting the sense, the "essence" of a message. In such a conception, the form becomes the outer shell, protecting the inner kernel of truth. And yet, does this conception not necessarily posit "form" as much as a "surface" as a "protective outer shell." Form becomes an obstacle, and translation becomes a kind of "transformation," which must enact something akin to a transmigration of the soul. Extraction becomes seizing the essential and cutting away the surface, or the superficial, the secondary, at any rate. All this is very spiritual, but the praxis of poetry translation brings us down with a bang because every undergraduate and lay reader perceives all too clearly that such a conception of translation simply doesn't work for poetry.

This would be somewhat simpler if poetry were just a question of rhythms and rhymes. If this were the case, we could simply find alternative rhymes and transpose French or German meters into English meters. But poems prove more subtle. Paradoxically, the free verse dogma tended to obscure two irrefutable truths that Eliot, one of the major exponents of free verse, saw right at the outset, when he argued that "the division between conservative verse and *Vers libre* does not exist, for there is only good verse, bad verse and chaos" (Eliot 91).

The first truth is that good free verse is patterned, and the form does matter, as much as the "matter" it engenders. The second truth is that rhymed metrical poems are also highly patterned, and their rhythms, sound-patterning, rhymes, and repetitions are highly specific, highly personal, and of great significance for the way each poem works as a meaningful expression, unfolding in motion. Catching that motion, which expresses and engenders emotion, is the hardest thing for the translator. That is what Ezra Pound meant when he suggested that "[r]hythm is the hardest quality of a man's style to counterfeit" (Pound 39).

That's all very well, says the defender of a hermeneutics of translation, the interpretive tradition defended by Seleskovitch and Lederer in *Interpréter pour traduire*. Those that espouse the interpretive act of penetrating and translating the meaning of the text are more than willing to concede that their theory of translation is impotent when it comes to translating poems. Laymen are often willing to celebrate poetry and praise its "magic," its "mystery," and its "music." But these three terms, "magic," "mystery," and "music" turn out to be intellectual cul-de-sacs, intended to annex and cordon off questions of a formal nature. They consolidate the age-old and wholly dysfunctional dichotomy of the "spirit" and the "letter," the "meaning" and the "content." Ultimately, they assign the praxis of poetry translation to a transcendental plane, while allowing a reductive semantics to set itself up in the vacuum and reign over a supposedly rigorous science of interpretation.

If translating poems were only a question of finding the right meter and the right rhymes, the number of great translators would be legion. I do not wish to underestimate the difficulties involved in finding formal equivalents, questions that Jiří Levý (1962, 2011), and Henri Meschonnic (1982, 1999) have contributed to elucidating and critically reappraising. Nevertheless, translating Shakespeare or Baudelaire will produce stilted results if we simply chop prose up into lines and round them off with a rhyme. The dynamism of Shakespeare's syntax, with its rapid turnabouts, his violent juxtapositions of short words, such as "Had, having and in quest to have extreme" (Shakespeare, *Sonnet* 129) will inevitably be lost or discarded by translators if that juxtaposition is not recognized for what it is—a dramatic moment of meaning. And if it is apprehended, then that moment of meaning must be reenacted. Otherwise, how can poetry translation hope to rise above interpretive prose, or stiff and hollow formalism?

There is a "poetry" within "poems" which cannot be reduced to "poetry," if we mean by that the formal definition used in treatises of versification. This will become all the more plain, if we remember that "versification" has always been used as a derogatory term for doggerel, or bad verse. That "poetry" within poems is exactly what good free verse intended to preserve. Besides, the whole argument used—rather disingenuously, in a project of self-promotion—to justify free verse, by even its greatest exponents, Pound and Eliot, was that poetry had become stuck in a neo-classical mode of formalism. This was tantamount to arguing that the form had become a hollow shell. If such were the case, those innovators argued, poets should strike out and innovate. "Make it New" was the call of modernist poets led by Pound, who invited his fellow poets to forge more meaningful, more personal, and more moving rhythms.

For obvious practical reasons, poetry translators have tended to side with free verse. In doing so, they allow themselves greater scope for handling the meaning. And such a practice enables them to allow metrical lines to ebb and flow in the translation in a way similar to the ideal that Eliot envisaged when he argued that "the ghost of some simple metre should lurk behind the arras in even the 'freest' verse; to advance menacingly as we doze, and withdraw as we rouse" (Eliot 90). This translation practice with meter freely coming and going, drifting in and fading out, is widespread in Britain and in the United States, and it proves to be the dominant translation practice in contemporary France.

Prose poems offer an ideal arena for this struggle to reestablish the meaningful movement that is constantly tugged in two directions: form and meaning. Prose poems should, in theory at least, allow the translator sufficient scope to reenact a free formal patterning that is satisfying at an aesthetic level and that highlights the meaningful links and oppositions between words and phrases, sounds and rhythms.

The Poetry of Plainness

Baudelaire's poetry is beautiful, of course, but there is more to his verse than simple unadulterated beauty. There is a paradoxically precious plainness in his poems. And this makes him a challenge for translators because, as the editors, Clark & Sykes point out, in their wonderful compilation of Baudelaire's poems *Baudelaire in English,* the "hardest thing for a translator to catch is the sheer simplicity of some of Baudelaire's lines" (Clark & Sykes xxvii). As Baudelaire translators themselves, Clark and Sykes were in a good position to appraise the difficulty of the task. Baudelaire has a predilection for commonplace monosyllables, such as *grand, beaux, doux,* and *bon.* But as Baudelaire demonstrates, no word is commonplace, when transformed within the dynamic activity of the poem. Just as the melody determines whether the note is beautiful, kitsch, or false, it is the phrasing of the poem which gives value and meaning to the word within the whole. Baudelaire's simplicity proves anything but simple. There is what Clark and Sykes rightly call an "inspired plainness" (xxvii) to Baudelaire's verse, which is all too evident in lines such as, *Riche, mais impuissant, jeune, et pourtant très vieux* (Baudelaire, *Œuvres Complètes* 74).

Translating that simplicity inevitably proves arduous. Lewis Piaget Shanks, for example, reproduces that plainness without managing to achieve the melancholy monotony of the original in his "—wealthy, but impotent, still young, but old—" (Clark & Sykes 92). Roy Campbell manages to maintain something more balanced with his "Grown impotent and old before my time" (Clark & Sykes 93). True, Campbell is forced to drop "rich." And this is not only a semantic loss, but also a loss in parallelism. Campbell thereby transforms the quadripartite, rising-falling opposition movement of the original into a binary, rising-falling lament. Robert Lowell, on the other hand, demonstrates that great poets do not always prove great (or consistently great) translators when he completely misses the measured tone and deforms the register of the original by proposing "rich / but sterile, young, but with an old wolf's itch" (Clark & Sykes 94). Among such versions as these, James McColley Eilers' internet-posted version, posted on the www.intranslation.brooklynrail.org site, comes as a welcome addition: "Rich, but powerless; young, yet feeling wintry."

Lowell proves far more convincing in re-enacting Baudelaire's profound simplicity in *Meditation,* his version of the opening lines of "Recueillement":

> Sois sage, ô ma Douleur, et tiens-toi plus tranquille,
> Tu réclamais le Soir, il descend; le voici,
> > (Baudelaire, *Œuvres Complètes* 140)

> Calm down, my Sorrow, we must move with care.
> You called for evening; it descends; it's here.
> > (Clark & Sykes 226)

Plain Prose

Baudelaire's plainness is of a paradoxically metaphysical nature. In Baudelaire, the sublime coexists with the commonplace. The abyss can rise out of an ashtray. The gutters can reflect the heavens. Even decomposition and moral decay can be transformed into magical flights of fancy. Conversely, magical flights of fancy often fall, like Icarus—one of Baudelaire's cherished motifs—into dismay and disenchantment. Poetic transports often return like a boomerang to torment the poet. Inspiration often transpires to be an impulse that turns in on itself. Elation, in Baudelaire's poems, turns into abuse of himself and others. Indeed, the very flight of fancy and the craving for stimulation in an imaginary realm, however vividly and enticingly

Baudelaire portrays it, remains the flipside of a much more somber and morose sensibility, spelling that malaise in Baudelaire's relation to the world here and now, which he summed up in the word he imported from English into French "spleen."

Baudelaire is always complex, always ambivalent, as reality itself and our perception of it. It is difficult now to grasp the originality of this quality for a poet of Baudelaire's times. There is a dynamic tension, a sense of irony, and a heightened sensitivity to both beauty and to contradictions, that makes Baudelaire a very "modern" poet. The poems of Keats and Tennyson remain unquestionably beautiful today. But who would call them "modern"? In contrast to their poems, Baudelaire's imagination seems to have seized upon something crucial and vital in the urban experience. The poet, for whom wandering the city streets and visiting fairs and bars was a meaningful aesthetic adventure, offers us a vision of the city that remains meaningful for us today and that has reshaped the imagination of those who spend any time reading his work. For poets, from Swinburne to T. S. Eliot, and for thinkers, such as the great German essayist of the first half of the twentieth century, Walter Benjamin, Baudelaire introduced a new mode of perception and a means of expression for the urban experience.

The plain and the prosaic break into poetic reverie. And poetic reverie can rise out of the muck in the gutter or the butt ends of Prufrock's days and ways. But once more, the intimate relationship we seem to have maintained with Baudelaire throughout the twentieth century proves problematic for English readers. For as Clark & Sykes, the two English editors of the Penguin collection rightly suggest, many of the most successful Baudelaires are American. Edna St. Vincent Millay, writing in the thirties, is only one example. Among the translators who are rightly praised by Clark & Sykes, we find F. P. Sturm (1879–1942), who, though he wrote, in standard English, was, nevertheless, born and bred in Aberdeen. And the great Baudelaire translator, Roy Campbell (1901–57), was from Durban, South Africa.

This testifies to a somewhat curious state of affairs. The English don't seem to like English translations of Baudelaire: or not any more. What is going on here? Are the English translations simply out-dated, and old-fashioned? It is commonplace to argue that translations are not like good wine: they do not age well. The French thinker and translator Meschonnic, however, liked to remind us that translations age badly not because language and styles go out of fashion. Nobody finds the language of great texts or great translations tasteless or ridiculous. Shakespeare and Shelley, Hardy and Dickens, or the King James Version are read today with the same enthusiasm as before. The language is strange, but powerfully strange. It draws us into its own realm, it does not repulse us. Translations, on the other hand, all too often soon seem worn-out and stilted or absurd. The mannerisms of the times—so palpable in the choice of words and the way they are put together—repel us. Meschonnic, amusingly, added that if we find ourselves having to "retranslate texts," it is because we translate badly, because we mimic and monkey the styles of our times. And our styles and times do go out of fashion, unless they manage to fashion their own individual, authentic, and meaningful style.

This may be so, but it does not account for what Clark & Sykes object to in the English translations of Baudelaire's poems by Arthur Symons (1865–1945). Why should they be so much more stilted and out of date than American translations of the 1930s?

I would argue that the English have a problem with translating French. It is not so much a problem of translating the French language itself, but rather of the perception of "French" that the English have that is interfering with the translation process. "French" for the English is very different from the French language for the French. Since we have assimilated so much French and since it shares with Latin a certain prestige linked with our own heritage and the style and register of official prose, it is difficult for the English to grasp that, for the French, words like "assimilation" and "descend," are banal, commonplace words. In English, they instantly appear as the elegant, refined terms for expressing something akin to "fitting in," or "going down." We navigate between words of Germanic and Gallic origin in English, using either kind to shape the tone and register we require. We might "descend into the depths of despair," but we "go down the hill on our bikes." The choice of words and phrasing trigger entirely different associations and connotations. One is poetical, the other is prosaic.

And yet, translators often choose to slavishly follow the French, translating directly the words and the phrasing. This produces stilted and unconvincing prose, which is curiously very different from the impression the original French language produces. This is plain enough if we compare the way Louise Varèse translates with Baudelaire's prose poetry:

> Every piece of furniture is of an elongated form, languid and prostrate, and seems to be dreaming, endowed, one would say, with a somnambular existence, like minerals and vegetables (Clark & Sykes 237).

> *Les meubles ont des formes allongées, prostrées, alanguies. Les meubles ont l'air de rêver; on les dirait doués d'une vie somnambulique, comme le végétal et le minéral* (Baudelaire, *Œuvres Complètes* 68).

Four things are going wrong here:

- The words themselves, "elongated," "languid," and "prostrate" are of an intellectual or elevated register. They are markedly unlike the equivalent terms that would be used in spoken English.
- The phrase "of an elongated form" belongs to the written language, but not to everyday spoken English, which would prefer "longish in shape" and might opt for a phrasal verb like "long drawn out."
- Rather than preserving the short sentences and appositions that form part of Baudelaire's snappy style, Varèse prefers to join the two sentences together in a way that conforms more to the style of written prose.
- Varèse translates *"on"* by "one": the former is familiar and commonplace, the latter belongs to an entirely different register.

Ironically, Varèse (1890–1989), the wife of the composer Edgard Varèse, was not English. She was American. But in her style, she conforms to the same aesthetics of translation as Symons when he opens his translation of *Le Beau Navire*, *The Beautiful Ship*, with:

My desire is to respire thy charms that are divine
And all in thee that is more beautiful than wine,

(Clark & Sykes 67).

Varèse does not stoop to "thy"—a hangover from nineteenth-century nostalgia, which was still clinging on in poetry translation at the start of the twentieth century. On the other hand, "respire" lifts Baudelaire out of the ordinary without preserving his pithy poetry of clashes and contrasts. Varèse and Symons both elevate Baudelaire, while Baudelaire was forever oscillating between the vulgar and the sublime. And sadly, their elevation impoverishes the poetry of the original.

The irony of it is that both translators evidently feel they are being "faithful" to Baudelaire. They do indeed perceive the sublime in his verse. But they are suffering from what I would call the "Swinburne syndrome": they are incapable of assimilating the vulgar and the plain into the poetic. (Swinburne claimed somewhat absurdly that *Les Litanies de Satan,* were among "the noblest lyrics ever written" [Clark & Sykes xxix]). For such critics, the poetic must be preserved, intact, untouched by earthly realities and by ugly bodily functions. At another level, translators like Varèse believe they are being faithful to the French by hanging onto it, word by word, line by line. In practice, this proves to be misguided for two reasons. Firstly, words, etymologically linked or formally identical, often turn out to evoke very different meanings. Secondly, analogous phrasing can often produce very different results in two different languages.

The case I am making here should not be overstated. Baudelaire proves so powerful, so invitingly beautiful, so sensitive, and indeed so neurotically, but fascinatingly, hypersensitive, that his poems and his poems in prose invariably meet with great praise among English readers. I will offer a few examples of the poignant and balanced poetic prose that Baudelaire's translators have produced. Nonetheless, a double danger threatens the translation process when it comes to his poems and prose poems. Some translators persist in believing that clinging to French syntax will produce the same results in a different language. Meanwhile, others inadvertently "elevate" the poet to their own dubiously "poetical" ideal, by choosing archaic, refined, or "prissy" diction.

A great translator, like Aleister Crowley (1875–1947), is not above concocting a contrived phrasing that is not only patently intellectual—where Baudelaire was spiritual and poetical. The results are predictably heavy and rather difficult to follow. The following sentence from Crowley's translation of *The Artist's Confiteor* should make this point:

> At the same time thoughts, whether they arise from myself or dart forth from things external, soon become too intense (Clark & Sykes 236).

The syntax is complex, "whether" belongs to rhetoric of prose argument, and the inversion "things external" is archaic, and, moreover, particularly confusing in a subordinate clause. A freer translation would no doubt have cleaved more closely to the movement of the soul that Baudelaire was following and bodying forth.

Successful Passages

Now we have clearly identified the danger, we must, in all fairness, do justice to some of the translators, who very often manage to avoid falling into the trap of mistakenly elevating and intellectualizing Baudelaire. In the following passages, each of the translators brings forth a Baudelaire that sings with the angels, while strolling in the gutters. Take, for instance, the fourth paragraph of Crowley's *Crowds:*

> The solitary and pensive stroller draws a singular intoxication from this universal communion. He who easily weds himself to the crowd becomes acquainted with feverish enjoyments, of which the egotist, closed up like a strong-box, and the idle man, shut up in his shell like a mollusc, are eternally deprived. He adopts as his own all the professions, all the joys, and all the miseries which chance brings under his notice (Clark & Sykes 242).

We might object to "He who…" and "which chance brings under his notice," as intellectual or non-colloquial prose, but these are merely small blemishes in a beautiful whole.

The great Celan translator, Michael Hamburger, produces an equally elegant poetic prose version of Baudelaire in his *Anywhere out of the World,* which begins:

This life is a hospital where every patient is possessed with the desire to change beds; one man would like to suffer in front of the stove, and another believes that he would recover his health beside the window.

It always seems to me that I should feel well in the place where I am not, and this question of removal, is one which I discuss incessantly with my soul (Clark & Sykes 254).

Symons' prose poem versions prove something of a surprise. To say that Clark's and Sykes' appreciation of his verse translations is tepid is something of a euphemism. They refer to his collection of Baudelaire poems as "a belated stillborn offspring of the relationship between the former's [Symons'] complex pessimism and the satanic posturings of the English *fin de siècle*" (Clark & Sykes xxxii). Nonetheless, Clark and Sykes do justice to Symons' translations of the prose poems, which they find "far more successful" (Clark & Sykes xxxii). Indeed there is a lyrical world-weariness in his version, which is made all the more poignant by Symons' strategic use of alliteration and delicate phrasing. This is certainly true of the two opening paragraphs of his *Evening Twilight*:

The day is over. A great restfulness descends into poor minds that the day's work has wearied; and thoughts take on the tender and dim colours of twilight.

Nevertheless from the mountain peak there comes to my balcony, through the transparent clouds of evening, a great clamour, made up of a crowd of discordant cries, dulled by distance into a mournful harmony, like that of the rising tide or of a storm brewing (Clark & Sykes 247).

These examples should give some insight into why Baudelaire lives on in English, while many of our own poets—even much more recent poets, poets like Yeats, or Dylan Thomas—for all their beauty and powerful rhythms, seem to call to us from further afield.

Scots as a Solution

The English have their Baudelaires. The Americans too. And World English has generated many other Baudelaires on the internet in recent years. But there is a lesser-known Scottish tradition, which has produced powerful results. James Robertson's versions, to my ear, remain among the most piercing voices that break though into modern English with a guttural, gutsy, but startlingly poetic lyricism.

For my own part, I believe Scots can serve as a means of avoiding a whole host of bad habits in translation. Scots poets are keenly aware of "orality," the trace of the oral tradition in written verse. They listen to the sound-patterning of phrases, and they assert rhythms of their own. Scots writers are very much in tune with an oral tradition, and because they are so preoccupied with rejecting the neutral stylized formality of Standard English, they have developed an ear for the original, the authentic, and the powerfully expressive. Scots poets are not simply interested in saying things, they are interested in saying them right. They are interested in making an impact. And that is part of the performance that is latent, but nevertheless very present in their written works.

As translators, Scots translators are making a difference. This is not so much a choice or a strategy as an inevitable fact of existence. By striving to bring the foreign home into a language appropriate to their public, they are upsetting standards and norms. They are therefore "faithfully deviant." They "pervert" accepted practices, while striving to make something sound "natural," natural to us Scots.

How are we to interpret this within contemporary debates on translation practices and the ethics of translating? Are Scots "domesticating" their authors? Are they making them strange? Are Scots translators "foreignizers," to use the terms of Lawrence

Venuti (1995)? Ultimately, they are doing both. They are making things strikingly strange and original by bringing them into a form acceptable to an audience which would most probably reject the flat colorless style of standard English prose.

For this reason, I have chosen to translate some of Baudelaire's poems in prose into Borders Scots. By firmly anchoring Baudelaire in dialect and in familiar language, I hope to make him accessible and plain, while allowing the irrepressible beauty of his prose poems to shine forth from that prosaic plainness. I will quote two examples from a co-edited book project for a Scots Baudelaire, on which Tom Hubbard and I are currently at work.

A Baudelaire for the Borders?

The Stranger

Whae dae ye love maist, ma strange wee maun, tell us: yer fither, yer mither, yer sister or yer brither?
I have nae fither, nae mither, nae sister nor nae brither.
Yer friends?
Now thair's a word, a dinae ken the meanin ov.
Yer country?
I dinae ken whit latitude that land lies upon.

I have tried to reproduce lyrical alliterations in the last line and made the most of like sounds in "brither" and "fither." And I have opted for speech rhythms that I have tried to reproduce in free-cadenced phrasing.

My translation will inevitably perturb English-speakers, and indeed Scots dialects are so numerous and so specific that other Scots might feel like tampering with some of my wording. But my intention is to bring Baudelaire back home to the Borders and to lift up the Borders to Baudelaire's lyricism.

One of the editors of *Baudelaire in English,* Carol Clark, includes her own version of the same prose poem. As one might expect, given her scathing criticism of Symons, she opts for plain neutral prose. But to my mind, she does not manage to avoid the

---

Latinate syntax and the diction of French origin, and these failings mar her translation, leaving it laborious and uninteresting.

The Stranger

"Whom do you love best, puzzling man, tell us: your father, your mother, your sister or your brother?"

"I have no father no mother, no sister and no brother."

"Your friends?"

"Now you are using a word whose meaning to this day remains unknown to me."

"Your country?"

"I do not know in which latitude it lies."

(Clark & Sykes 235)

By rights, Clark's translation should be closer to us than the works of Baudelaire's other translators. It should be closer to us than the American versions of the thirties. And yet, Clark seems to fall prey to the failing of following the syntax. She tries to translate neither Baudelaire nor his French. And she ends up translating his French into "French," that rather hollow-sounding, elevated English prose that seems to derive from no place, no dialect, and nobody. In the final analysis, I would ask whether her translation is not "voiceless."

Lest this should appear to be turning into another round of the Border Wars between the Scots and the English, I should stress that a Geordie or a Yorkshire translator might equally produce a dialect translation that avoids Clark's failings and produces a more convincing and more poetic prose. As we have seen, many translators manage to avoid producing a poetical offering that clings to the ideal of an elevated and dignified "Frenchified" English prose. Scots is simply one strategy among others. Scots produces one more Baudelaire among many voices that are making the poet heard in various varieties of English today.

I will end with one longer extract from a translation of Baudelaire's *Le Mauvais Vitrier* (1975) and let readers decide whether dialect translation helps the translator get out of the rut of slavishly reproducing a diction and syntax that proves inappropriate in English. The idea is to make a voice heard, in new rhythms, new sounds, but in rhythms and sounds that work within the prose poem as a whole and that work within the linguistic community into which the poet is being invited. I have highlighted these rhythms by opting for line-by-line free verse. In this passage, about a mean, practical prank that a layabout plays on a glazier, the lyrical subject ponders the nature of his malicious desires. This takes him into the realm of analytical contemplation. But as the intellectual carves up and examines his own soul, the prose must remain both personal and abstract. The language must not fall into that nostalgic melancholy poetry that the English associate with the Scots. It should reproduce the hard analytical pithy poetry; that form of contemplation, which is both down to earth, but capable of precision, a style of thinking and expression that Burns made famous. The reader must judge to what extent my effort succeeds.

> Please understand me weel, there's a state of mystification
> That cannot be explained or analyzed.
> That sudden state of surprise cannot be broken doon
> Or attributed tae reflection. "Hysterical"
> The doctors call it. And thase that have mare intuition
> speak of "satanic malice." Whatever!
> That ardent desire drains all our energy and sends us
> Catapultin' towards calamitous actions
> and the abuse of conventions.

The narrator gloats over the fact that he has wasted the window-framer's time by making him heave his wares up to the garret flat where he lives. And he takes malicious pleasure in haranguing him for not bringing any color into the lives of the poor by offering stained glass windows. The diatribe must be both supercilious and ridiculous, despicable and base, and it must smack of the bitterness of back-street brawls. At least, this is the tone I have tried to achieve.

> Apen moothed and heavin hard he stared,
> As I apened up the door, awaitin me
> Tae inspect his pretty range of panes, But I
> Frowned, wrathful, and exclaimed: "The very nerve!
> Ye should be ashamed! Not a single coloured pane!

Nae pink, nae red, nae blue, nae magic colours
Or panes fri paradise? Ye geet limmer!
Hoo dare ye insult the puir, strollin roon this squalor
Withoot the wares tae display life in a' its colour."
With that I booted him a'er the threshold 'n halfway
Doon the stairs tae the fifth flair.

This is not a Frenchman speaking, but a Scot. The question is whether that Scot speaks with the same verve and energy as the perverted poet, who rejoiced in malice with that magical gift of dissecting his own guts and offering up his findings to the amusement of his audience.

Works Cited

Baudelaire, Charles. *Œuvres Complètes*. 1975. Vol. 1. Ligugé: Gallimard (Pléiade edition), 1997. 2 vols.

_____. *The Flowers of Evil*. 1993. Trans. James McGowan. Oxford, UK: Oxford World's Classics, 1998.

_____. *Frae the Flouers o Evil: Baudelaire in Scots*. Trans. James Robertson. Kingskettle, Fife: Kettillonia, 2001.

Clark, Carol & Robert Sykes, eds. *Baudelaire in English*. New York: Penguin Books, 1997.

Eliot, T. S. *Selected Prose*. London: Penguin, 1953.

Levý, Jiří. *Umění Překladu* (Art of Translation). Prague: State Publishing House, 1963.

_____. *Die literarische Übersetzung: Theorie einer Kunstgattung*. Frankfurt am Main: Athenäum, 1969.

_____. *The Art of Translation*. Trans. Patrick Corness. Philadelphia: John Benjamins Press, 2011.

Meschonnic, Henri. *Critique du rythme: anthropologie historique du langage*. Paris: Verdier, 1982.

_____. *Poétique du traduire*. Paris: Verdier, 1999.

Pound, Ezra. *Selected Poems 1908–1969*. London: Faber & Faber, 1975.

Scott, Clive. *Translating Baudelaire*. Exeter: Exeter UP, 2000.

Seleskovitch, Danica & Marianne Lederer. *Interpréter pour traduire*. Paris: Didier, 1984.

Shakespeare, William. *The Sonnets*. Ed. M. R. Ridley. London: Everyman's Library, 1988.

Supervert, ed. *Charles Baudelaire's Fleurs du mal/Flowers of Evil*. Supervert 32C, Inc., New York. 1 Feb. 2004. Web. 17 Feb. 2014. <www.fleursdumal.org>.

Venuti, Lawrence. *The Translator's Invisibility: A History of Translation*. London, Routledge, 1995.

Overcoming Despair: "Le Voyage" and its Ethical Implications_____

Edward K. Kaplan

> Tout homme qui n'accepte pas les conditions de la vie, vend son âme.
> —Baudelaire, *Les Paradis artificiels*,
> *Œuvres Complètes*, 1: 438

In my adult cohabitation with Baudelaire and his works, I have found most illuminating, and sustaining, this approach of Yves Bonnefoy:

> Ainsi, donnant la valeur suprême à ce qui n'est que mortel, dressant les êtres dans l'horizon de la mort and par la mort, je puis dire, je crois, que Baudelaire invente la mort, sachant désormais qu'elle n'est pas cette négation de l'Idée qu'aimait en secret Racine, mais un aspect profond de la présence des êtres, en un sens leur seule réalité (114).

Yves Bonnefoy—faithful to his post-Christian "reinvention" of hope—has defined Baudelaire's ethical thrust: his love of mortal, fallible, even sinful human beings. An ethical reading of Baudelaire assumes the preciousness of "la présence des êtres," real persons in the world.

Especially germane are Søren Kierkegaard's analyses of three dimensions of human experience: the aesthetic, the ethical, and the religious. Briefly put, for Baudelaire, (1) the "aesthetic" includes voluptuous pleasure, sensory or imaginative; (2) the "ethical" involves reality as such and especially relationships with (autonomous) human subjects; (3) the "religious" confronts the question of God and transcendent meaning. These conceptual distinctions can help readers interpret Baudelaire's various masks— his provocations, his ambivalence, his sentimentality or genuine compassion; the positive values are often disguised by what I call

---

"ethical irony" (Kaplan, "Baudelaire and the Vicissitudes..." & "Baudelaire through Kierkegaard...").

My contention is that the underlying premise of the entire collection is condensed in the word "Death" as metaphor of human finitude. The concluding section of *Les Fleurs du mal*, "La Mort," recapitulates a conversion from otherworldly, Romantic idealism through disillusion to arrive at an ethical realism. The three poems Baudelaire added in 1861 force us to reinterpret the three visionary sonnets of the 1857 conclusion ("La Mort des amants," "La Mort des pauvres," and "La Mort des artistes"). Three poems added in 1861—"La Fin de la journée," "Le rêve d'un curieux," and especially "Le Voyage"—focus on the brute facts of human mortality (Kaplan, "Courage of Baudelaire..." & "Baudelaire and the Battle..."). In Kierkegaard's terms: Baudelaire eschews the aesthetic and the religious for the ethical. (It echoes the other grand poem of self-examination, "Un Voyage à Cythère," which surpasses despair as it strives toward religious hope, or personal redemption.)

"Le Voyage" conveys a spiritual itinerary that can serve as a hermeneutical key to the 1861 edition of *Les Fleurs du mal*. First and foremost, architecturally, it is the longest poem (144 lines), and it marks the book's conclusion. Along with inevitable repetitions and inconsistencies, the poem's thematic structure is linear. The poem itself, however, develops a sort of spiral motion, its eight numbered parts echoing previous voyages, such as the first and longest section, "Spleen et Idéal" (Lawler, Runyon).

"Le Voyage" not only recapitulates unsuccessful quests for the Ideal throughout *Les Fleurs du mal*; it elaborates complex emotions that allow poet (and readers) to integrate what are, in strict logic, irreducible contradictions. Poetic emotions display a cognitive function greater than ideas or ideologies (Kaplan, "Courage of Baudelaire"; Ricœur).

Inner and Outer Worlds

Our "ethical" reading begins with a clear recognition of the limits of desire. The six stanzas of Part I posit the duality of experience

---

versus imagination, the mental versus the objective dimensions of the human condition, as it begins:

Pour l'enfant, amoureux de cartes et d'estampes,
L'univers est égal à son vaste appétit.
Ah! Que le monde est grand à la clarté des lampes!
Aux yeux du souvenir que le monde est petit! (1–4).

The chiasmus codifies the idealized "cartes," "estampes," "lampes" versus lived experience ("le souvenir").

Monde grand lampes
Souvenir   monde petit

For the child, free imagination is primary. Adult dreamers are often impelled by the need to escape.

That is why positive and negative emotions are mixed from the very start. In an act of solidarity, the poet associates himself with all humankind driven by desire ("nous partons"):

Un matin nous partons, le cerveau plein de flamme,
Le cœur gros de rancune et de désirs amers,
Et nous allons, suivant le rhythme de la lame,
Berçant notre infini sur le fini des mers (5–8).

So far, the dreamer-voyagers remain free. Yet, dissatisfied adults soon discover that their creative passions ("le cerveau plein de flamme") are first motivated by an admixture of resentment ("rancune") a bitterness or anger ("désirs amers") that chains them to the world. At the same time, passivity and trust seem to provide some confidence, "suivant le rhythme de la lame, / Berçant notre infini sur le fini des mers" (7–8). Ironically, imagination can feel infinite in relation to the sea, a conventional image of a natural infinite.

The remainder of Part I emphasizes the inherent conflict between desire and experience. It is a sad story, although the poet repeatedly acknowledges the persistence of passion. The heart's alloy of anger and hope expresses the fundamental ambiguity of desire, either seeking absolute freedom within imagination or gratification within the world.

The next stanzas evoke various attempts to be free, while stressing the dangers of imaginative autonomy. There are two types of voyagers: escapists, who fall prey to Circe (the enchantress of *The Odyssey*), sensuality, and false ideals, "astrologues noyés dans les yeux d'une femme" (11); and realists, "vrais voyageurs . . . qui partent pour partir" (17), those who are able to detach themselves from specific goals. Here, "Le Voyage" follows, not a didactic, linear structure, but a spiral, in which analogous situations recur, and then again progress, but without achieving a definitive resolution.

There are good reasons to seek escape, such as political alienation ("une patrie infâme") or dysfunctional families ("Horreur de leur berceau," 9–10). A symbolic Woman summarizes the temptations of voluptuous pleasures, sensual or drug induced: "La Circé tyrannique aux dangereux parfums" (12). According to Baudelaire's notorious misogyny, Woman represents artificial paradises, the "aesthetic," and its ecstatic though temporary release from Time: "Pour n'être pas changés en bêtes, ils s'enivrent / D'espace et de lumière et de cieux embrasés"(13–14). The key word here is "s'enivrer," for such intoxication is fleeting and fictitious.

The last two stanzas of Part I define the authentic quest, anticipating the poem's "lesson." Baudelaire favors the gratuitous journey, independent of preordained goals:

> Mais les vrais voyageurs sont ceux-là seuls qui partent
> Pour partir; cœurs légers, semblables aux ballons,
> De leur fatalité jamais ils ne s'écartent
> Et, sans savoir pourquoi, disent toujours: Allons! (17–20).

True voyagers are able to combine mental freedom with a tragic sense of its limits ("leur fatalité"). Incorporating these contradictory perceptions may help cultivate the courage to strive without guarantees, to take risks, "cœurs légers . . . sans savoir pourquoi [ils] disent toujours: Allons!". The not-yet-known (the mystery) challenges the imagination and suggests that the most meaningful goals are unknowable. (These images reappear at the poem's conclusion.)

The next two stanzas reiterate the process, spiraling back thematically. Aesthetic freedom appears in the poetic lexicon of reverie: "ceux-là . . . qui rêvent . . . / De vastes voluptés, changeantes, inconnues, / Et dont l'esprit humain n'a jamais su le nom!" (23–24). (This insight is echoed by the capitalized "Inconnu" in the poem's very last line.)

Anatomy of Desire

The voyagers now denounce the utopian ideologies of the century. (With irony, Baudelaire dedicated the poem to Maxime Du Camp, traveler and friend of Flaubert, and, unlike Baudelaire, a believer in Progress.) Goaded by direct experience, the poet diagnoses civilization as afflicted with a pervasive *ennui*, a pathological apathy (akin to boredom, the usual translation)—but, more accurately, *ennui* is a clinical depression and an antecedent to suicidal despair.

Part II of "Le Voyage" inaugurates a methodical demolition of several ideals that remain beyond reach. The positive quest is first stimulated by humankind's most rudimentary motivation, "Curiosité" (27). A ship typifies the pursuit of easy answers: "Notre âme est un trois mâts cherchant son Icarie" (33), referring to a book by the utopian Étienne Cabet, titled *Voyage en Icarie* (1840). But, once again, fantasy cannot supplant objective reality.

Echoing previous situations, Part II lists more failures. Hyperbolic illusions are evoked and immediately crushed: "'Amour!... gloire... bonheur!' Enfer, c'est un écueil!" (36). The dialectic of hope/despair is condensed in these maritime images: "Un Eldorado promis par le Destin; / L'Imagination qui dresse son orgie / Ne trouve qu'un récif aux clartés du matin" (37–40).

Imagination, here, carries a negative valence, conveyed by images of drunkenness, inebriation, not free inspiration; and so experience yields only "pays chimériques" (41). As mirages brutally collapse, human existence itself becomes poisoned, making "le gouffre plus amer" (44), spilling into an overwhelming pessimism.

Yet, there remains an implicit optimism within Baudelaire's grim diagnosis. Hope persists, despite repeated failures. The poet even announces "Hope"—a propitious humanism, a substitute for religion or ideology as defined by the modern mind in search of absolute meaning: "L'Homme, dont jamais l'espérance n'est lasse" (31). Why do we persist? Why not succumb to despair?

Human solidarity introduces a solution, as the poet initiates a dialogue with the experienced travelers. The two stanzas of Part III (49–57) become more analytical as they evoke an energizing mixture of emotions. The poet is surprised by the courage of these "Étonnants voyageurs!"(49), who, nevertheless, serve up yet another series of shattered illusions. Echoing the poem's opening stanza, the poet celebrates another inspired boat (a sort of proleptic "bateau ivre" of Rimbaud). Poet, voyagers, and readers exclaim as one:

> Nous voulons voyager sans vapeur et sans voile!
> Faites, pour égayer l'ennui de nos prisons,
> Passer sur nos esprits, tendus comme une toile,
> Vos souvenirs avec leurs cadres d'horizons (53–56).

Seasoned, experienced voyagers recognize that such ecstasies are of no avail: "Nous avons vu des astres / Et des flots; /. . . Et . . . / Nous nous sommes souvent ennuyés, comme ici" (57–60). Line sixty both summarizes past failures and inaugurates yet another, but more realistic, departure.

Cognitive Mixtures

Part IV introduces a new focus, and a new interpretive paradigm. No longer are we stymied by the rigid, unsubtle dialectic of illusion/disillusion. Poetry is especially apt at integrating conflicting ideas and emotions. Poetry can convey the inchoate complexities of existential struggle, the quest for meaning in spite of overwhelming opposition or indifference. Contrary perceptions of the world can somehow be reconciled, but never eliminated.

Two metaphors of desire evoke the energies inherent in the "curiosité" (27) (or dissatisfaction) with which humankind is both afflicted and blessed. Images of fire had activated the original, naïve departure, "le cerveau plein de flamme" (5). Now the experienced voyagers, from their mature viewpoint, report a positive force within: "La gloire des cités . . . / Allumaient dans nos coeurs une ardeur inquiète / De plonger dans un ciel au reflet alléchant" (61–64). The words "allumer," "ardeur," and "plonger" are emotionally powerful and affirmative, while the underlying passion or "ardeur" remains mixed, "inquiète."

Such oxymorons attest to the complexity of the voyagers' self-awareness, the affective mixture that energizes the entire poem—as well as the final section, "La Mort." (In addition, "inquiète" [63] is emphasized by the diaeresis, forming a diphthong [in-qui-yete] and preparing us for *sou-ci-yeux* [68]). These images all reappear at the conclusion of "Le Voyage," repeating "plonger," a forceful verb that could signify, according to its context, either enthusiastic self-assertion or surrender—suicide.

These internal contradictions give rise to a complex analysis, through metaphor, of anxiety. The premise: "Et toujours le désir nous rendait soucieux!" (68). The negative pole of "soucieux" (which I translate here as "anxious") is likewise highlighted by the extra syllable.

The next stanza develops an extended metaphor of anxiety-motivated desire. First, the tenor, the basic meaning: "—La jouissance ajoute au désir de la force" (69). The metaphorical vehicle elaborates this relationship between energy and desire: "Désir, vieil arbre à qui le plaisir sert d'engrais, / Cependant que grossit et durcit ton écorce, / Tes branches veulent voir le soleil de plus près!" (69–71) Gratification ("le plaisir") both exhausts and stimulates; while the excrement "engrais" fertilizes *Les Fleurs du mal*.

Ennui can thus play a positive role in the poet's resistance to despair. A crust of insensitivity to ennui (or existential anxiety) develops—for the "écorce of apathy" is a defensive detachment from adverse feelings—from despair, or from fear of change as such. Energy can prevail over inhibitions: "Grandiras-tu toujours, grand arbre plus vivace que le cyprès?" (73–74). The words "toujours" and "vivace" and the repeated "grand" and "grandir" are assertive, as are the positive epithets of the cypress tree: "immortel," "incorruptible," and "religieux." They are also funereal.

A Grim Hypothesis

In Part VI, these and additional exotic journeys lead to an utterly pessimistic conclusion, as the experienced voyagers challenge the still naïve "cerveaux enfantins" (84) of readers.
Another stage has been completed, as the voyagers attest:

> "Pour ne pas oublier la chose capitale,
> Nous avons vu partout, et sans l'avoir cherché,
> Du haut jusques en bas de l'échelle fatale,
> Le spectacle ennuyeux de l'immortel péché:" (85–88).

Baudelaire has translated ennui into an audacious theological claim, compatible with the authoritative Joseph de Maistre. To be human is to be inherently contaminated with Original Sin. Desire appears to be irremediably corrupt. Men and women are equally perverse. Baudelaire seems to have modified his notorious misogyny as he reviles the will to power of all persons:

> La femme, esclave vile, orgueilleuse et stupide,
> Sans rire d'adorant et s'aimant sans dégoût;
> L'homme, tyran goulu, paillard, dur et cupide,
> Esclave de l'esclave et ruisseau dans l'égout; (89–92).

Humankind takes pleasure in torturing itself. The poet lists some of the culprits: "Le bourreau qui jouit, le martyre qui sanglote" (83), politicians, "Le poison du pouvoir énervant le despote,/ Et le peuple amoureux du fouet abrutissant" (95–96); religion as an opportunity for depraved sensuality; even remorse, on the path to self-purification, can be corrupted: "La Sainteté, / Comme en un lit un délicat se vautre, / Dans les clous et le crin cherchant la volupté"(98–100).
The next stanza names and then invalidates two solutions: (1) rebel against God: "'Ô mon semblable, ô mon maître, je te maudis!'" (104); or (2) escape into fantasy or madness, "dans

l'opium immense!" (107). The insight that civilization supports no transcendent values leads to this devastating diagnosis: "—Tel est du globe entier l'éternel bulletin" (108). The image of the human condition as a hospital summarizes the dreadful enslavement of will, even of the will to live.

The Wisdom of Finitude

Three sections remain, all recapitulating the preceding examples, while passing beyond. The foundational insight: voyagers (and poet) gain an "amer savoir," a bitter wisdom. Now ennui can become a springboard to hope and a realistic faith.

The first stanza of Part VII recapitulates the pessimistic view:

> Amer savoir, celui qu'on tire du voyage!
> Le monde, monotone et petit, aujourd'hui,
> Hier, demain, toujours, nous fait voir notre image:
> Une oasis d'horreur dans un désert d'ennui! (109–112).

On the level of imagery, we have returned to the initial departure, motivated, as it was, by negative emotions: "le coeur gros de rancune et de désirs amers" (6). The difference is that now, renouncing illusory goals, the experienced voyagers gain wisdom. In a word, they no longer deny reality.

The first two stanzas of Part VII (109–116) consolidate a major turning point. We achieve a radical transformation of consciousness—from idolatrous pursuit of idealized goals—absolute desire—to an acceptance of humankind's finite condition. We acknowledge the unconquerable power of Time, of mortality, symbolized in Baudelaire's poetic lexicon by the word "Death" (Bonnefoy).

However, the remaining stanzas of Part VII do not develop this logical trajectory in a didactic fashion, as a syllogism would produce a conclusion. Rather, they dwell upon the central problem, the meaning of mortality. Our interpretation of the poem, the section, and the entire collection depends upon our understanding of these words (Time, Death):

Faut-il partir? Rester? Si tu peux rester, reste;
Pars, s'il le faut. L'un court, et l'autre se tapit
Pour tromper l'ennemi vigilant et funeste,
Le Temps! Il est, hélas! des coureurs sans répit (113–116).

The mature voyagers do not evade or deny anxiety; they reinterpret it. Ennui motivates action instead of apathy. Their tragic wisdom contains a new type of bitterness, which fortifies self-assertion. We are released from overly specific goals and so overcome our fear of failure. We accept Death, the finitude of body and mind that is part and parcel of life.

The poet cites examples of those (who like himself) have conquered their fear of death: "Comme le juif errant et comme les apôtres" (117). Time is a "rétiaire infâme" (119), an existential gladiator as it were, conquered by the courageous poet.

This wisdom, first and foremost, inspires courage, far beyond the impulse to escape. Parallel lines of Parts VII and VIII trace a tragic joy that arises from heroic battles with finitude. Time, the "ennemi vigilant et funeste" (115), becomes the dependable "vieux capitaine" (117). Time as "enemy" embodies the inescapable limits of a person's life. Baudelaire repeats the contrast: "Lorsque enfin il [le Temps] mettra le pied sur notre échine" (112), becomes "Ô Mort, vieux capitaine, il est temps! Levons l'ancre!" (137). These final exclamations reflect the affirmative charge of Part VII: "Nous pourrons espérer et crier: En avant!" (122). (Cf. "sans savoir pourquoi, disent toujours: Allons!" 20).

Now everything seems possible. The verbs are in the future tense; the heart remains joyful, though it may still include a heavy burden of disillusionment. Indeed, realistic confrontation with the implacable world must subsume both terror and joy: "Nous nous embarquerons sur la mer des Ténèbres / Avec le cœur joyeux d'un jeune passager" (125–126). The verbs focus the energy of this courageous faith.

Even so, spiraling back, the wise traveler remains vulnerable to distractions, such as the Lotus Eaters who deny death, inviting oblivion though psychotropic drugs: "Venez vous eniverer de la douceur étrange / De cette après-midi qui n'a jamais de fin" (131–132). Even friendship can compromise free will: Pylades or Electra, "A l'accent familier nous devinons le spectre" (133).

Finally, the great, ambiguous conclusion. The two stanzas of Part VIII recall previous departures and return to their inception. But ambivalence is no longer paralyzing. Rationality cleansed of illusions can still arouse fear, even anguish; specific solutions remain in the dark. Yet somehow the heart is liberated. A new departure echoes the original one:

> Ô Mort, vieux capitaine, il est temps! Levons l'ancre!
> Ce pays nous ennuie, ô Mort! Appareillons!
> Si le ciel et la mer sont noirs comme de l'encre,
> Nos coeurs que tu connais sont remplis de rayons!
>
> Verse-nous ton poison pour qu'il nous réconforte!
> Nous voulons, tant ce feu nous brûle le cerveau,
> Plonger au fond du gouffre, Enfer ou Ciel, qu'importe?
> Au fond de l'Inconnu pour trouver du *nouveau*! (137–144).

Readers must make crucial interpretive decisions: the meaning and valence of the words "Mort" and "poison." As I have suggested, "Death" in the lexicon of *Les Fleurs du mal* can refer both to the universal fragility of human existence (e.g., the limits of desire) or to the cessation of biological function. Likewise, the "poison" that fortifies us can be construed either as a marker of suicide or the risks of inspiration, as in Baudelaire's essay on hashish (*Œuvres complètes*, 1: 429–30).

In "Le Voyage" life conquers death. Creative energy takes over. "Le ciel" and "la mer" are two images of the infinite, which also represent the Ideal. The earth is still blanketed with ennui. No escape is possible. The liberated mind illuminates the ink-blankness of "la mer des Ténèbres," i.e. meaninglessness (or mystery). More precisely, this image evokes the act of writing, the medium of Baudelaire's most objective confrontation with existence. The poet now forcefully entrusts himself to the Unknown. This personification points to an ultimate meaning, elusive, but within reach.

The italicized *"nouveau"* is Baudelaire's final word: it is both an aesthetic and an ethical category. Our artistic vision must be free from preconceptions, as we see abundantly in Baudelaire's art criticism. The unspecified "nouveau" conveys openness to whatever the world might bestow. The poet now trusts himself, and with a mixture of joy and terror, embraces whatever life—or art—has to offer.

Overcoming Despair

"Le Voyage" helps us understand other poems that confront despair. One example must suffice: "Le Jeu," number ninety-six in the section "Fleurs du mal," depicts a choice between life or death, existential courage versus suicidal anguish. In "Le Voyage," "la mer des Ténèbres" rejects death as such. "Le Jeu," by contrast, also asks if life is worth living at the edge of despair.

"Le Jeu" depicts an allegory of the human condition as a den of dying gamblers and prostitutes, to which he silently, passively submits ("taciturne," "muet"). The poet then takes center stage as he interprets "le noir tableau":

> Moi-même, dans un coin de l'antre taciturne,
> Je me vis accoudé, froid, muet, enviant,
>
> Enviant de ces gens la passion tenace,
> De ces vieilles putains la funèbre gaîté,
> Et tous gaillardement trafiquant à ma face,
> L'un de son vieil honneur, l'autre de sa beauté! (15–20).

The poet is surprised and then inspired by their stubborn will to live, their "passion tenace," as he exclaims with frosty irony:

> Et mon cœur s'effraya d'envier maint pauvre homme
> Courant avec ferveur à l'abîme béant,
> Et qui, soûl de son sang, préférerait en somme
> La douleur à la mort et l'enfer au néant! (21–24).

Suffering and humiliation (simulacra of lapsed love) are stronger than death! This is an astounding conclusion (provisional, of course) to a forty-year-old poet, who had more than once attempted suicide and whose apparent pessimism can overwhelm vulnerable readers. The poet repeats the word "envy" three times, and it stands out in the enjambement. Herein lies the irony that saves the poem from mere didacticism: one can "envy" (or wish for) such a degraded life only in contrast to annihilation.

Baudelaire concludes: Being is more worthy than non-being. Finite life is sacred. The poet's strange, twisted, but compassionate insight is but one glimpse of this affirmation, articulated by theologian Abraham Heschel (84): "Just to be is a blessing. Just to live is holy."

Note

This essay extends and refines previous analyses in Kaplan 1978, 1979, 1993.

Works Cited

Baudelaire, Charles. *Œuvres complètes*. Ed. Claude Pichois. Paris: Gallimard, Bibliothèque de la Pléiade, 1975.

Bonnefoy, Yves. "L'acte et le lieu de la poésie." *L'Improbable et autres essais*. Paris: Mercure de France, 1980: 105–31.

Heschel, Abraham Joshua. "To Grow in Wisdom." *The Insecurity of Freedom*. New York: Farrar, Straus & Giroux, 1966.

Kaplan, Edward K. "The Courage of Baudelaire and Rimbaud: The Anxiety of Faith," *The French Review* 70.2 (December 1978): 294–306.

_____. "Baudelaire and the Battle with Finitude: "'La Mort,' Conclusion of *Les Fleurs du mal*." *French Forum* 4.3 (September 1979): 219–31.

_____. "Baudelaire and the Vicissitudes of Venus: Ethical Irony in *Les Fleurs du mal*." Ed. Emanuel Mikel Jr. *The Shaping of Text: Style, Imagery, and Structure in French Literature*. Lewisburg: Bucknell UP, 1993: 113–30.

_____. "Baudelaire through Kierkegaard. Art, Fallibility, and Faith." Ed. Joseph Acquisto. *Thinking Poetry. Philosophical Approaches to*

Nineteenth-Century French Poetry. New York: Palgrave Macmillan, 2013: 9–24.

Lawler, James R. *Poetry and Moral Dialectic: Baudelaire's Secret Architecture*. Madison, NJ: Fairleigh Dickenson UP, 1997.

Runyan, Randolph. *Intratextual Baudelaire: The Sequential Fabric of* Les Fleurs du mal *and* Le Spleen de Paris. Columbus: Ohio State UP, 2010.

Ricoeur, Paul. *Fallible Man*. Trans. Charles Kelbley. Chicago: Henry Regnery, 1965.

RESOURCES

Chronology of Charles Baudelaire's Life————

1821	Charles Baudelaire is born on April 9 at 13 rue Hautefeuille, Paris, to Joseph-François Baudelaire and Caroline Dufayis.
1827	Joseph-François dies on February 10, at age 66. Charles' mother is 33.
1828	November 8: Caroline Baudelaire marries Commandant (later General) Jacques Aupick.
1832	Charles and his mother move to Lyon, where Aupick is stationed. In October, Charles enrolls at the Collège de Lyon, as a boarder.
1836	March 1: Baudelaire returns to Paris where he enrolls at the Lycée Louis-le-Grand, again as a boarder.
1838	Baudelaire visits the Pyrenees with his mother and Aupick.
1839	April 18: Baudelaire is expelled from the Lycée Louis-le-Grand for lack of discipline. August 12: he finishes his studies at the Pension Levêque et Bailly and receives his bachelor's degree.
1841	Baudelaire is pursuing a wayward existence in Paris. His family disapproves of his reluctance to take up any career apart from that of a writer and are anxious to detach him from his bohemian lifestyle. Accordingly, they send him on a voyage to Calcutta (Kolkata) in India. However, Baudelaire stops at the islands of Réunion and Mauritius and chooses not to proceed to India. He is now seriously writing poems, but many of

the pieces dating from this time are not published until much later.

1842	Baudelaire arrives back in France on February 15. He forms friendships with the poets Théophile Gautier and Théodore de Banville and with the photographer Nadar. He begins his lifelong relationship with Jeanne Duval, his "Black Venus," the mulatto actress who is the subject of most of his love poems. He's in debt—and will continue to be for the rest of his life.
1843	Baudelaire rents an apartment at the Hôtel Pimodan (formerly the Hôtel du Lauzun, though it has remained known by that name), at 17 quai d'Anjou, Paris.
1844	Baudelaire's extravagance provokes his family into nominating the lawyer Narcisse Ancelle as trustee of his inheritance from his father.
1845	April: his seventy-two-page review of the year's Salon is published: it praises the painter Delacroix, who is a key influence on Baudelaire's aesthetics. His translations of Edgar Allan Poe begin to appear. On June 30, he makes a failed attempt at suicide.
1846	May: Baudelaire's essay on the Salon of 1846 is published; on the back of the volume, it is announced that that a collection of his poems is forthcoming; it is to be entitled *Les Lesbiennes*. Eleven years later, this will appear as *Les Fleurs du mal*.
1847	In January, his short story "La Fanfarlo" is published. He falls in love with Marie Daubrun, an actress. The Salon of 1847 rejects Courbet's portrait of Baudelaire.
1848	Aupick is posted to Constantinople; before setting out, he rebukes Baudelaire for not ending his relationship

with Jeanne Duval. Baudelaire breaks with his mother. February: France is in revolution; there are further uprisings in June. Baudelaire is seen on the barricades, threatening to shoot General Aupick. He joins a newspaper venture, *Le Salut publique*, but only two issues are published. His translation of Poe's *Magnetic Revelation* is published. A collection of poems, *Les Limbes*, is announced—it was previously announced as *Les Lesbiennes* and is the future *Les Fleurs du mal.*

1850	Baudelaire is in Dijon, believed to be fleeing his creditors, or seeking a job on a local newspaper. On January 9, he is joined there by Jeanne Duval. Baudelaire has secondary symptoms of syphilis, contracted some years before.
1851	His *Les Limbes* poems, that will later appear in *Les Fleurs du mal*, are published in April in the *Messager de l'Assemblée.* In May, his first study of wine and hashish is published. June: the Aupicks return from Constantinople; his mother finds Baudelaire living in squalor. She later joins Aupick in Madrid. December 2: Coup d'état; Louis-Napoléon, France's first President, declares himself Emperor and takes the title of Napoléon III.
1852	In March and April, Baudelaire's first essay on Poe is published. He breaks with Jeanne Duval, promises to oversee her financial affairs, but insists that he will never see her again. He begins his friendship with Madame Apollonie Sabatier.
1853	Translations of Poe's tales are published. Baudelaire is in a state of physical and mental collapse; Jeanne Duval is ill and penniless.

1854	Baudelaire sends poems (anonymously) to Mme. Sabatier.
1855	June 1: Eighteen poems, under the title *Les Fleurs du mal*, are published in the periodical *La Revue des deux mondes*. July 8: Baudelaire's essay *De l'essence du rire* is published.
1856	March: publication of Poe translations as *Histoires extraordinaires*. There is another break-up of the on-off relationship with Jeanne Duval. In December, Baudelaire signs a contract with the publisher Poulet-Malassis for a book-length collection of his poems, *Les Fleurs du mal*.
1857	January–February: trial of Flaubert and his novel *Madame Bovary*. March: publication of further Poe translations as *Nouvelles histoires extraordinaires*. Gen. Aupick dies on April 28. June 25: *Les Fleurs du mal* is published, in an edition of 1,300 copies. August 20: *Les Fleurs du mal* and its author are on trial for offending public morals. Baudelaire is fined 300 francs; six of the poems are suppressed. Victor Hugo praises the book. Baudelaire's essay on Flaubert, a kindred spirit, appears on October 18.
1858	May: publication of Baudelaire's translation of Poe's novel, *The Narrative of Arthur Gordon Pym of Nantucket*. September: the first part of *Les Paradis artificiels* is published. His health worsening, Baudelaire joins his mother in Honfleur, where she has been living since the death of Gen. Aupick. He resumes his relationship with Jeanne Duval; it is stormy, but they remain together.
1859	Many new poems are published this year, including "L'Albatros" and "Le Voyage." Baudelaire embarks

on the prose work *Mon cœur mis a nu*, a collection of mainly short prose paragraphs and jottings. In June/July his "Salon de 1859", one of his major essays in art criticism, is published.

1860	January 1: Baudelaire sells to his publishers Poulet-Malassis and de Brosse the second and expanded edition of *Les Fleurs du mal*, as well as *Les Paradis artificiels* and his essays on literary and art criticism. He suffers a minor stroke; generally, his health is in decline.
1861	February: publication of second edition of *Les Fleurs du mal*. April/May: publication of *Richard Wagner et Tannhauser à Paris*, in which he praises Wagner zealously. He begins to publish his prose poems. His essay on Hugo also appears. Further symptoms of syphilis. December 11: Baudelaire unsuccessfully applies for membership of the Académie Française. His financial situation deteriorates. Jeanne Duval is hospitalized.
1862	September: Algernon Swinburne publishes his highly favorable essay on Baudelaire in *The Spectator*; this is the first serious appreciation of the poet in English. Also in September, Baudelaire publishes an essay praising the painters Whistler and Manet. November: Baudelaire's publisher, Poulet-Malassis, is bankrupt and is gaoled for non-payment of a printer.
1863	January 13: Baudelaire sells the exclusive rights to publish a third and enlarged edition of *Les Fleurs du mal*, as well as his *Petits poèmes en prose* to the firm of Hetzel (these rights had been previously sold to Poulet-Malassis). Baudelaire takes the money, but Hetzel doesn't receive the manuscripts. Essay on Delacroix, who had recently died on August 13. *Le Peintre de la*

vie moderne is published in *Le Figaro* over November and December.

1864	*Le Figaro*, having published six prose poems as *Le Spleen de Paris*, won't take any more. April 24: Baudelaire, having had enough of France, arrives in Brussels. He remains in Belgium, though he soon comes to loathe the country and its people. He undertakes a disastrous series of lectures and readings in Brussels. In December, *Le Revue de Paris* publishes six new prose poems as *Le Spleen de Paris*. Health and money problems worsen.
1865	Publication of the fifth volume of his translations of Poe's stories as *Histoires grotesques et sérieuses*. In articles, Baudelaire's major successors in French poetry, Mallarmé and Verlaine praise his work.
1866	March: Baudelaire visits the Belgian city of Namur and has a fall at the church of Saint-Loup. On March 30, his right side is paralyzed; he loses the power of speech. He is hospitalized in a Brussels sanatorium. His mother arrives in Brussels and nurses him. April: Poulet-Malassis, now in Belgium, publishes 260 copies of Baudelaire's collection, *Les Épaves*, with a frontispiece by the Namur-based artist Félicien Rops. On July 2, Baudelaire is brought back to Paris.
1867	August 31, 11 a.m.: Baudelaire dies in his mother's arms. On September 2, he is buried in the cemetery of Montparnasse, beside Gen. Aupick.
1868	December. Michel Lévy begins publishing Baudelaire's complete works.

Works by Charles Baudelaire

Poetry
Les Fleurs du mal, 1857 (and subsequent expanded editions)
Les Épaves, 1866
Le Spleen de Paris / Petits poèmes en prose, 1869

Short Fiction
La Fanfarlo, 1847

Translations
Five volumes of Baudelaire's translations of Edgar Allan Poe's works were published
between 1856 and 1865.

Nonfiction
Salon de 1845, 1845
Salon de 1846, 1846
De l'essence du rire, 1855
Les paradis artificiels, 1860
Richard Wagner et Tannhauser à Paris, 1861
Réflexions sur quelques-uns de mes contemporains, 1861
Le peintre de la vie moderne, 1863
Curiosités esthétiques, in *Œuvres complètes*, 1868–70
L'art romantique, in *Œuvres complètes*, 1868–70
Journaux intimes: Fusées; Mon cœur mis à nu; various posthumous editions
Pauvre Belgique, 1953

Major Collected Editions
Œuvres complètes, ed. Jacques Crépet, 1922–53
Œuvres complètes, ed. Claude Pichois, 1975–76

Correspondence

Correspondance, ed. Claude Pichois and Jean Ziegler, 1973

Nouvelles lettres, ed. Claude Pichois, 2000

Bibliography

The secondary literature on Baudelaire is vast, and the following bibliography lists only book-length works with the name Baudelaire in their titles, or which discuss his work at some length. Readers should be aware that there is also much excellent work on the poet in journals and in composite works, as well as in books on nineteenth-century French literature generally (for example, in recent work by Damian Catani and Greg Kerr). The following bibliography should be used together with the Works Cited sections following each essay in the present work and with attention to the various emerging Baudelaire scholars cited in the introduction ("About This Book") in the present work.

An online annual bibliography is issued by the W. T. Bandy Center for Baudelaire and Modern French Studies at Vanderbilt University in Nashville, Tennessee, at http://www.library.vanderbilt.edu/bandy/publications.shtml .

Abbott, Helen. *Between Baudelaire and Mallarmé: Voice, Conversation and Music.* Farnham: Ashgate, 2009.

_____. *Parisian Intersections: Baudelaire's Legacy to Composers.* Oxford: Peter Lang, 2012.

Aggeler, William F. *Baudelaire Judged by Spanish Critics, 1857–1957.* Athens: U of Georgia P, 1971.

Austin, Lloyd James. *L'Univers poétique de Baudelaire: symbolisme et symbolique.* Paris: Mercure de France, 1956.

Baer, Ulrich. *Remnants of Song: Trauma and the Experience of Modernity in Charles Baudelaire and Paul Celan.* Stanford, CA: Stanford UP, 2000.

Benjamin, Walter. *Charles Baudelaire: A Lyric Poet in the Era of High Capitalism.* London: NLB, 1973.

Blin, Georges. *Baudelaire.* Paris: Gallimard, 1939.

Blood, Susan. *Baudelaire and the Aesthetics of Bad Faith.* Stanford, CA: Stanford UP, 1997.

Bonnefoy, Yves. *Baudelaire: la tentation de l'oubli.* Paris: Bibliothèque nationale de France, 2000.

Brunel, Pierre. *Baudelaire et le "puits des magies."* Paris: Corti, 2003.

Burt, Ellen S. *Regard for the Other: Autobiography and Autothanatography in Rousseau, De Quincey, Baudelaire, and Wilde.* Bronx: Fordham UP, 2009.

Calasso, Roberto. *La folie Baudelaire.* Trans. Alastair McEwen. New York: Farrar, Straus & Giroux, 2012.

Carpenter, Scott. *Acts of Fiction: Resistance and Resolution from Sade to Baudelaire.* University Park: Pennsylvania State UP, 1995.

Carrier, David. *High Art: Charles Baudelaire and the Origins of Modernist Painting.* University Park: Pennsylvania State UP, 1996.

Catani, Damian. *Evil: A History in Modern French Literature and Thought. [On Balzac, Baudelaire and later writers]* London: Bloomsbury Academic, 2013.

Chambers, Ross. *The Writing of Melancholy: Modes of Opposition in Early French Modernism. [Flaubert, Baudelaire and others]* Chicago: U of Chicago P, 1993.

Chesters, Graham. *Baudelaire and the Poetics of Craft.* Cambridge, England: Cambridge UP, 1988.

Compagnon, Antoine. *Baudelaire devant l'innombrable.* Paris: Presses universitaires de Paris IV-Sorbonne, 2003.

Coven, Jeffrey. *Baudelaire's Voyages: The Poet and his Painters.* Boston: Little, Brown, 1993.

Crépet, Jacques. *Propos sur Baudelaire.* Paris: Mercure de France, 1957.

DalMolin, Eliane. *Cutting the Body: Representing Woman in Baudelaire's Poetry, Truffaut's Cinema, and Freud's Psychoanalysis.* Ann Arbor, MI: U of Michigan P, 2000.

Evans, David. *Rhythm, Illusion and the Poetic Idea: Baudelaire, Rimbaud, Mallarmé.* Amsterdam & New York: Rodopi, 2004.

Evans, Margery A. *Baudelaire and Intertextuality: Poetry at the Crossroads.* Cambridge: Cambridge UP, 1993.

Fairlie, Alison. *Baudelaire: Les Fleurs du mal.* London: Edward Arnold, 1960.

Hannoosh, Michele. *Baudelaire and Caricature: From the Comic to an Art of Modernity.* University Park: Pennsylvania State UP, 1992.

Hemmings, F. W. J. *Baudelaire the Damned.* London: Hamish Hamilton, 1982.

Hiddleston, James A. *Baudelaire and the Art of Memory*. Oxford: Oxford UP, 1999.

Hilton, Frank. *Baudelaire in Chains: Portrait of the Artist as Drug Addict*. New York: Peter Owen, 2004.

Howells, Bernard. *Baudelaire: Individualism, Dandyism, and the Philosophy of History*. Oxford: Legenda, 1996.

Hyslop, Lois Boe. *Charles Baudelaire Revisited*. New York: Twayne, 1992.

Jackson, John E. *Baudelaire*. Paris: Le Livre de Poche, 2001.

_____. *Baudelaire sans fin: essais sur "Les Fleurs du mal"*. Paris: Librairie José-Corti, 2005.

Johnson, Barbara. *Défigurations du langage poétique: la seconde révolution baudelairienne*. Paris: Flammarion, 1979.

Jones, Percy Mansell. *Baudelaire*. New Haven: Yale UP, 1952.

Kaplan, Edward K. *Baudelaire's Prose Poems: The Esthetic, the Ethical and the Religious in "The Parisian Prowler."* Athens: U of Georgia P, 1990.

Kopp, Robert. *Baudelaire: le soleil noir de la modernité*. Paris: Gallimard, 2004.

Krueger, Cheryl L. *The Art of Procrastination: Baudelaire's Poetry in Prose*. Newark: U of Delaware P, 2007.

Labarthe, Patrick. *Baudelaire et la tradition de l'allégorie*. Geneva: Droz, 1999.

Lawler, James R. *Poetry and Moral Dialectic: Baudelaire's "Secret Architecture."* Madison: Farleigh Dickinson UP, 1997.

Leakey, F. W. *Baudelaire and Nature*. Manchester: Manchester UP, 1969.

_____. *Baudelaire: Collected Essays, 1953–1988*. Cambridge, UK: Cambridge UP, 1990.

Lévy, Bernard-Henry. *Les derniers jours de Charles Baudelaire*. Paris: Editions Grasset, 1988.

Lloyd, Rosemary. *Baudelaire's World*. Ithaca: Cornell UP, 2002.

_____, ed. *The Cambridge Companion to Baudelaire*. Cambridge, UK: Cambridge UP, 2005.

MacInnes, John W. *The Comic as Textual Practice in "Les Fleurs du mal."* Gainesville: U of Florida P, 1988.

Maleuvre, Didier & Cathérine Nesci. *L'Œuvre d'identité: essais sur le romantisme de Nodier à Baudelaire.* Montreal: Université de Montréal, Département d'études françaises, 1997.

Marder, Elissa. *Dead Time: Temporal Disorders in the Wake of Modernity (Baudelaire and Flaubert).* Stanford, CA: Stanford UP, 2001.

Meltzer, Françoise. *Seeing Double: Baudelaire's Modernity.* Chicago: U of Chicago P, 2011.

Mills, Kathryn Oliver. *Formal Revolution in the Work of Baudelaire and Flaubert.* Newark, DE: U of Delaware P, 2012.

Miner, Margaret. *Resonant Gaps: Baudelaire and Wagner.* Athens, Georgia: U of Georgia P, 1995.

Murphy, Margueritte S. *Material Figures: Political Economy, Commercial Culture and the Aesthetic Sensibility of Charles Baudelaire.* Amsterdam, New York: Rodopi, 2012.

Murphy, Steve. *Logiques du dernier Baudelaire: lectures du "Spleen de Paris."* Paris: Champion, 2003.

Peyre, Henri, ed. *Baudelaire: A Collection of Critical Essays.* Englewood Cliffs, NJ: Prentice Hall, 1962.

Pia, Pascal. *Baudelaire par lui-même.* Paris: Editions du Seuil, 1952.

Pichois, Claude. *Baudelaire: études et témoignages.* Neuchâtel: La Baconnière, 1967.

Raiser, Timothy Bell. *Poetics of Art Criticism: The Case of Baudelaire.* Chapel Hill, NC: U of North Carolina P, 1989.

Richardson, Joanna. *Baudelaire.* New York: St. Martin's Press, 1994.

Robb, Graham. *La poésie de Baudelaire et la poésie française 1838–1852.* Paris: Aubier, 1993.

Runyon, Randolph. *Intratextual Baudelaire: The Sequential Fabric of the* Fleurs du mal *and* Spleen de Paris. Columbus: Ohio State UP, 2010.

Sartre, Jean-Paul. *Baudelaire.* Paris: Gallimard, 1947.

Sanyal, Debarati. *The Violence of Modernity: Baudelaire, Irony and the Politics of Form.* Baltimore: John Hopkins UP, 2006.

Schlossman, Beryl F. *Objects of Desire: The Madonnas of Modernism. [Baudelaire, Flaubert, and Others]* Ithaca, NY: Cornell UP, 1999.

_____. *The Orient of Style: Modernist Allegories of Conversion. [Baudelaire, Flaubert, Proust]* Durham, NC: Duke UP, 1991.

Scott, Clive. *Translating Baudelaire.* Exeter: U of Exeter P, 2000.

Scott, Maria C. *Baudelaire's "Le Spleen de Paris:" Shifting Perspectives*. Farnham, England: Ashgate, 2005.

Starkie, Enid. *Baudelaire*. Harmondsworth: Penguin, 1971.

Starobinski, Jean. *La Mélancholie au miroir: trois lectures de Baudelaire*. Paris: Julliard, 1989.

Stephens, Sonya. *Baudelaire's Prose Poems: The Practice and Politics of Irony*. Oxford: Oxford UP, 1999.

Thélot, Jérôme. *Baudelaire, violence et poésie*. Paris: Gallimard, 1993.

Thompson, William J., ed. *Understanding "Les Fleurs du mal:" Critical Readings*. Nashville: Vanderbilt UP, 1997.

Thum, Reinhard H. *The City: Baudelaire, Rimbaud, Verhaeren*. New York: Peter Lang, 1994.

Verhaeren, Emile. *De Baudelaire à Mallarmé*. Lausanne: L'Age d'Homme, 2008.

Wanner, Adrian. *Baudelaire in Russia*. Gainesville: UP of Florida, 1996.

Ward, Patricia & James S. Patty. *Baudelaire and the Poetics of Modernity*. Nashville: Vanderbilt UP, 2001.

Wright, Barbara & David H.T. Scott. *Baudelaire, "La Fanfarlo" and "Le Spleen de Paris."* London: Grant & Cutler, 1984.

Zimmerman, Melvin. *Baudelaire & Co.* Toronto: Editions de GREF, 2009.

About the Editor

Tom Hubbard is a Scottish novelist, poet, and itinerant scholar who has worked in many countries. He has been a visiting professor at the Universities of Budapest (ELTE), Connecticut (where he was Lynn Wood Neag Distinguished Visiting Professor of Scottish Literature in 2011) and Grenoble (as Professeur invité), and a writer in residence at the Château de Lavigny in Switzerland. His short book, *The Integrative Vision: Poetry and the Visual Arts in Baudelaire, Rilke and MacDiarmid* (1997), was based on lectures to students of design at Glasgow School of Art. He was the first librarian of the Scottish Poetry Library, from 1984 to 1992. His novel *Marie B.* (Ravenscraig Press, 2008), based on the life of the Ukrainian-born painter Marie Bashkirtseff, was longlisted for a Saltire Society Book Award. His recent book-length poetry collections are *The Chagall Winnocks* (2011) and *Parapets and Labyrinths* (2013), both from Grace Note Publications, as well as a pamphlet collection, *The Nyaff* (2012), from Windfall Books. An essay on the Scottish poet Harvey Holton (1949–2010) was published as a pamphlet by Fras Publications as *Harvey Holton: Bard, Makar, Shaman* (2013). A second novel, *The Lucky Charm of Major Bessop*, is due to appear from Grace Note in 2014, and he has recently made English and Scots versions of poems by the nineteenth-century Russian poet Lermontov for a forthcoming anthology *After Lermontov*, edited by Peter France and Robyn Marsack (Carcanet 2014). He is on the editorial board of the journal *Scottish Affairs* and is an honorary visiting fellow at the University of Edinburgh Institute of Governance, where he is working on a "Scotland and Europe" project with Dr. Eberhard Bort.

Between 2000 and 2010, he was research fellow and editor of major bibliographical projects: BOSLIT (the Bibliography of Scottish Literature in Translation, University of Edinburgh and the National Library of Scotland, at http://boslit.nls.uk [2000–2005]) and BILC (the Bibliography of Irish Literary Criticism, National University of Ireland Maynooth, at http://bilc.nuim.ie [2006–2010]).

Contributors

Helen Abbott is senior lecturer in French studies at the University of Sheffield (UK). She specializes in the relationship between words and music in nineteenth-century France, with particular emphasis on the concepts of voice, performance, rhetoric, and poetics. She has published on the poetry of Baudelaire, Mallarmé, Rimbaud, Verlaine, and Villiers de l'Isle-Adam, and on song-settings of their poems by composers, such as Berg, Britten, Debussy, Duparc, Fauré, and Vierne. Helen is also a classically-trained soprano and regularly gives solo and consort recitals. She coaches professional singers who are working on French song, including Sophie Bevan, Mary Bevan, and David Webb, and she has a long-standing research collaboration with the Oxford Lieder Festival. Her research blog is at: http://helenabbott.wordpress.com.

David Evans is senior lecturer in French studies at the University of St. Andrews (Scotland). He works on music, poetry, and aesthetic value in nineteenth-century France and has published *Rhythm, Illusion and the Poetic Idea: Baudelaire, Rimbaud, Mallarmé* (Rodopi, 2004) and *Théodore de Banville: Constructing Poetic Value in Nineteenth-Century France* (Legenda, 2014). He has edited three volumes on French literature and culture with Kate Griffiths—*Haunting Presences*, *Pleasure and Pain*, *Institutions and Power*—an issue of *Paragraph* with Peter Dayan, *Literature as Rhythm after the Crisis in Verse*, and an issue of *Dix-Neuf* on Banville.

Frances Fowle is reader in history of art at the University of Edinburgh and senior curator of French art at the Scottish National Gallery. A specialist in French and British nineteenth-century art, she has curated a number of major international exhibitions for the National Galleries of Scotland, including *Van Gogh to Kandinsky: Symbolist Landscape in Europe 1880–1910* (2012), *Impressionism and Scotland* (2008), and *Van Gogh and Britain: Pioneer Collectors* (2006). Other publications include *Van Gogh's Twin: The Scottish Art Dealer Alexander Reid* (2010) and *Monet and French Landscape* (2006).

Edward K. Kaplan studies the interconnections of aesthetic, ethical, and religious experience. He is Kaiserman Professor in the Humanities at Brandeis University, where he has taught French and comparative literature and religious studies since 1978. He has published books on Jules Michelet and *Baudelaire's Prose Poems* (Georgia UP, 1990); a prize–winning translation, *The Parisian Prowler* (Georgia UP, 1989); a classroom edition of *Les Fleurs du Mal* for speakers of English (European Masterpieces, 2010); articles on Baudelaire, Hugo, Rimbaud, Nerval, Desbordes-Valmore, Jabès, Bachelard, Yves Bonnefoy; and a two-volume biography of the Jewish theologian and activist, Abraham Joshua Heschel (Yale UP, 1998, 2007).

Rosemary Lloyd is Rudy Professor emerita at Indiana University Bloomington; fellow emerita at Murray Edwards College, University of Cambridge; and adjunct professor at University of Adelaide. She has published three studies on Baudelaire—*Baudelaire et Hoffmann: affinities et influences* (Cambridge University Press, 1978), *Baudelaire's Literary Criticism* (Cambridge University Press, 1981), and *Baudelaire's World* (Cornell University Press, 2002)—and was editor of the *Cambridge Companion to Baudelaire* (Cambridge University Press, 2005). She also translated *La Fanfarlo et Petits Poèmes en Prose* (Oxford University Press, 1991).

Kathryn Oliver Mills has published a number of articles on Baudelaire relating to *Le Peintre de la vie moderne* and its modernist aesthetic, *Les Fleurs du mal* in contrast with *Le Spleen de Paris,* Baudelaire's exploitation of poetic form, and Baudelaire's connection with the linguistic philosophy of Joseph de Maistre, as well as on the origins and aesthetics of detective fiction. Her book, *Formal Revolution in the Work of Baudelaire and Flaubert* (University of Delaware Press, 2012), brings many of those themes together. Mills has just edited the *Selected Poems* of Wilmer Mills, her husband (University of Evansville Press, 2013), and is currently writing critically about the roles that both faith and doubt play in his view of language and of poetry.

Mario Relich, whose MA is from McGill University and whose PhD is from the University of Edinburgh, is associate lecturer in the English and postcolonial literature MA program for the Open University. In the past, he has also lectured on European and American Film at Edinburgh College of Art and Edinburgh Napier University. He is a regular contributor to the Scottish/American periodical, *The Dark Horse,* and the cultural/sociological quarterly, *Scottish Affairs.* Currently, he is on the executive committee of *Scottish PEN* and Secretary of the *Poetry Association of Scotland.* His own poems have been published both in Britain and in Canada, including the Scottish magazines *Fras* and *Southlight* and in *The Antigonish Review.* His first collection will be published by Grace Note in 2014.

Randolph Paul Runyon, professor of French at Miami University of Ohio, has analyzed the hidden structural elements of literary collections in *Intratextual Baudelaire* (Ohio State University Press, 2010), *Order in Disorder: Intratextual Symmetry in Montaigne's "Essays"* (Ohio State University Press, 2013), *The Art of the Persian Letters* (University of Delaware Press, 2005), *In La Fontaine's Labyrinth* (Rookwood Press/EMF Monographs, 2000), *La Fontaine's Complete Tales in Verse, an Illustrated and Annotated Translation* (McFarland, 2009), *Ghostly Parallels: Robert Penn Warren and the Lyric Poetic Sequence* (University of Tennessee Press, 2006), and *Reading Raymond Carver* (Syracuse University Press, 1992).

Beryl F. Schlossman is professor of comparative literature, film, and media studies at the University of California, Irvine, and has published widely on modern literature and the arts. Her books include *Joyce's Catholic Comedy of Language*; *The Orient of Style: Modernist Allegories of Conversion*; and *Objects of Desire: The Madonnas of Modernism*. Her poetry and prose fiction have been published on both sides of the Atlantic, including *Angelus Novus* and several artists' books. New projects include a volume of poetry, a study of Baudelaire, essays on travel writing, and short fiction.

Maria Scott is a lecturer in French at the University of Exeter. Her first book was on the subject of Baudelaire's prose poetry, *Baudelaire's 'Le Spleen de Paris': Shifting Perspectives* (Ashgate, 2005). It won the Gapper Book Prize for the best book published that year on a French studies theme by a UK- or Ireland-based scholar. Maria has published a number of articles on Baudelaire and particularly on his prose poetry. She has also published numerous articles and, in 2013, a book on Stendhal

Juliet Simpson is professor of art history and visual culture at Buckinghamshire New University, UK and is a research member of Wolfson College, Oxford. She is a specialist in French art, visual culture, and art criticism, with a particular interest in Symbolism and transnational *fin-de-siècle* visual cultures. She has published extensively in this area, including the books *Aurier, Symbolism and the Visual Arts* (1999); *Jules Flandrin: The Other Fin-de-Siècle* (2001); and, with co-editor Carol Adlam, *Art Criticism of the Eighteenth and Nineteenth Centuries in Russia and Western Europe* (2009). Her most recent articles include studies on Mallarmé and English art in the 1870s (2012), the Goncourts' "Symbolist" *maison d'art* (2011), and "Paul Bourget's Oxford Aesthetes: Towards Decadent Cosmopolitanism" (2013).

James W. Underhill is full professor, lecturing on translation, poetics, stylistics and the philosophy of language at Rouen University, France. He has published widely throughout the world on metaphor, translation, versification, and language theory. His work on language brings together cognitive theories of metaphor with Wilhelm von Humboldt's conception of languages as worldviews. He is currently working on two books. One of these, which will be co-written with Mariarosaria Gianninoto, a sinologist, will consider the assimilation into Chinese of Western concepts of the people, the individual, and the citizen. Another will concern the way space is conceived in language and the way we translate space from one language to another. Underhill has translated poems from Czech, German, and mostly French. Tom Hubbard and he are currently working on a series of publishing projects to bring Baudelaire not only into "standard" Scots, but also into a variety of Scots registers.

Lois Davis Vines is professor of French and distinguished teaching professor of humanities at Ohio University, where she teaches French literature, language, and culture. The author of *Valéry and Poe: A Literary Legacy* (New York UP, 1992) and *Poe Abroad: Influence, Reputation, Affinities* (U of Iowa P, 1999) she has also published numerous articles on literature, the French media, and teaching. She was named *Chevalier dans l'Ordre des Palmes Académiques* by the French government in 1993.

Index

Watson, George 229
Watteau, Antoine 161
Watt, Ian P. xxi
Weber, Carl Maria von 163, 189
Weltanschauung 90
Werner, Alfred 165
West Indies 116
Wetherill, Peter M. 105
What Is Art? 60, 66
White, Edmund 26
White, Ruth 208
Whitman, Walt 22
Wilde, Oscar xiv, 8, 59
William Blake: A Critical Essay
    xxi
Wing, Nathaniel 94
Witches Sabbath, The 162

Women if Algiers, The 27
Wordsworth, William 9
Works of Edgar Allan Poe, The 29
*Writer of Modern Life: Essays on
    Charles Baudelaire, The* 79,
    125

Yeats 241
Yorick 15
Youens, Susan 208

Ziegler, Jean 20, 64, 177, 193,
    207, 270
Zimmerman, Melvin 19
Zohn, Harry 64, 79, 93, 125
Zola, Émile 3